CT 105 E25 1970
S0-DUI-159

MAKERS OF FREEDOM

GEORGE SHERWOOD EDDY
and KIRBY PAGE

MAKERS OF FREEDOM

BIOGRAPHICAL SKETCHES IN SOCIAL PROGRESS

BY

GEORGE SHERWOOD EDDY

AND

KIRBY PAGE

"With a great price obtained I this freedom."

Essay Index Reprint Series

BOOKS FOR LIBRARIES PRESS

FREEPORT, NEW YORK

Reprinted 1970 by arrangement with
Harper & Row, Publishers, Inc.

INTERNATIONAL STANDARD BOOK NUMBER:
0-8369-1803-7

LIBRARY OF CONGRESS CATALOG CARD NUMBER:
79-117786

PRINTED IN THE UNITED STATES OF AMERICA

FOREWORD

"*With a great price obtained I this freedom*," said the Roman officer to the apostle Paul. And all of us must likewise admit that the liberty which we now enjoy was purchased at stupendous cost. Primitive man was everywhere in fetters. Throughout his whole history man has been enslaved—by the uncontrolled elements of nature and disease, by hunger and poverty, by ignorance and superstition, by custom and tradition, by tyranny and mob violence, and by his own appetites and passions. The record of man's struggle for freedom is a story of sweat and tears, of bloodshed and boundless sacrifice. In no realm has liberty of thought or action been achieved without the toil and suffering of the pioneer. We owe an incalculable debt to these prophetic and heroic men and women who patiently endured pain and persecution for the sake of liberty. With a great price indeed have we secured our freedom!

Biography is perhaps the best medium through which to reveal the cost of that measure of freedom which is now our common heritage. The present volume is an attempt briefly to interpret the lives of eight men and women who well deserve the title "Makers of Freedom." Our choice of characters does not, of course, include all the great leaders in reform movements. The reader will at once detect conspicuous omissions, some of whom were not included because their lives are already so well known. In our treatment of each character portrayed, we have sought light upon six questions: (1) What kind of world did he live in? (2) What did he do? (3) What did he say? (4) What happened to him? (5) What kind of man was he? (6) What were the results of his life?

It is obvious that the age-long effort to achieve liberty has not yet been fully achieved. We have, therefore, included a section on "The Present Struggle for Freedom," in which we have sought to analyze some prevailing attitudes, practices and institutions which are now enslaving mankind, and have faced the question as to what an individual can do to make more effective the present crusade for the complete emancipation of the human spirit.

Sherwood Eddy
Kirby Page

▼

CONTENTS

MAKERS OF FREEDOM

Chapter 1

FREEDOM FROM SLAVERY

William Lloyd Garrison

1. WHAT KIND OF A WORLD DID GARRISON LIVE IN?

William Lloyd Garrison was born at an hour when human slavery was still regarded as a divine institution by millions of his countrymen. At the time of his death it had been banished as a legalized institution from the civilized world. The story of its abolition is one of the most dramatic and significant in the whole history of social progress.

Traffic in human flesh is older than the written records of man. Everywhere in ancient times captives in war were killed or enslaved. Indeed, as has often been pointed out, slavery was more merciful than slaughter. Civilization began with the crack of the whip. The glories of ancient Egypt, Greece and Rome rested upon slave labor. Single individuals owned from 5,000 to 10,000 slaves. Slavery did not die out in Europe during the middle ages, although in many places it took the milder form of serfdom.

The modern slave traffic has been confined chiefly to Negroes. As early as 1434 a Portuguese captain landed on the Guinea Coast and carried away some Negro boys. In 1562 Queen Elizabeth legalized the purchase of black slaves by English subjects. In 1620 Dutch traders landed black slaves at Jamestown in Virginia. By the end of the century the slave traffic was a well-established and highly profitable business. Between 1680 and 1786 more than 2,000,000 Africans were imported into America and the West Indies. The Peace of Utrecht, which was signed in 1713, gave England a practical monopoly in the slave trade from West Africa to America. This treaty was celebrated in St. Paul's

Cathedral in London by the singing of a *Te Deum* specially composed by Handel for the occasion.

There is no blacker page in modern history than that containing the record of the European slavers during this period. With insatiable greed and terrible cruelty they raided the jungles of Africa and carried into captivity multitudes of these helpless peoples. Language is inadequate to describe the horrors of the passage to America. Shackled with heavy irons, chained together, crowded like animals into vile quarters, with foul air, indescribable filth and loathsome disease, they were subjected to a degree of torture which has rarely been equaled in the whole history of man's cruelty to man.

Concerning the question as to how slaves were treated by their masters, it is not safe to generalize. The slave code was constantly changing and was never uniform throughout the country. Some states went much further than others in protecting slaves. Moreover, many owners treated their slaves far better than was required by law. *It would be grossly untrue to say that all slaves were in practice denied the fundamental rights of human beings.* There was a basis in fact for the vivid picture contained in "Uncle Tom's Cabin," but this was by no means the whole story of slavery. There is no doubt but that on the better plantations the slaves were well fed and clothed, were not overworked, and on the whole were contented and happy. But at best slavery was highly paternalistic and depended upon the good pleasure of the master. At its worst it was hideous cruelty and barbarous inhumanity.

Grounds on Which Slavery Was Defended

Slavery could never have been so thoroughly incorporated into the law of the land if it had not rested upon a well-defined philosophy which was widely accepted. Included in this philosophy of slavery were the following elements:

1. *African slaves are an inferior race and are therefore doomed to servitude.* The doctrine of inferior peoples is of ancient origin. Aristotle believed that "nature endeavors to

make the bodies of freemen and slaves different; the latter strong for necessary use, the former erect and useless for such operations, but useful for political life. . . It is evident, then, that by nature some men are free, others slaves, and that in the case of the latter, slavery is both beneficial and just." On this point Chancellor William Harper said: "It is as much in the order of nature that men should enslave each other, as that other animals should prey upon each other. . . The Creator did not intend that every individual human being should be highly cultivated, morally and intellectually, for, as we have seen, he has imposed conditions on society which would render this impossible."

2. *Slavery is necessary and is the cornerstone of civilization.* In 1835 Governor McDuffie sent an official message to the Legislature of South Carolina, which contained the following sentiment: "Domestic slavery, therefore, instead of being a political evil, is the cornerstone of our republican edifice." One writer said: "Destroy our Slavery and you put a stop to all progress, all improvement at the South: you throw it back to its primitive state, in which it is only fit for the residence of beasts of prey. Abolish slavery and you throw back society into a state of barbarism—you dry up its resources—the means of its prosperity—and check civilization for centuries to come."

3. *Slavery is a blessing for the slaves themselves.* In going through the literature on this subject one is impressed with the frequency with which this argument occurs. Hundreds of quotations along this line could easily be gathered together. The following utterances are typical of many others: "Negroes in a state of slavery are comfortable and prosperous beyond any peasantry in the world, and even beyond the most opulent serfs of Europe; but emancipate them and you irretrievably consign them to barbarism." The spiritual contribution of slavery to the African is frequently emphasized: "Slavery has tamed, civilized, Christianized, if you please, the brutal negroes brought to our shores by New England kidnappers; it has elevated them physically, mentally, morally, and therefore is a proven

blessing to them and ought to be perpetuated. Really, the only way to civilize and Christianize Africa is to annex that vast continent to the United States, and let our people reduce them to slavery, set them to work, and thus develop the resources of Africa." The fourth point in a sermon on slavery by a Richmond minister in 1856 was that "the institution of slavery is full of mercy. . . In their bondage here on earth, they have been much better provided for, and great multitudes of them have been made the freemen of the Lord Jesus Christ, and left this world rejoicing in the hope of the glory of God."

4. *Slavery is a divine institution.* Literally hundreds of books were written to prove this point. Professor Taylor, of Yale College, said that "if Jesus Christ were now on earth, he would under certain circumstances become a slaveholder." Governor Hammond said: "I firmly believe that American slavery is not only not a sin, but especially commanded by God through Moses, and approved by Christ through his apostles." Governor McDuffie expressed the opinion that "no human institution is more manifestly consistent with the will of God than domestic slavery, and no one of his ordinances is written in more legible characters than that which consigns the African race to this condition."

On Thanksgiving Day in 1860 the pastor of the First Presbyterian Church in New Orleans preached a sermon entitled: "Slavery a Divine Trust—the Duty of the South to Preserve and Perpetuate the Institution as It Now Exists." In this sermon Dr. Palmer said: "In this great struggle we defend the cause of God and religion. The abolition spirit is undeniably atheistic." The fourfold argument of his sermon "establishes the nature and solemnity of our present trust to preserve and transmit our existing system of domestic servitude, with the right, unchanged by man, to go and root itself wherever Providence and nature may carry it. The position of the South is at this moment sublime. If she has grace given her to know her hour, she will save herself, the country, and the world."

Slavery Upheld by Leading Citizens

On such grounds as these slavery was defended by most Southern people and many who lived in the North, including many of the most prominent, best educated and most religious men of the nation. In 1857 Hinton Rowan Helper pointed out that the Presidency of the United States had been held for forty-eight years by slaveholders, as against twenty years by non-slaveholders. George Washington, Patrick Henry and many other fathers of the Constitution owned slaves. Numerous governors of states were advocates of the institution. A majority of the members of the United States Supreme Court at the time of the famous Dred Scott decision were slaveholders. Many college presidents and professors in educational institutions were numbered with the defenders of slavery.

A large proportion of the several hundred books in defence of slavery now in the New York Public Library were written by ministers and theological professors. The great evangelist Whitefield said: "As to the lawfulness of keeping slaves I have no doubt." In 1855 Dr. N. L. Rice, Moderator of the Presbyterian General Assembly, said: "God has permitted slavery for wise reasons in order to the accomplishment of some great and important ends."

A clergyman by the name of Spring expressed the conviction that "if by one prayer I could liberate every slave in the land, I would not dare to offer it." In 1840 the Rev. James Smylie wrote: "If the buying, selling and holding of a slave for the sake of gain is a heinous sin and scandal, then verily three-fourths of all the Episcopalians, Methodists, Baptists and Presbyterians in eleven States of the Union are of the devil. They hold, if they do not buy and sell slaves."

In the Mercier Luminary, J. Cable wrote: "Those who know anything about slavery, know that the worst kind is jobbing slavery—that is, the hiring out of slaves from year to year. What shocked me more than anything else was that the church engaged in this jobbing of slaves. The college church which I attended, and which was attended by all the students of Hamden Sydney College and Union Theological Seminary (Virginia) held slaves enough to pay their pastor, Mr. Stanton, one thousand dollars a year. The slaves, who had been left to the Church by some pious mother in Israel, had increased so as to be a large and still increasing fund. They were hired out on Christmas day of each year, the day in which they celebrate the birth of our blessed Saviour, to the highest bidder. There were four other churches near the college church that supported the pastor, in whole or in part, in the same way."

2. WHAT DID GARRISON DO ABOUT SLAVERY?

For thirty-five years Garrison was editor of the Liberator and through its columns thundered his message of immediate emancipation of the slaves. The crusading spirit of the man is revealed in the following memorable words taken from the first issue, January 1, 1831: "I will be as harsh as truth, and as uncompromising as justice. On this subject I do not wish to think, or speak, or write, with moderation. No! No! Tell a man whose house is on fire to give a moderate alarm; tell him to moderately rescue his wife from the hands of the ravisher; tell the mother to gradually extricate her babe from the fire into which it has fallen;—but urge me not to use moderation in a cause like the present. I am in earnest—I will not equivocate—I will not excuse—I will not retreat a single inch—and I will be heard."

Garrison was only twenty-six when he wrote these ringing words. He was born on December 10, 1805, in Newburyport, Massachusetts, next door to the parsonage in which Whitefield, the great evangelist, died. His father was a sea captain. When William Lloyd was not quite three years old his father deserted his family and never returned. One of his brothers followed the father in the pathway of drunkenness and debauchery. His mother, thus compelled to provide for herself and the three children, turned to the occupation of nursing. During the period of bitter poverty in his boyhood, Garrison learned the lesson of self-denial and self-reliance which were manifested to such a marked degree later in life. His mother was a very religious woman. She was a Baptist, and at that time in that section it required courage to be a "dissenter." From her William Lloyd received the elements of religion which remained with him throughout his life.

At the age of nine he was apprenticed to a shoe manufacturer in Lynn, where his mother was nursing. Later he was apprenticed to a cabinet-maker in Haverill. In 1815 he began work as a printer's boy in the shop of the Newburyport Herald, where sixty years later he handled type for the last time. While still in his teens Garrison was made foreman of the Herald office. In this capacity he contributed anonymously to his employer's paper. In June, 1823, shortly after his sister's death, he went to Baltimore to join his mother, whom he had not seen for seven years. Within a few weeks his mother, weakened by overwork and privation, died.

In 1826 Garrison was for a short time editor and publisher of the Free Press in Newburyport. During the following year he worked as a compositor in four different shops. In 1828 he became co-editor and publisher of the National Philanthropist and began his career as a reformer. Vigorous attacks were launched against intemperance, lotteries, infidelity and Sabbath breaking. In March occurred the momentous meeting with Benjamin Lundy, which was to mean so much to the future of the emancipation movement. Lundy was a Quaker itinerant solderer, who for thirteen years had been talking and writing continuously against human slavery. He was an "earnest, undersized peripatetic, devoid of the charms of oratory, and afflicted with the infirmity of deafness." Some years before he had founded the Genius of Universal Emancipation at Mount Pleasant, Ohio.

Later in the year Garrison became editor of the Journal of the Times, at Bennington, Vermont. In March, 1829, he gave up this position to become co-editor of the Genius with Lundy. In his last editorial in the Journal, Garrison wrote: "I trust in God that I may be the humble instrument of breaking at least one chain, and restoring one captive to liberty; it will amply repay a life of severe toil." Through the columns of the Genius, Garrison opposed the liquor traffic, denounced the breaches of faith with the Georgia Indians and advocated a boycott of the products of slave labor. When he accused Francis Todd, of Newburyport, of engaging in the domestic slave trade between Baltimore and New Orleans, he found himself engaged in a libel suit, which he lost. Unable to pay the fine and costs of about one hundred dollars, he was imprisoned for seven weeks in the Baltimore jail. Shortly after this experience his partnership with Lundy was dissolved, and a little later he launched the Liberator.

The story of the early days of the Liberator is one of the most thrilling in the whole journalistic history of social reform. It was launched with practically no capital, with no subscribers and at a time when the doctrine of immediate emancipation was regarded as social heresy if not actual treason. The type for the first three issues was borrowed, and then some second-hand type was secured from a foundry. The paper was printed by a hand-press. For a year and a half Garrison and his partner, Isaac Knapp, lived in the printing office. In these humble quarters they ate their meagre food procured from a neighboring bakery, slept on the floor, and issued their publication. Garrison was an expert typesetter and fortunately was able to set up his editorials directly into his composing stick, thus saving much time and energy. Aided only by a Negro assistant, they carried on all the processes necessary to composing, proofreading, printing and distributing the paper. For fourteen hours a day they labored at their task. They lived in the utmost simplicity, often having only bread and water as their fare. Within a very few months their efforts began to attract widespread notice. The vicious and slanderous attacks upon Garrison which began at this time did not cease until emancipation was achieved and continued in some sections for a long time thereafter.

In May, 1831, Garrison urged that a national anti-slavery

society be formed, and he was one of the leading figures at the meeting in Boston where the New England Anti-Slavery Society was launched. In fact, he became its corresponding secretary. Of the twelve original members of this society it was said that "not more than one or two could have put a hundred dollars into the treasury without bankrupting themselves!" In 1832 Garrison published an exceedingly able and influential pamphlet on "Thoughts on African Colonization," in which he severely attacked the policies of the American Colonization Society.

At this period he was married to Miss Ellen Benson, of Providence, daughter of a Quaker abolitionist. Of his wife it was said that Garrison "might have looked in vain for a sweeter woman or a better helpmate to stand by him in the arduous years to come." It required great courage and faith to begin a home at such a period in Garrison's life. The Liberator was in almost desperate financial straits. Two thousand dollars were due from unpaid subscriptions. Garrison's own friends and supporters were being alienated by his harsh language, and for a time it looked as if the paper would have to be discontinued. In fact, in January, 1835, Garrison "went home to write his valedictory, and to advertise to the world the downfall of the Liberator."

His already very heavy burden was increased by the arrival of George Thompson, an English abolitionist. In August, 1835, there was a meeting "of great respectability" in Boston to protest against the spread of abolitionism. A Concord crowd nearly mobbed Thompson. About this time a protest meeting was held by the Whigs of New York. The bitterness against Thompson increased, and his meetings were broken up with violence. It was during this period that Garrison had his famous experience with the Boston mob, narrowly escaping with his life. At this time of crisis the continuance of the Liberator was made possible by the generous aid of Samuel E. Sewall. Another powerful ally for the abolition cause now appeared in Wendell Phillips, of brilliant intellect and courageous heart.

By 1840 the emancipation movement had taken deep root

in all sections of the North, and the tide was powerfully and irrevocably turning against slavery. During the two momentous decades which followed Garrison poured out his soul against this vile institution through a never-ceasing stream of articles, pamphlets and books. He travelled widely throughout many sections of the country and made innumerable speeches. He was one of the most effective organizers in the whole abolitionist movement and helped to launch many anti-slavery societies, local and national.

A vivid summary of Garrison's activities during these years has been given by John Jay Chapman, in the following words: "It was between 1830 and 1840 that the real work of Garrison was done. At the beginning of that decade Abolition was a cry in the wilderness: at the end of it, Abolition was a part of the American mind. Garrison's occupation throughout the epoch was to tend his engine—his Liberator—and to assist in the formation of Anti-slavery societies. Every breath of the movement was chronicled in the Liberator, every new convert wrote to Garrison for help. Garrison was the focus, the exchange, the center and heart of Anti-slavery activity. . . It was Garrison who caused the heat-lightning of 1825 to turn into the thunderbolts of 1835. His gift of doing this was his greatness. We must imagine Garrison then, as always, behind and underneath the machinery and in touch with all the forces at work, writing away at his terrible Liberator—fomenting, rebuking, retorting, supporting, expounding, thundering, scolding. The continuousness of Garrison is appalling, and fatigues even the retrospective imagination of posterity: he is like something let loose. I dread the din of him. I cover my head and fix my mind on other things; but there is Garrison hammering away, till he catches my eye and forces me to attend to him. If Garrison can do this to me, who am protected from dread of him by eighty years of intervening time, think how his lash must have fallen upon the thin skins of our ancestors."

3. WHAT DID GARRISON SAY ABOUT SLAVERY?

Garrison's message is simple, direct and unmistakable The record of his writings and speeches is extraordinarily voluminous, but one clear note runs through it all: *Slavery is sinful and should be abolished immediately.* His attack was many-sided, and in his use of illustrations he was exceedingly versatile, but in it all he was saying just one thing.

There were a good many persons who believed in the abolition of slavery by a process of "gradualism." As contrasted with this policy, Garrison believed in immediate and complete abolition. In the first issue of the Liberator, he wrote: "I shall strenuously contend for the immediate enfranchisement of our slave population." In 1832, Garrison published a vigorous 240-page onslaught on the colonization of slaves in Liberia and Haiti. Concerning those persons who advocated colonization, he wrote: "My complaint is that they content themselves with representing slavery as an evil—a misfortune—a calamity which has been entailed upon us by former generations—*and not as an individual CRIME,* embracing in its folds robbery, cruelty, oppression and piracy. *They do not identify the criminals;* they make no direct, pungent, earnest appeal to the consciences of men-stealers."

Concerning the wisdom and practicability of immediate abolition, he said: "The question of expedience has nothing to do with that of right, and it is not for those who tyrannize to say when they may safely break the chains of their subjects. As well may a thief determine on what particular day or month he shall leave off stealing, with safety to his own interest." On another occasion he said: "It appears to us a self-evident truth, that, whatever the gospel is designed to destroy at any period of the world, being contrary to it, ought NOW to be abandoned."

Garrison did not hesitate to attack anything that stood in the way of abolition. We, therefore. find him making vigorous attacks on the Constitution of the United States, on the ground that it sanctioned slavery. In the Liberator in 1832, he wrote: "There is much declamation about the sacredness of the compact which was formed between the free and slave States, on the adoption of the Constitution. A sacred compact, forsooth! We pronounce it the most bloody and heaven-daring arrangement ever made by men for the continuance and protection of a system of the most atrocious villainy ever exhibited upon the earth." In 1842, he declared that "slavery is a combination of Death and Hell, and with it the North have made a covenant and are at agreement." In 1854, he publicly burned a copy of the Constitution, as a means of calling attention to its sanction of slavery.

Garrison often attacked the churches of his day on the ground that many of them sanctioned slavery. In a letter to a friend in 1830, he said: "Is not the fact enough to make one hang his head, that Christian men and Christian ministers (for so they dare to call themselves) are slave-owners? . . . The Gospel of Peace and Mercy preached by him who steals, buys or sells the purchase of Messiah's blood!—Rulers of the Church making merchandise of their brethren's souls!—and Christians trading the persons of men!"

In this connection, Professor A. B. Hart says: "When Garrison began his work, he thought nothing was more like the spirit of Christ than to relieve the oppressed, and preach the gospel to the benighted, and to bring a whole race of people out of sin and debasement; but he soon found that neither minister nor Church anywhere in the lower South continued to protest against slavery; that the cloth in the North was arrayed against him, and that many northern divines entered the lists against abolition."

In 1830 Garrison wrote from Baltimore to a friend: "I found the minds of the people strangely indifferent to the subject of slavery. Their prejudices were invincible—stronger if possible, than those of slave-owners. Objections were started on every hand; apologies for the abominable system constantly saluted my ears; obstacles were industriously piled up in my path." In the first number of the Liberator, he wrote: "The apathy of the people is enough to make every statue leap from its pedestal, and to hasten the resurrection of the dead."

In his attacks upon the enemies of immediate abolition, Garrison used strong and vehement language. "For myself," he said, "I hold no fellowship with slave-owners. I will not make a truce with them even for a single hour. I blush for them as countrymen—I know they are not Christians; and the higher they raise their profession of patriotism or piety, the stronger is my detestation of their hypocrisy. They are dishonest and cruel—and God, and the angels, and devils and the universe know that they are without excuse."

This use of strong language was deliberately adopted and vigorously defended. "But why so vehement?" he asked, "so unyielding? so severe? Because the times and the cause demand vehemence. An immense iceberg, larger and more impenetrable than any which floats in the Arctic Ocean, is to be dissolved, and a little extra heat is not only pardonable, but absolutely necessary. . . . With reasonable men, I will reason, with humane men, I will plead; but to tyrants I will give no quarter, nor waste arguments where they will certainly be lost."

In an address in 1833 he said: "How, then, ought I to feel, and speak, and write, in view of a system which is red with innocent blood, drawn from the bodies of millions of my countrymen by the scourge of brutal drivers;—which is full of all uncleanness and licentiousness;—which destroys the life of the soul;—and which is too horrible for the mind to imagine, or the pen to declare? How ought I to feel and speak? As a man! as a patriot! as a philanthropist! as a Christian! My soul should be, as it is, on fire. I should thunder—I should lighten. I should blow the trumpet of alarm, long and loud. I should use just such language as is most descriptive of the crime. I should imitate the example of Christ, who, when he had to do with people of like manners, called them sharply by their proper names—such as, an adulterous and perverse generation, a brood of vipers, hypocrites, children of the devil who could not escape the damnation of hell. . . . I will not waste my strength in foolishly endeavoring to beat down this great Bastile with a feather. . . . I am for digging under its foundations, and springing a mine that will not leave one stone upon another."

In strong contrast with his denunciatory words is his message concerning the weapons which are to be used in abolishing slavery. Garrison was an extreme non-resistant.[1] He not only objected to all wars, he was a total disbeliever in force and coercive measures. In replying to Henry Ward Beecher, he said: "We know not where to look for Christianity if not to its founder; and, taking the record of his life and death, of his teaching and example, we can discover nothing which even remotely, under any conceivable circumstances, justifies the use of the sword or rifle on the part of his followers . . . We believe in his philosophy; we accept his instruction; we are thrilled by his example; we rejoice in his fidelity."

No better summary of his attitude toward war could be found than the statement which he made in 1858: "When the anti-slavery cause was launched, it was baptized in the spirit of peace. We proclaimed to the country and the world that the weapons of our warfare were not carnal, but spiritual, and we believed them to be mighty through God to the pulling down even of the stronghold of slavery; and for several years great moral power accompanied our cause wherever presented. Alas! in the course of the fearful developments of the Slave Power, and its continued aggressions on the rights of the people of the North, in my judgment a sad change has come over the spirit of anti-slavery men, generally speaking. We are growing more and more warlike, more and more disposed to repudiate the principles of peace . . . I will not trust the war-spirit anywhere in the universe of God, because the experience of six-

[1]See William Lloyd Garrison on Non-Resistance, by Fanny Garrison Villard and Oswald Garrison Villard.

thousand years proves it not to be at all reliable in such a struggle as ours."

4. WHAT HAPPENED TO GARRISON?

Garrison was the most bitterly hated man of his generation. Few men have ever suffered the amount of abuse which was heaped upon him. At the age of twenty-five he was convicted of libel for denouncing the transfer of slaves between Baltimore and New Orleans in a ship belonging to Francis Todd. He was sentenced and served a term in the Baltimore jail. In 1831 the Legislature of Georgia offered a reward of $5,000 to anyone who would arrest and bring him to trial.

Two years later he narrowly escaped from the hands of a mob in New York City. In 1835 he was led about with a rope around his body by a Boston mob, which included "many gentlemen of property and influence." Garrison tells us that at the conclusion of an address in Pennsylvania Hall in Philadelphia, which was attended by some three thousand persons, "a furious mob broke into the hall yelling and shouting as if the very fiends of the pit had suddenly broke loose." The next evening the mob succeeded in burning the great hall to the ground.

At an anti-slavery meeting in the Broadway Tabernacle in 1850, Garrison was threatened by the so-called Rynders Mob. Prior to the meeting the New York Herald had advised the breaking up of the meeting by violence. Concerning Garrison, the Herald said: "Never, in the time of the French Revolution and blasphemous atheism, was there more malevolence and unblushing wickedness avowed than by this same Garrison. Indeed, he surpasses Robespierre and his associates, for he has no design of building up. His only object is to destroy."

A Southern writer in 1836 expressed his opinion of Garrison in the following words: "His religious madness, his vehement cant and violence of spirit naturally gained for him the mastery in their councils. His writings have been blackened with the vilest slanders, and the most vindictive abuse. Indeed, so vehement, rancorous and fiend-like have been his exhibitions of passion against his opponents, that most persons have considered, and do still consider, him insane."

Garrison was constantly denied freedom of speech and press. "When free discussion does not promote the public good," said the New York Herald, "it has no more right to exist than a bad government that is dangerous and oppressive to the common weal. It should be overthrown. On the question of usefulness to the public of the packed, organized meetings of these abolitionists, socialists, Sabbath-breakers, and anarchists, there can be but one result arrived at by prudence and patriotism. They are dangerous assemblies—calculated for mischief, and treasonable in their character and purposes."

The abolitionists often had extreme difficulty in obtaining the use of a hall for their meetings. It is recorded that in 1835, "The hostility of the Churches and the timidity of public-hall owners now began to be a most serious embarrassment to the Abolitionists in their oral propaganda. The New England Convention was shut out of seven churches, of the Masonic Temple, and of every hall in the city but two."

In upholding the postmaster of Charleston, S. C., for refusing to deliver anti-slavery publications, and the postmaster of New York for refusing to forward such papers, Amos Kendall, Postmaster-General of the United States, said: "We owe an obligation to the laws, but a higher one to the communities in which we live; and if the former be perverted to destroy the latter, it is patriotism to disregard them." The New York Tribune, of which Horace Greeley was the editor, was pronounced incendiary by the Attorney General of Virginia and excluded from many postoffices. On February 28, 1860, J. M. Ferguson, Postmaster at Wayne, Virginia, wrote to the editor of the Western Christian Advocate as follows: "Sir, you will please discontinue sending your paper to this office, as it has been found to contain incendiary matter, and burnt."

So acute did this situation become that the New York

Tribune wrote: "There exists at this moment throughout the Southern States, an actual Reign of Terror. No Northern man, whatever may be his character, his opinions, or his life, but simply because he is a Northern man, can visit that region without the certainty of being subjected to a mean espionage over all his actions, and a rigid watchfulness over all his expressions of opinions; with the risk of personal indignity, and danger even to life and limb."

Garrison once wrote to George Benson: "I have just received a letter written evidently by a friendly hand, in which I am apprised that 'my life is sought after, and a reward of $20,000 has been offered for my head by six Mississippians.'"

The evidence is incontrovertible that throughout most of Garrison's lifetime, abolitionists were regarded by many people as dangerous malefactors and were treated accordingly.

5. WHAT KIND OF A MAN WAS GARRISON?

We cannot get an accurate picture of Garrison from his enemies. We cannot even get such a picture from a study of his own writings and speeches. He deliberately adopted strong language as a means of rousing his fellowmen to a realization of the evils of slavery. But he was wholly opposed to violence as a means of freeing the slaves, and his personal character was exactly opposite from that pictured by those against whom he was arrayed.

Garrison made mistakes, many of them, and some that were serious. That was because he did things. These mistakes need not be excused. They should be understood. When Mr. Samuel J. May was taken to task by Dr. Channing, he replied, "I am tired of these complaints. The cause of suffering humanity, the cause of our oppressed, crushed, colored countrymen, has called as loudly upon others as upon us Abolitionists. It was just as incumbent upon others as upon us to espouse it. We are not to blame that wiser and better men did not espouse it long ago. The cry of millions, suffering cruel bondage in our land, had been heard for half a century and disregarded. 'The wise and prudent' saw the terrible wrong, but thought it not wise and prudent to lift a finger for its correction. The priests and Levites beheld their robbed and wounded countrymen, but passed by on the other side. . . We Abolitionists are what we are—babes, sucklings, obscure men, silly women, publicans, sinners, and we shall manage this matter just as might be expected of such persons as we are. It is unbecoming in abler men who stood by and would do nothing to complain of us because we do no better."

Harriet Martineau has described Garrison in these words: "His aspect put to flight in an instant what prejudices his slanderers had raised in me. I was wholly taken by surprise. It was a countenance glowing with health, and wholly expressive of purity, animation and gentleness." A friend who spent several weeks with the Garrisons in Europe wrote: "As to Mr. Garrison himself, he is the most delightful man I have ever known—magnanimous, generous, considerate, and, as far as I can see, every way morally excellent."

There is no doubt that Garrison was a deeply religious man. His departure from orthodox ways of expressing his religion gave his enemies an opportunity to call him an atheist and led many clergymen to attack him as an enemy of the church. But no man of his day was further from being an atheist or an enemy of real religion than was Garrison. "The source of Garrison's power," says one of his biographers, "was the Bible. From his earliest days he read the Bible constantly. It was with this fire that he started his conflagration." Concerning the charge that he was an infidel, Garrison wrote to a friend in 1841: "I need not say to you that the charge is both groundless and malicious."

Concerning Garrison's character, Wendell Phillips wrote: "I have seen him intimately for thirty years, while raining on his head was the hate of the community, when by every possible form of expression malignity let him know that it wished him all sorts of harm. I never saw him unhappy.

I never saw the moment that serene abounding faith in the rectitude of his motive, the soundness of his method, and the certainty of success did not lift him above all possibility of being reached by any clamour about him."

Oliver Johnson, lifelong friend of Garrison, bears this testimony: "His heart was all aflame with enthusiasm for his cause . . . A faith so absolute in the sacredness and power of moral principles, a trust in God so firm and immovable as his, I have never seen exhibited by any other man. Never for an instant did he doubt the success of the movement to which, upon his knees, with his Bible open before him, he had consecrated his life. Whoever else might yield to discouragement, he never . . . How often did I hear him speak in tenderest pity of the deluded men who stood ready to take his life at the first opportunity."

Mr. John Jay Chapman has summarized his impression of Garrison's character in the following vivid paragraph: "If you take the great political agitators of the world, like Luther, Calvin, Savonarola, Garibaldi, or certain of the English church reformers, you will find that these men always live under a terrible strain, and they generally give way somewhere. No one can imagine how fierce is the blast upon a man's nervous system, when he stands in the midst of universal antagonism, solitary and at bay. . . There is generally something to forgive in the history of such men. Now Garrison is almost perfect: he is perfect in his lack of personal ambition, in his indifference to power, in his courage, his faith, his persistence, his benevolence. When he breaks down it is in driblets, and every day—in the bad taste and self-indulgence of a disgusting rhetoric, in his inability to 'shut up' about anything, in his use of the personal pronoun."

6. WHAT WERE THE RESULTS OF GARRISON'S LIFE?

There are conflicting estimates of the results of Garrison's life. In the opinion of some persons Garrison was the chief cause of the Civil War, while others deny this and say that to him, more than to any other person, the freedom of the slaves is due. Abraham Lincoln, in response to words of gratitude from Daniel H. Chamberlain for his great deliverance of the slaves, said: "I have been only an instrument. The logic and moral power of Garrison, and the Anti-Slavery people of the country, and the army have done all." Wendell Phillips, himself one of the greatest of the abolitionists, said in 1865: "I have never met the man or woman who had struck any effectual blow at the slave system in this country whose action was not born out of the heart and conscience of William Lloyd Garrison." One of his biographers says of Garrison's influence: "The history of the United States between 1800 and 1860 will some day be rewritten with this man as its central figure."

While the present writers recognize an element of truth in the adverse view of Garrison's work, they believe that on the whole the other estimate is the more correct one. It cannot be questioned that Garrison irritated and enraged the defenders of slavery and thus contributed to the bitterness of the struggle. It is also beyond dispute that his severity and harshness alienated many genuine supporters of the anti-slavery movement. But the question keeps recurring, could the deadened consciences of that day have been aroused without the reformer's stinging words? Are there times when the scathing rebuke of a prophet is absolutely necessary? If not, then Elijah and Jeremiah, Jesus and Paul, Savonarola and Luther were wrong in their use of denunciatory language. Consider these words from the lips of Jesus: "Woe unto you, scribes and Pharisees, hypocrites! . . . ye fools and blind . . . for ye are like unto whited sepulchres, which indeed appear beautiful outward, but are within full of dead men's bones . . . ye serpents, ye generation of vipers, how can ye escape the damnation of hell?" (Matt. 23.) Was Jesus to blame for the anger, hatred and violence with which his words were received? Is Gandhi, of sainted life and non-resistant spirit, responsible for the violence which has occasionally resulted from his policy of non-co-operation with the British?

If ever the use of vehement language in denouncing sin

was justifiable, surely the blindness, complacency and selfishness of the American public with regard to slavery, justified Garrison in his uncompromising attack upon so vile an institution. It is probably true that Garrison was unduly extreme and that his influence would have been even greater if he had avoided gross intemperance of speech. Nothing is to be gained by refusing to admit that great damage to the cause resulted from his excesses. But if we are to arrive at a correct estimate of his influence we must keep vividly in mind the appalling lethargy concerning the evils of slavery which everywhere prevailed, and the further fact that Garrison was on fire. All about him were men who were frozen with apathy, whose perceptions and consciences were so dull and insensible that they were blind to the terrible nature of slavery.

The horrors of slavery were never absent from Garrison's mind. He could never forget the millions of his fellow beings who were held in bondage, with no right to gain freedom or to protect their own lives or the virtue of their wives and daughters, with no right of property, education or religious instruction, many of whom were subjected to inhuman toil and barbarous cruelty. He could never forgive the indifference and cowardice of his fellowmen in the presence of such hideous injustice. His soul burned within him. His words were like molten lava. For forty years they poured upon the frozen hearts of his countrymen. Finally, the conscience of America was awakened. Is it too much to say that Garrison, more than any other person, was responsible for *the change in public opinion* which ultimately resulted in the freeing of the slaves in the United States?

CHAPTER 2

FREEDOM FROM IGNORANCE AND POVERTY

Booker T. Washington

1. WHAT KIND OF A WORLD DID WASHINGTON LIVE IN?

Booker T. Washington was born as a slave, and was about seven years old when the Civil War ended. The formative years of his life were, therefore, spent in the atmosphere of war and the terrible days of reconstruction which followed. To understand the significance of Washington's life and work it is necessary to keep in mind the outstanding political and economic facts of the period following the war of secession.

The Political Situation

The Thirteenth Amendment completed the abolition of slavery and insured the personal freedom of the Negroes. The Fourteenth Amendment guaranteed the rights of citizenship to Negroes, while the Fifteenth Amendment was intended to safeguard their right of suffrage. At the same time many Confederate officials and soldiers were temporarily disfranchised. Not until 1872 were their political disabilities removed and even then about 750 leaders were permanently disfranchised. The former state governments in the South were not recognized or allowed to function. Five governors were imprisoned, and in all the Southern States provisional governors were appointed by the President. Garrisons of Federal troops were stationed throughout the South and dominated the situation. The last of these troops were not removed until 1877. Swarms of "carpet-baggers" swooped down from the North and were assisted by southern "scalawags" in their efforts to exploit the defeated whites. In many electorates the Negro voters were in a majority. They were for the most part illiterate and were, of course, wholly inexperienced in the art of government. Many ignorant blacks were used as tools by the unprincipled "carpet-baggers." Under such circumstances it was inevitable that excesses should occur. Negro governments were set up throughout the South. In South Carolina, eight years after the war ended, two-thirds of the Legislature and four out of five Congressmen were Negroes. Two Negroes were elected to the United States Senate from Mississippi, Senator Bruce serving until 1881. As late as 1876 South Carolina, North Carolina, Florida, Alabama, Mississippi and Louisiana were represented in the House by one or more Negroes. Wild extravagance, gross corruption and extreme inefficiency everywhere prevailed. Taxes were increased at a terrific rate, and yet state debts piled higher and higher. In South Carolina taxes increased 500 per cent from 1860 to 1871, while the taxable value decreased nearly 300 per cent during the same period. The state debt of South Carolina increased 600 per cent. from 1868 to 1872, while the debt of Louisiana increased more than 700 per cent. during these four years. In some states the amount of the state debt was unknown, since no record of bond issues had been preserved. The impoverished planters were unable to carry the intolerable burden of taxes, and in large numbers gave up their lands to be sold by the sheriff. In Mississippi twenty per cent. of the total acreage of the state was forfeited for taxes. The tables were being turned on the former slave-owners with a vengeance.

Picture the situation for a moment. Men never lived who had more pride than the leaders of the old South. In spite of gallant resistance and unbounded self-sacrifice, they had been overpowered by superior force. Almost to a man they believed their cause to have been just and looked upon the North as the aggressor and violator. Now they found themselves defeated, with many of their leaders imprisoned or disfranchised, with an army of occupation stationed on their soil, with the government in the hands of former slaves and hated Yankees. Their bitterness was greatly intensified by the presence of a large number of black troops in the army of occupation. Under these circumstances the whites resorted to intimidation and violence against the Negroes. The Ku Klux Klan spread like wildfire throughout the Southern States. They took the law into their own hands and sought by intimidation and violence to do what they were unable to do by ballot or processes of orderly government. Houses were surrounded in the night and burned, and the inmates shot as they fled. Tar and feathers were frequently applied to Negroes and "carpetbaggers." Riots were not uncommon. "Between 1866 and 1879 more than three thousand Negroes were summarily killed." Bitterness was further intensified by the ruthlessness with which General Grant suppressed the Klan in certain sections.

By 1876 the southern whites had recovered control of their state governments and were dominant in the House at Washington. That this result was accomplished by intimidating Negroes to such an extent that large numbers of them were afraid to vote cannot be denied. "Before the close of the decade," says Brawley, "by intimidation, the theft, suppression or exchange of the ballot boxes, the removal of the polls to unknown places, false certifications, and illegal arrest on the day before an election, the Negro vote had been rendered ineffectual in every state of the South." In 1890 began a series of electoral qualifications which in actual practice barred most Negroes from the polls. Poll-tax and educational restrictions reduced the number of Negroes who registered in 1890 to 8,615 out of 147,000 Negroes of voting age. In 1898 Louisiana invented the so-called "grandfather clause," which excused from her disfranchising act all descendants of men who had voted before the Civil War, thus admitting to suffrage most white men who were illiterate and without property and excluding most Negroes. Thus, in one way or another, in actual practice most Negroes are to-day barred from the polls.[1]

The Economic Situation

The first significant fact to keep in mind is that the entire South was almost in bankruptcy at the end of the war. The expense of the war had been exceedingly heavy, the devastation in the invaded areas was stupendous, the normal processes of production and distribution had ceased to function, the railways were sadly dilapidated, slave property to the extent of two billion dollars had been swept away, the gentlemen of the South were almost wholly unaccustomed to manual labor. "Throughout the first winter after the war the whole South was on the verge of starvation."

It is not surprising that when fear of the whip was removed many former slaves took a holiday and refused to work any harder than was absolutely necessary to keep alive. Throughout the South manual toil and slavery had so long been linked that it was difficult to get either whites or blacks to regard physical labor as an honorable or respectable activity. Large numbers of Negroes wandered aimlessly about the country. Thieving was common.

Immediately after the war the provisional governments passed the so-called Black Code, which, by establishing a rigid apprentice system and by severe vagrancy laws, reduced many Negroes to what was actual slavery. This code, however, was practically overthrown by the operation of the Federal Government's Freedmen's Bureau. The wage system was then tried, but in general proved to be unsatisfactory both to whites and blacks. The rental system worked better, but was often unsatisfactory to the Negro because of the high rents charged. The share system, which became the most general of all systems, was open to serious abuse because it was usually necessary for the owner to advance

[1] For a summary of the laws which disqualify most Negro voters see Benjamin Brawley, A Short History of the American Negro, pp. 153-155. See also an excellent article by W. A. Dunning, The Atlantic Monthtly, Vol. 88, pp. 437-449.

provisions to the tenant until the crop was harvested. This opened the way for exorbitant charges, and it is not a serious exaggeration to say, as does a recent writer, that at harvest time the Negro "always came out just a few dollars behind." Thus he would begin each year in debt to the land-owner. In many cases he was led by easy stages into a degree of peonage which was not far removed from slavery.

Severe vagrancy laws persisted throughout the South. There can be no doubt that the presence of large numbers of idle Negroes was a distinct menace to a community. Some of the vagrancy laws were exceedingly drastic. In some cases the laws were so extreme that "a man could not stop work without technically committing a crime." Long sentences for trivial offences were a common occurrence. The large number of prisoners constantly in custody led to the custom of leasing convicts for outside labor. The chain-gang soon became a common sight in many communities. Since most of the prisoners were Negroes, race feeling was intense, and it is not surprising that gross abuses occurred. Cruelty was frequently shown to prisoners, and the mortality rate was exceedingly high. Moreover, mob violence was often resorted to without waiting for due process of law. The number of Negro lynchings has been appalling, numbering a total of 3,182 between the years 1885 and 1925.

2. WHAT DID WASHINGTON DO?

The life of Garrison marks the first milestone in the advance of the Negro race in America, in its release from slavery. The life of Booker T. Washington marks the second, in the heroic struggle of the Negro for economic freedom and racial uplift. As we are fortunate in possessing an autobiography of Mr. Washington, we shall as far as possible let him tell his own story.[2]

[2] We are chiefly indebted for the account of Mr. Washington's early life to his "Up From Slavery," and for his later life to "Booker T. Washington, Builder of a Civilization," by Emmett J. Scott and Lyman Beecher Stowe, as well as to Mr. Washington's other works. Since frequent breaks in the narrative become a typographical irritation to the reader, such omissions will not ordinarily be indicated.

"I was born a slave," he says, "on a plantation in Franklin County, Virginia. I am not quite sure of the exact place or exact date of my birth. The year was 1858 or 1859. The earliest impressions I can now recall are of the plantation and the slave quarters. My life had its beginning in the midst of the most miserable, desolate, and discouraging surroundings. I was born in a typical log cabin, about fourteen by sixteen feet square. In this cabin I lived with my mother and a brother and sister till after the Civil War, when we were all declared free.

"In the slave quarters, and even later, I heard whispered conversations of the tortures which the slaves suffered in the slave ship while being conveyed from Africa to America. Of my father I know even less than of my mother. I do not even know his name. Whoever he was, I never heard of his taking the least interest in me or providing in any way for my rearing. There was no wooden floor in our cabin, the naked earth being used as a floor. I cannot remember having slept in a bed until after our family was declared free by the Emancipation Proclamation. Three children—John, my older brother; Amanda, my sister, and myself—slept in a bundle of filthy rags laid upon the dirt floor. There was no period of my life that was devoted to play. From the time that I can remember anything, almost every day of my life has been occupied in some kind of labor. I had no schooling whatever while I was a slave."

As soon as they were free, the mother and her children started on foot a journey of several hundred miles, to join her husband in West Virginia. Here as a child Booker began tending a furnace. He had an intense longing to get an education, which had always been denied the slaves; but there was not at the time a single Negro in the district who could read or write. With no one to teach him, he began to devour an old spelling book. When a young Negro arrived who could teach, the new day-school, night-school and Sunday-school were always crowded, and Booker began to attend at night. When the roll was first called he had no second name, so promptly invented one, and gave his name as "Booker Washington." Soon after, he was forced, through poverty, to leave the school and begin work in a coal mine. He continues: "One day, while at work in the coal mine, I happened to overhear two miners talking about a great school for colored people somewhere in Virginia. In the darkness of the mine I noiselessly crept as close as I could. It seemed to me that it must be the greatest place on earth, and not even Heaven presented more attractions for me at that time than did the Hampton Normal and Agricultural Institute in Virginia, about which these men were talking. This thought was with me day and night."

In order to save money to attend this school he began to work for a New England woman, who was the wife of General Ruffner, at five dollars a month. Here for a year and a half he learned the lessons of industry, cleanliness, punctuality, orderliness and honesty, upon which his character and work were afterward founded.

Finally the great day came, and he started for Hampton on foot, on this long journey of five hundred miles. In Richmond, Virginia, he walked the streets penniless and hungry and slept on the ground under a sidewalk at night. He reached Hampton with fifty cents in his pocket with which to get an education, only to find the school crowded and a gloomy prospect of being refused admission.

"As soon as possible after reaching the grounds of the Hampton Institute, I presented myself before the head teacher for assignment to a class. Having been so long without proper food, a bath and a change of clothing, I felt I could hardly blame her if she got the idea that I was a worthless loafer or tramp. After some hours had passed, the head teacher said to me: 'The adjoining recitation-room needs sweeping. Take the broom and sweep it.' It occurred to me at once that here was my chance. I swept the recitation-room three times. Then I got a dusting-cloth and I dusted it four times. All the woodwork around the walls, every bench, table and desk, I went over four times with my dusting-cloth. When I was through, I reported to the head teacher. She went into the room and inspected the floor and closets; then she took her handkerchief and rubbed it on the woodwork about the walls, and over the table and benches. When she was unable to find one bit of dirt on the floor, or a particle of dust on any of the furniture, she quietly remarked, 'I guess you will do to enter this institution.' I was one of the happiest souls on earth. The sweeping of that room was my college examination. Miss Mary F. Mackie, the head teacher, offered me a position as janitor. This, of course, I gladly accepted. I had to rise by four o'clock in the morning, in order to build the fires and have a little time in which to prepare my lessons.

"Life at Hampton was a revelation to me; was constantly taking me into a new world. The matter of having meals at regular hours, of eating on a tablecloth, using a napkin, the use of the bathtub and of the toothbrush, as well as the use of sheets on the bed, were all new to me. The greatest benefits that I got out of my life at the Hampton Institute, perhaps, may be classified under two heads: First, was contact with a great man, General S. C. Armstrong, who was, in my opinion, the rarest, strongest, and most beautiful character that it has ever been my privilege to meet. Second, at Hampton, for the first time, I learned what education was expected to do for an individual. I not only learned that it was not a disgrace to labor, but learned to love labor, not alone for its financial value, but for labor's own sake and for the independence and self-reliance which the ability to do something which the world wants done, brings. At that institution I got my first taste of what it meant to live a life of unselfishness. The great and prevailing idea that seemed to take possession of every one was to prepare himself to lift up the people at his home. No one seemed to think of himself. And the officers and the teachers, what a rare set of human beings they were! They worked for the students night and day, in season and out of season.

"The education that I received at Hampton out of the textbooks was but a small part of what I learned there. Perhaps the most valuable thing that I got out of my second year was an understanding of the use and value of the

Bible. The lessons taught me in that respect took such a hold upon me that at the present time, when I am at home, no matter how busy I am, I always make it a rule to read a chapter or a portion of a chapter in the morning, before beginning the work of the day."

Booker was graduated from Hampton as penniless as he had entered it, and returned to his former home in Malden to teach his people. Here his day-and-night-school was crowded, as were also the reading room and the debating society which he started. When it was observed that the students sent by him were the best prepared of those coming to Hampton, he was called back to the institution as a teacher. In his invaluable association with General Armstrong he was assigned the charge of the poorer students in the night-school.

As he did with all his might each duty assigned him, there soon came what later proved to be the great opportunity of his life, to open a new institution at Tuskegee. At first sight it did not seem very promising to open a school with thirty poor colored students, without land, buildings, or teachers, on a deserted plantation, equipped with a kitchen, a stable and a hen-house which had to serve as classrooms. Mr. Washington found Tuskegee a little town of two thousand inhabitants, in the Black Belt of the South. About half of the town and three-quarters of the county were colored people. During the first month he explored the county on foot, looking for pupils. Conditions were depressing. Most of the colored farmers' crops were mortgaged and they were in debt. Whole families lived in one room.

On July 4, 1881, Mr. Washington, undaunted, opened his school with thirty pupils, most of whom were public school teachers, some of them nearly forty years of age. But they were in earnest. As there was no provision for land, buildings or apparatus, Mr. Washington began the school in a dilapidated shanty and the colored Methodist Church. When it rained a student had to hold an umbrella over the teacher.

As the accommodations were utterly inadequate, they found an old abandoned plantation of a thousand acres for sale at five hundred dollars, or about fifty cents an acre. The house had burned down, and there was nothing on that old barren hill but sand and clay. But it was just such poor soil that his students would often be compelled to cultivate if they ever got any land, and it would be a good place on which to overcome obstacles.

Accordingly, Booker borrowed $250 from a Hampton friend and took possession. The old stable and hen-house were used as recitation rooms. To clear the land, Washington proposed a "chopping bee," but this went against the grain of the former slaves, who had come there "to be educated and not to work." However, Booker shouldered his own axe, and by setting an example of working every afternoon with the entire school, finally cleared some twenty acres and planted a crop.

They had to contend not only with obstacles on the plantation, but all about them. Because Mr. Washington looked upon the task "as an economic one instead of a theological one," he was at first met with suspicion and almost universal opposition from the leaders of his own race. Many of the white men believed he was "spoiling the niggers by education." Only sixteen years previous a Negro could not be taught from books without the teacher receiving the condemnation of the law or of public opinion.

From the first, Washington inculcated the principle that they were "to learn by doing." They were being educated not only to make a living, but to make a life; and they were to learn by living, then and there. They now began to erect the first of the forty buildings that were constructed in the next twenty years by student labor. After repeated failures in brickmaking, Booker finally pawned and lost his own watch to make the last experiment, which was finally successful.

"The principle of industrial education has been carried out in the building of our own wagons, carts, and buggies, from the first. The plan of having the students make the furniture is still followed. After the student has left the night-school he enters the day-school, where he takes academic branches four days in a week, and works at his trade two days. No student, no matter how much money he may be able to command, is permitted to go through school without doing manual labor. In fact, the industrial work is now as popular as the academic branches." All this came with the growth of the boarding department, where the students could be trained in having regular meals well cooked and served by themselves. Here students, who at home had never sat down to a regular meal in their lives, could be influenced during all their waking hours."

But the rapid growth of the school created a pressing financial problem. In order to raise funds, General Armstrong proposed to make a tour of the North with Booker Washington, with the object of introducing him to the people of that section. With the General's characteristic selfless generosity, all the money was to go to Tuskegee.

At this time Mr. Washington walked two miles in a storm to spend three hours with a gentleman in New England who gave him nothing. Two years later, unasked, he sent him $10,000. Collis P. Huntington first gave him two dollars, but on his last visit he gave $50,000. When Mr. Washington first saw Andrew Carnegie, he seemed to take little interest in the school. After years of cultivation, he gave the money for a library building and $600,000 for the endowment fund.

When the expenses of Tuskegee rose to some $300,000 a year, Mr. Washington was responsible for raising about half of that sum. After hearing him speak in Madison Square Garden, Mr. H. H. Rogers, then the active head of the Standard Oil Company, wired for Mr. Washington to come to his office and, unasked, gave him $10,000. He later helped to finance the rural school extension work in the great task of race-building. An anonymous donor, after reading the school's annual report, offered $250,000 towards the building fund.

Booker Washington finally developed not only as a

financier and executive, but as a really great orator. His first notable speech was in Madison, Wisconsin, before the National Educational Association, to an audience of some four thousand. The Southerners present were surprised to hear no single word of abuse in his address, where full credit was given the South for whatever help it had given the Negro. Mr. Washington's conviction was that progress could best be gained by co-operation, by bringing the races together in friendly relations for the benefit of both, instead of fighting in bitterness.

In 1893 he traveled two thousand miles to speak for five minutes to an audience of two thousand southern white people. Following this came the Atlanta Exposition in 1895 Booker Washington was asked to speak at the opening meeting. This was the first time in history that a Negro had been asked to speak on the same platform with a southern white man on an important national occasion. It was a great audience of northern and southern whites and Negroes all together, and a single unfortunate remark might have put back for years the clock that marked the advance in race relationships.

Mr. Washington thus tells the story of this epoch-making speech: "Almost the first thing that I heard when I got off the train in that city was an expression something like this, from an old colored man near by: 'Dat's de man of my race what's gwine to make a speech at de Exposition to-morrow. I'se sho' gwine to hear him.' I did not sleep much that night. The next morning, before day, I went carefully over what I intended to say. I also kneeled down and asked God's blessing upon my effort. I make it a rule never to go before an audience, on any occasion, without asking the blessing of God upon what I want to say.

"The first thing that I remember, after I had finished speaking, was that Governor Bullock rushed across the platform and took me by the hand, and that others did the same. When I went into the business part of the city I was surprised to find myself pointed out and surrounded by a crowd of men who wished to shake hands with me. This was kept up on every street. The editor of the Atlanta Constitution telegraphed to a New York paper: 'Professor Booker T. Washington's address yesterday was one of the most notable ever delivered to a southern audience. The address was a revelation. The whole speech is a platform upon which blacks and whites can stand with full justice to each other.'"

Mr. James Creelman, the war correspondent, wrote in the New York World: "While President Cleveland was waiting to send the electric spark that started the machinery of the Atlanta Exposition, a Negro Moses stood before a great audience of white people and delivered an oration that marks a new epoch in the history of the South. With his whole face lit up with the fire of prophecy, Clark Howell said, 'That man's speech is the beginning of a moral revolution in America.' Professor Booker T. Washington must rank from this time forth as the foremost man of his race in America. There was a remarkable figure: tall, bony, straight as a Sioux chief, high forehead, straight nose, heavy jaws, and strong, determined mouth, with big white teeth, piercing eyes, and a commanding manner. . . The whole audience was on its feet in a delirium of applause. I have heard the great orators of many countries, but not even Gladstone himself could have pleaded a cause with more consummate power than did this angular Negro. Most of the Negroes in the audience were crying."

Mr. Washington was later invited by the Governor and City Council to address the citizens of Charleston, near his birthplace. In Richmond, Virginia, the former capital of the southern Confederacy, where twenty-five years before he had slept in poverty under the sidewalk night by night on his way to school, the State Legislature and City Council attended in a body the great meeting in the Academy of Music. Probably the two events which gave Mr. Washington his wide reputation were his Atlanta address and the publication of his book, "Up From Slavery," in 1900. Ten thousand copies of the book were soon sold, and it was published widely in European languages. One anonymous donor upon reading the book sent Mr. Washington $1,000, and later, unasked, contributed $250,000 toward the building fund.

Twenty years after beginning in a broken-down shanty and an old hen-house, Booker Washington had built up at Tuskegee a great institution of sixty-six buildings and 2300 acres of land, one thousand of which were cultivated by the students. The property and endowment were valued at $1,700,000. The number of students had grown from thirty to 1,400, drawn from twenty-seven states. He had disproved the assertion that the Negro was essentially and necessarily inferior, slipshod and lazy, by conducting an institution—now almost as large as Yale, running like clockwork long after his death—without a single white man connected with the organization. Tuskegee is a masterpiece of administration, and has furnished a model for hundreds of institutions among the white people and in other lands. Visitors from Oxford and Cambridge, educators from Europe and Asia, often visit Tuskegee and Hampton for models of a new type of education.

The work of Booker Washington had long been projected beyond Tuskegee. He soon learned that 85 per cent. of the Negroes of the Gulf States lived on the land and were dependent on agriculture. Accordingly, he began to go out on Sundays to give the people simple talks on how to improve their lot. Mr. Washington and his teachers went weekly to the churches, schools, farms and homes of the people to show them "how they could make their farms more productive, their homes more comfortable, their schools more useful and their church services more inspiring." They invited the farmers to come to the school farm to learn deep-plowing, and a variety of crops to supplement their sole reliance on cotton. Mrs. Washington also gathered the idle women into women's clubs to teach them to improve their homes and living conditions. She established a model country school, or farm home, where the pupils and the people of the community are taught how to live on a farm. Soon these schools were multiplied throughout the South under the Rural School Extension Department. Julius Rosenwald became deeply interested in the uplift of the Negro. He offered $300 for every similar amount given by the Negroes in rural communities for new, modern school-houses. The work is still spreading. Mr. Rosenwald also offered $25,000 to every city in America that would raise three times this amount for a colored Y. M. C. A. building. Some fifteen cities have already taken advantage of his generous offer.

The extension work of Tuskegee began long before that of the demonstration agents of the United States Department of Agriculture. One of the first colored farmers to adopt the new method of deep-plowing got speedy results. He soon bought five hundred acres of land and was prospering. In a community where the average production of sweet potatoes had been only forty-nine bushels to the acre, one of the Tuskegee graduates produced 266 bushels to the acre. Such practical results soon laid the foundation of better economic conditions upon which the whole uplift of the race had to be founded.

The agents of Tuskegee from their model farm were soon introducing better breeds of cattle, hogs and chickens. They sent out the first "Jessup wagon," as a kind of traveling farmers' school. They took samples of their better-bred stock, seeds, corn and cotton. They soon printed and distributed pamphlets prepared by the Tuskegee Agricultural Research Department on such subjects as school gardening, improvement of country schools, cotton-growing, how to fight insect pests, etc. Every January for two weeks the people were invited to the Farmers' Short Course at the school. Then followed the annual farmers' conference. Mr. Washington and others addressed them on such questions as, "What kind of a house do you live in?" "What kind of schoolhouse have you?" "What kind of a church?" "Where does your pastor live?" Prizes were offered for the greatest progress.

Next came the summer school for teachers, attended by some five hundred teachers gathered from over fifteen states. They are instructed not only in teachers-training courses, but also in practical subjects like canning, basket- and broom-making, needlework and various forms of manual training.

Following the plan which Booker Washington studied in Denmark, the graduates of the agricultural department are helped to settle on the land on forty-acre farms and are given ten years in which to pay for the land. It is proposed to follow the Denmark plan for a co-operative dairy, fruit-growing, poultry and live-stock association. From the first, Booker Washington was engaged not only in conducting a school, but in educating a race. Methods were improved, mortgages were paid off, land bought and men began to witness the slow but steady uplift of the Negro.

Extension schools are now conducted throughout the state in agriculture and home economics. These are advertised like a country circus. As one result, the changed condition of the farmers of Mason County may be taken. When Mr. Washington began here the soil was exhausted, the Negroes were mostly shiftless and ignorant, and less than a hundred in the county owned their own land. Today 95 per cent. of the 3800 Negroes who are farmers in this county operate their own farms, either as cash tenants or owners, with an average of 122 acres per farmer.

Following the extension work in Alabama, Mr. Washington made wide tours through nine of the Southern States to widen his work for the race. In 1884 he founded the Teachers' Institute. In 1891 the Annual Tuskegee Negro Conference was called into existence. Then followed the Greenwood Hospital. In 1893 he started the Ministers' Night School, conducted by the Bible Training School of the Institute. In 1895 the Building and Loan Association was established, and a movement for better homes is steadily progressing. The Town Library and Reading Room were followed by the County Fair in 1898, to stimulate the farmers. In 1900 he organized the National Negro Business League and served as its president until his death.

The terrific pace at which Mr. Washington worked began finally to tell upon even his iron constitution. In twenty years he took but one vacation, when in 1889 some personal friends put money into his hands and forced him and his wife to spend three months in Europe. He was so tired that on the voyage over he slept for fifteen hours a day. In Europe he made a tour of Holland, Belgium, France and England. At Windsor Castle he was the guest of Queen Victoria at tea. His interview with Henry M. Stanley convinced him that there was no hope for the American Negro in Africa. At this time the Duke and Duchess of Sutherland became permanent friends of the work at Tuskegee.

In 1910 Mr. Washington made a second journey through Europe to study the backward peoples and classes. The result of his researches he records in "The Man Farthest Down." Here he studied the Labour Movement in Great Britain, the conditions of industrial and agricultural labor in Italy, Hungary and Austria; and among the Poles, Russians and other races. His most interesting chapter is on the rise of the farmers of Denmark through their wonderful Co-operatives.

Emmett Scott, his former secretary, gives us the picture of a typical day's work of this physical, intellectual and moral giant. As usual, he rose at six, visited his poultry and pigs and rode on horseback over the grounds and farm, inspecting buildings, crops and conditions until eight o'clock. He now went to his office, attended to his morning's mail and dictated replies for an hour. He then caught the train to Atlanta, where he arrived at two in the afternoon and shook hands with some four hundred persons gathered to meet him. Arrived at the Government Building, he shook hands with another throng. He next dined with Negro leaders and made a tour of the city by motor, visiting several Negro schools and making a half-hour address at each, with all the earnestness of his nature. After supper he spoke to twelve hundred people in the Armory for an hour and a half. Following this he spoke for twenty minutes at a banquet given in his honor. Interviews with various leaders kept him up until one o'clock. After four hours' sleep, he caught an early train which brought him to the school again at ten-thirty. He at once began work in his office and continued until the late afternoon, when he went for his daily ride. His incoming mail averaged over a hundred and twenty-five letters and his out-going over five hundred letters a day. After supper he presided at the Executive Council and then attended the chapel exercises. At ten o'clock he inspected the grounds and buildings before going to bed.

In addition to his close supervision of Tuskegee, his public speaking all over the United States, and his time spent in raising hundreds of thousands of dollars, he found time in his crowded life to write not less than a dozen volumes. His "Up From Slavery" was supplemented by "Working with the Hands," "The Story of My Life and Work," and "My Larger Education." His practical chapel talks were collected in his "Character Building." "The Story of the Negro" is told in two large volumes. He wrote also "The Future of the American Negro," "Sowing and Reaping", "Tuskegee and Its People" and "The Negro in Business."

3. WHAT DID WASHINGTON SAY?

Mr. Washington's first contribution was in the field of practical education. Here he saw the way to eliminate ignorance and its resultant crime. Mr. Washington writes, "In nine cases out of ten the crimes which serve to give an excuse for mob violence are committed by men who are without property, without homes, and without education except what they have picked up in the city slums, in prisons, or on the chain-gang. The individuals who commit crimes of violence and crimes that are due to lack of self-control are individuals who are, for the most part, ignorant. The decrease in lynching in the Southern States is an index of the steady growth of the South in wealth, in industry, in education, and in individual liberty."[3]

[3] In the Outlook of March 14, 1914, Mr. Washington wrote, "A few weeks ago three of the most prominent white men in Mississippi were shot and killed by two colored boys. Investigation brought to light that no one had taught these boys the use of books, but some one had taught them, as mere children, the use of cocaine and whiskey. These two ignorant boys created a 'reign of murder,' in the course of which three white men, four colored men and one colored woman

Under its great president, Tuskegee came to incarnate the identity between real education and actual life. Concerning this, Mr. Washington said in an article in the Annals of the American Academy of Political and Social Science for September 1913, "If I were asked what I believe to be greatest advance which Negro education has made since emancipation I should say that it has been in two directions: first, the change which has taken place among the masses of the Negro people as to what education really is; and, second, the change that has taken place among the masses of the white people in the South toward Negro education itself. The Negro learned in slavery to work but he did not learn to respect labor. On the contrary, the Negro was constantly taught, directly and indirectly during slavery times, that labor was a curse. The Negro thought freedom must, in some way, mean freedom from labor. The students at Tuskegee are divided into two groups: the day students who work in the classroom half the week and the other half on the farm and in the shops, and the night students who work all day on the farm or in the shops and then attend school at night. The great majority of the day students have fought their way in from the night school. All students of both groups receive in the course of a week a fairly even balance between theory and practice."

Professor Paul Monroe of the Teachers College of Columbia University says, "My interest in Tuskegee and a few similar institutions is founded on the fact that here I find illustrated the two most marked tendencies which are being formulated in the most advanced educational thought, but are being worked out slowly and with great difficulty. These tendencies are: first, the endeavor to draw the subject matter of education, or the 'stuff' of schoolroom work, directly

---

met death. As soon as the shooting was over a crazed mob shot the two boys full of bullet-holes and then burned their bodies in the public streets. Now this is the kind of thing, more or less varied in form, that takes place too often in our country. Why? The answer is simple: it is dense ignorance on the part of the Negro and indifference arising out of a lack of knowledge of conditions on the part of the white people."

from the life of the pupils; and second, to relate the outcome of education to life's activities, occupations and duties. This is the ideal at Tuskegee, and, to a much greater extent than in any other institution I know of, the practice; so that the institution is working along not only the lines of practical endeavor, but of the most advanced educational thought. To such an extent is this true that Tuskegee and Hampton are of quite as great interest to the student of education on account of the illumination they are giving to educational theory as they are to those interested practically in the elevation of the Negro people and in the solution of a serious social problem."

Mr. Washington believed that education was a matter of character expressed in concrete habits of industry, honesty and right conduct. Speaking before the National Council of Congregational Churches on October 25, 1915, Mr. Washington said, "There is sometimes much talk about the inferiority of the Negro. In practice, however, the idea appears to be that he is a sort of super-man. He is expected with about one-fifth or one-tenth of what the whites receive for their education to make as much progress as they are making. Taking the Southern States as a whole, about $10.23 per capita is spent in educating the average black child."

Mr. Washington concludes the last volume of his "Story of the Negro" as follows: "In slavery the progress of the Negro was a menace to the white man. The security of the white master depended upon the ignorance of the black slave. In freedom the security and happiness of each race depends, to a very large extent, on the education and the progress of the other. The problem of slavery was to keep the Negro down; the problem of freedom is to raise him up . . . The story of the Negro, in the last analysis, is simply the story of the man farthest down; as he raised himself he raised every other man who is above him."

Mr. Washington's second great message was on the breaking down of race prejudice, by means of co-operation and justice in race relations. Before his great Atlanta Exposition address Mr. Washington wrote, "The thing that was uppermost in my mind was the desire to say something that would cement the friendship of the races and bring about hearty co-operation between them." On that occasion, he said in part: "One-third of the population of the South is of the Negro race. No enterprise seeking the material, civil, or moral welfare of this section can disregard this element of our population and reach the highest success. . . This is a recognition that will do more to cement the friendship of the two races than any occurrence since the dawn of our freedom. . . A ship lost at sea for many days suddenly sighted a friendly vessel. From the mast of the unfortunate vessel was seen a signal, 'Water, water; we die of thirst!' The answer came back from the friendly vessel at once, 'Cast down your bucket where you are.' . . To those of my race who depend on bettering their condition I would say: 'Cast down your bucket where you are'—cast it down in making friends in every manly way of the people of all races by whom we are surrounded. Cast it down in agriculture, mechanics in commerce, in domestic service, and in the professions. . . In the great leap from slavery to freedom we may overlook the fact that the masses of us are to live by the productions of our hands, and fail to keep in mind that we shall prosper in proportion as we learn to dignify and glorify common labor. It is at the bottom of life we must begin, and not at the top.

"To those of the white race I would repeat, 'Cast down your bucket where you are! Cast it down among the millions of Negroes whose habits you know, whose fidelity and love you have tested in days when to have proved treacherous meant the ruin of your firesides. Cast down your bucket among these people who have, without strikes and labor wars, tilled your fields, cleared your forests, builded your railroads and cities . . . the most patient, faithful, law-abiding, and unresentful people that the world has seen. *In all things that are purely social we can be as separate as the fingers, yet one as the hand in all things essential to mutual progress.* There is no defence or security for any of us except in the highest intelligence and development of all."

In the New Republic he wrote strongly against segregation laws which were being passed in the South. He did not, however, favor race amalgamation, and wrote, "I have never looked upon amalgamation as offering a solution of the so-called race problem, and I know very few Negroes who favor it, or even think of it, for that matter. What those whom I have heard discuss the matter do object to are laws which enable the father to escape his responsibility, or prevent him from accepting and exercising it, when he has children by colored women." Yet he felt that the Negro could not be neglected or degraded without dragging down both races, as he said, "One cannot hold another in a ditch without himself staying in a ditch." He said, "The time will come when the Negro in the South will be accorded all the political rights which his ability, character, and material possessions entitle him to. I believe in universal, free suffrage, but I believe that in the South we are confronted with peculiar conditions that justify the protection of the ballot in many of the states; but whatever tests are required, they should be made to apply with equal and exact justice to both races."

Mr. Washington never disputed about what seemed to him the academic question of social equality. He pleaded for justice and intercourse in commercial and civil relations, saying, "What is termed social recognition was a question I never discussed." He says, in "My Larger Education," "the only way to hold people together is by means of a constructive, progressive program. It is not argument, nor criticism, nor hatred, but work in constructive effort, that gets hold of men and binds them together in a way to make them rally to the support of a common cause."

If he were alive today, he would greatly rejoice to see the rise and rapid growth of the movement known as The Commission on Interracial Co-operation, founded by John J. Eagan and organized by his southern white and colored associates with "the avowed intention of securing for the Negro in every community fair and just treatment under the law as well as an equitable share in all privileges and benefits for which he is taxed as a citizen." Over a thousand interracial committees of white and colored men throughout the cities, towns and counties, where the two races are found side by side, are helping to solve the race problem whose final solution can only be found not in conflict but in co-operation.

4. WHAT HAPPENED TO WASHINGTON?

Booker Washington's long life was one unbroken series of overcoming terrific obstacles. He began in slavery, poverty and ignorance, not as a man popular and successful. "For many years he had to fight his way inch by inch against the bitterest opposition, not only of the whites but also of his own race."

It must never be forgotten that the problem of race relations has been aggravated and embittered by the Civil War and the days of the Northern "carpet-baggers" during the miserable Reconstruction period. Great Britain freed her slaves without a civil war, paying fair compensation for every slave that was freed. The result is that there is no such bitterness and hostility between the two races in the West Indies, for instance, as is found in some parts of America.

Mr. Washington was one of the first to bridge the gulf of racial antagonism and maintain an unbroken attitude of persistent goodwill toward the white man, whatever injustice his race had suffered in the past or present. In his Atlanta address, he had said, "The wisest among my race understand that the agitation of questions of social equality is the extremest folly, and that progress in the enjoyment of all the privileges that will come to us must be the result of severe and constant struggle rather than of artificial forcing."

Such sentiments were bitterly resented by a portion of his own people, and he was accused of encouraging a policy of submission to injustice. Some Negroes were smarting under the memory of the long-continued wrongs suffered by their race and of still continued personal humiliation and frequent insult. It is no wonder if they and their race are bitter.

They have abundant reason to be. But Booker Washington found a yet more excellent way. He found that love works better than hate, even when hatred is justified. If his race follows him it may prove that you cannot build a great reform on the dogmatism of hatred, but that in the end love never fails.

We do not mean, however, to criticize the more radical wing of the movement among the colored people, especially in the North. There are many who are prepared to use every lawful means of fighting for their rights and of opposing their wrongs. This policy will have its place just as the outspoken agitation of Garrison had. The white man at least, who has so long used force in his relation to the darker and more backward races all over the world, can hardly ask that an oppressed and handicapped race shall rise above his own ethical standards. He can hardly expect that a large proportion of the colored people shall, like Booker Washington, in the matter of character, intelligence, education, magnanimity and persistent goodwill in the face of indignity or injustice, be superior to the large majority of the white race. But he should at least appreciate the great work done by leaders of both races, like Booker Washington and John J. Eagan, to bring the two peoples into closer co-operation.

For nothing was Mr. Washington so bitterly attacked as when he was invited to dinner with President Roosevelt and his family at the White House. Feeling was so deeply stirred over this incident that both the President and Mr. Washington received many threats against their lives. A Negro confessed later that he came to Tuskegee in the pay of a group of white men in Louisiana to assassinate Mr. Washington. He was hurt in jumping from the train and being kindly nursed for some weeks in Mr. Washington's hospital at the Institute, never fulfilled his commission. Mr. Washington says, "The public interest aroused by this dinner seemed all the more extraordinary and uncalled for because, on previous occasions, I had taken tea with Queen Victoria at Windsor Castle; I had dined with the governors of nearly every state in the North; I had dined in the same room with

President McKinley at Chicago at the Peace-jubilee dinner; and I had dined with ex-President Harrison in Paris, and with many other prominent public men."

Under abuse, misrepresentation and opposition, Mr. Washington usually remained silent. He says, "My experience convinces me that the thing to do when one feels sure that he has said and done the right thing and is condemned, is to stand still and keep quiet." While Mr. Washington was misunderstood and opposed by some, few men have received such endorsement and recognition. Booker Washington was the first man of his race to receive an honorary M.A. degree at Harvard. When President Eliot visited Tuskegee at its twenty-fifth anniversary, he said, "The oldest and now largest American institution of learning was more than two hundred years in arriving at the possession of much less land, fewer buildings, and a smaller quick capital than Tuskegee has come to possess in twenty-five years."

Mr. Washington was on friendly relations with or well-known personally to five Presidents—Benjamin Harrison, Grover Cleveland, William McKinley, Theodore Roosevelt, and William Howard Taft. President Cleveland congratulated him upon his Atlanta address and had him in his home in Princeton. President McKinley and his cabinet officers paid a special visit to Tuskegee. The Alabama State Legislature adjourned in a body and with the Governor, the state officials and several generals back from the Spanish-American War, attended the exercises at Tuskegee. President McKinley said, "The Tuskegee Normal and Industrial Institute is ideal in its conception. This unique educational experiment has attracted the attention and won the support even of conservative philanthropists in all sections of the country. . . To speak of Tuskegee without paying special tribute to Booker T. Washington's genius and perseverance would be impossible." Mr. Long, then Secretary of the Navy, said, "God bless the orator, philanthropist, and disciple of the Great Master—who, if he were on earth, would be doing the same work—Booker T. Washington." President Roosevelt visited Mr. Washington at Tuskegee and frequently corresponded with him or conferred with him regarding appointments in the South, and the progress of the Negro.

Roosevelt, Cleveland and President Eliot served on a committee to raise a memorial fund for Tuskegee. Mr. Washington made a deep impression on Prince Henry of Prussia. He dined with the King and Queen of Denmark and speaks amusingly of the sensations of the former slave boy who had eaten his syrup from a tin plate, then taking dinner upon dishes of gold. He had the confidence and friendship of John D. Rockefeller and Andrew Carnegie, H. H. Rogers and many industrial leaders.

5. WHAT KIND OF A MAN WAS WASHINGTON?

His remarkably few faults and many virtues stand out with transparent clarity. Coupled with his titanic energy and enormous capacity for work were his patience, tenacity, thoroughness and indefatigable industry. He combined dignity with humility. It was of great consequence that in his position as leader and mediator between two races he had such magnanimity, absence of bitterness, indomitable goodwill, determination to co-operate, and patient silence under abuse and misrepresentation. He was never carried away by the crowd into saying on any platform in the North what he would not say on any platform in the South, or wish to have printed in any paper there. The qualities that marked him for leadership were his quiet self-confidence, his absence of personal vanity, his passion for service and the consuming desire for the uplift of his race. With these he combined great executive ability, grasp of detail, capacity for organization, the ability to lead and inspire others, indefatigable optimism, and the courage of attacking and overcoming obstacles.

On one occasion he wrote: "It is now long ago that I learned this lesson from General Armstrong, and resolved that I would permit no man, no matter what his color might be, to narrow and degrade my soul by making me hate him. With God's help, I believe that I have completely rid myself of any ill feeling toward the southern white man for any wrong that he may have inflicted upon my race. While writing upon this subject, it is a pleasure to add that in all my contact with the white people of the South I have never received a single personal insult. . ."

His magnanimity, his generous nature, quick to forgive, eager to overlook a fault and find common ground for reconciliation, found abundant illustration in his daily life. In Birmingham, Alabama, being forced to ride in the elevator for colored people marked "For Negroes and Freight," instead of allowing himself to be moved to venomous sarcasm, in his address at the theatre to members of both races, he pleaded with the Negroes to look upon their southern white neighbors as friends; and, speaking to the white portion of the audience with regard to the elevator sign, said, "Now, my friends, that is mighty discouraging to the colored man." At once white people sprang to their feet and shouted their approval. He had so spoken the truth in love that he had won the members of the other race who might be either potential friends or enemies.

At Tuskegee, when a former white Congressman was called upon to speak he was irritated by the preceding colored speaker who had praised the people of New England who had so generously helped in the education of the colored people after the war. The ex-Congressman said, "I want to give you niggers a few words of plain talk and advice. No such address as that you have just listened to is going to do you any good; it's going to spoil you. You had better not listen to such speeches. You might just as well understand that this is a white man's country, as far as the South is concerned, and we are going to make you keep your place. Understand that. I have nothing more to say to you." Without a word of anger or resentment, Mr. Washington rose and closed the meeting with these simple words: "Ladies and Gentlemen: I am sure you will agree with me that we have had enough eloquence for one occasion. We shall listen to the next speaker at another occasion, when we are not so fagged out. We will now rise, sing the doxology, and be dismissed."

In Boston, after a dinner when some of the more talented and more highly educated men of his own race had poured abuse and bitter contempt upon him, they told him to go on with his industrial education and "leave to us the matters political affecting the race." Without a single word of resentment or even of self-defense, Mr. Washington thanked them for their candor and simply told them for half an hour of the work Tuskegee was doing. Such magnanimity was a mark of true greatness and marked the trail of a pathfinder who was leading the way for both races to come together in closer co-operation. At his death the brilliant colored lawyer who had told him to go back to mind his business in the South wrote, "He was unselfish and generous to a fault; he was modest yet masterful; he was quiet yet intense; his common sense and sagacity seemed uncanny, such was his knowledge of human nature. His was a great soul in which no bitterness or littleness could even find a lurking place. His was the great heart of Lincoln, with malice toward none and charity for all. He loved all men and all men loved him. My humble prayer is that his torch has lighted another among the dark millions of America, to lead the race onward and upward."

His jaded body finally collapsed under the domination of his giant will and indomitable spirit. He was taken by his New York trustees to St. Luke's Hospital where he was told that he had but a few hours to live. He refused to die and insisted on starting for home at once, saying, "I was born in the South, I have lived and labored in the South, and I expect to die and be buried in the South." This remark when sent out in the Associated Press dispatches announcing his death, touched the South as nothing else could have done. No Negro was ever eulogized in the Southern press as he was.

His spirit rose as he neared Tuskegee and he reached home in triumph. The next morning, November 14, 1915, he died at the age of fifty-seven. One of his former students, the president of Tuskegee Alumni Association, spoke at the memorial exercises for thousands of his graduates and millions of his race when he said, "And yet our Principal is not buried out yonder. It is his tired body which is resting just beyond that wall; but he is not buried in that grave. The real Dr. Washington is buried in the graduates who sat at his feet and imbibed his spirit, and he lives in them."

6. WHAT WERE THE RESULTS OF WASHINGTON'S LIFE?

To Booker T. Washington more than to any other one man is due the very great progress that has been achieved by the Negro race since the Civil War. Colonel Henry Watterson, the great Southern editor, said: "The world has never witnessed such progress from darkness into light as the American Negro has made in the period of forty years." Since his emancipation the Negro has increased his homes owned from 12,000 to 650,000, his farms operated from 20,000 to 1,000,000, his business enterprises successfully conducted from 2,000 to 65,000, his literacy from 10 per cent to 80 per cent, the number of teachers from 600 to 44,000, voluntary gifts for the education of Negroes from $80,000 to $2,700,000, his churches from 700 to 45,000, and the value of his church property from $1,500,000 to $90,000,000. Tuskegee Institute now has 3,000 students, property valued at $2,145,000, and an endowment of $2,907,425.

William Henry Lewis, a brilliant colored lawyer, Harvard graduate and football star, and Assistant Attorney-General of the United States under President Taft, said: "Booker Washington has always been from fifteen to twenty years ahead of any other leader of his race. . . While most of us were agonizing over the Negro's relations to the State and his political fortunes, Booker Washington saw that there was a great economic empire that needed to be conquered. He saw an emancipated race chained to the soil by the Mortgage Crop System and other devices, and he said, 'You must own your own land, you must own your own farms'—and forthwith there was a second emancipation. He saw the industrial trades and skilled labor pass from our race into other hands. He said, 'The hands as well as the heads must be educated,' and forthwith the educational system of America was revolutionized. He saw the money earned by the hard toil of black men passing into other men's pockets. He said, 'The only way to save this money is to go into business—sell as well as buy.' He saw that if the colored race was to become economically self-sufficient, it must engage in every form of human activity. Himself a successful business man as shown by Tuskegee's millions, he has led his race to economic freedom. . . In 1900 there was one league with 50 members, and a few businesses represented. Today I am told there are 600 leagues, nearly 40,000 members, who represent every branch and variety of business, trade and finance."

Mr. Washington told the story of Wat Terry, who began as a coachman on a capital of twelve cents. After saving money by working in a shoe factory, he began to buy and sell real estate. Within a decade he had an income of some $7000 a month and owned 222 buildings in Brocton. Another, J. H. Blodgett, an ex-slave, started on $1.10 in Jacksonville, Florida, and was inspired when as a bricklayer working at $1.25 a day, he heard Booker Washington speak. He now owns a Packard and has built 208 houses of his own. Most of all, Booker Washington's character became re-incarnated in the hearts of his students, and his work was extended by them throughout the South.

Another typical example of Mr. Washington's projected influence is found in Professor George W. Carver, the eminent agricultural chemist, a full-blooded African. Mr. Washington found him a promising boy in the Agricultural Department of the Iowa State College. As he came fresh from his college chemical laboratory, Mr. Washington could offer him no costly equipment, but asked him to tackle the barren old hill on which Tuskegee stands. There was nothing on that hill but sand and clay. Out of that sand, Professor Carver has developed some eighty-five chemical and commercial products. From the common clay he has discovered more than two hundred. That thin sandy soil, purchased at fifty cents an acre, would yield at first only peanuts and sweet potatoes. Out of the peanuts Professor Carver has made over one hundred products, and from the sweet potato a hundred and twelve. Several of these have great commercial and financial possibilities.[4]

The parable is plain. Booker Washington saw more in that barren hill, more in the boy Carver, more in every boy of his race, than the multitudes about him, blinded by race prejudice. He saw more in them than they had ever seen, or dreamed, in themselves; more than he had ever realized in his own life as an ignorant and undeveloped slave boy.

In speaking of Booker T. Washington, Andrew Carnegie said: "To me he seems one of the foremost of living men because his work is unique. The Modern Moses, who leads his race and lifts it through Education to even better and higher things than a land overflowing with milk and honey—History is to know two Washingtons, one white, the other black, both Fathers of their people." While Theodore Roosevelt declared that he was "a great American. For twenty years before his death he had been the most useful, as well as the most distinguished, member of his race in the world. . . I profited very much by my association with Booker T. Washington. I owed him much along many different lines. I valued greatly his friendship and respect; and when he died I mourned his loss as a patriot and an American." No one can deny that he deserved to be ranked as an eminent Maker of Freedom.

---

[4] "In his book, 'The Negro in the New World', Sir Harry Johnston says, 'Professor Carver, who teaches scientific agriculture, botany, agricultural chemistry, etc., at Tuskegee, might be professor of botany, not at Tuskegee but at Oxford or Cambridge.'" "My Larger Education" p. 225.

Chapter 3.

FREEDOM FROM MATERIALISM

Francis of Assisi

1. WHAT KIND OF A WORLD DID FRANCIS LIVE IN?

The first half of the thirteenth century, in which Francis lived, was characterized by gross materialism and incessant strife. Both had invaded the Church, whose allegiance was divided between mammon and God. This was a cause of grief to the spiritual leaders of the Church itself. Of the higher officials of the Roman *curia* of the day it was said, "They are stones for understanding, wood for justice, fire for wrath, iron for forgiveness; deceitful as foxes, proud as bulls, greedy and insatiate as the minotaur." Bishops extorted money from the simple priests and among their recognized revenues was the "collagium," the payment of which secured to the clergy the right to keep a concubine. Many of the priests in turn sought to accumulate benefices, to seize inheritance from the dying and by despicable means to procure support for their illegitimate children. In spite of this they kept the people in deadly terror of their power of miracle-working in the present, and of life and death in the world to come. Public worship was often a matter of dead ritual of magic formula, and the pulpit was open only to the bishops. "The monks were, in great majority, deserters from life, who for motives entirely aside from religion had taken refuge behind the only walls which at this period were secure." Some monasteries sought to draw the crowds by fair grounds with jugglers and courtesans. The papal bulls of the period reveal constant appeals made to the court of Rome against the priests, who were beyond the reach of the secular jurisdiction, with constant reference to assassination, violation, incest and adultery. Even Innocent III, the powerful prince of the Church who ruled Italy with an iron hand, speaks with discouragement of prevailing conditions for which he can see no remedy but fire and sword. Men seemed to have gone mad for money and pleasure.

And it was an age of war and strife. "Emperor was opposed to Pope, prince to king, village against village and burgher against noble." From the twelfth century there had been bitter feuds and frequent war between Assisi and her more powerful and war-like neighbor, Perugia. At the age of seventeen Francis had feverishly worked with his fellow-citizens to build and later defend the city walls and towers of Assisi. The common people, or "minores," who did the work, thus learned their own power and importance and finally rose in revolt against the proud nobles living in their fortified residences. Civil war broke out, which threatened the downfall of the nobility.

The nobles turned for aid to their powerful enemy, Perugia, which eagerly seized the occasion to advance and conquer divided Assisi and reduce it to subjection. In the battle that followed between the two cities, Francis was taken prisoner in 1202 and was kept in a separate prison in Perugia with the young nobles of Assisi for a year—an association which had a marked influence on his after life. Such wars between towns, factions, castles and petty states were incessant all over Italy. Sabatier says, "Let us picture to ourselves the Italy of the beginning of the thirteenth century with its divisions, its perpetual warfare, its depopulated country districts, the impossibility of tilling the fields except in the narrow circle which the garrisons of the towns might protect; all these cities from the greatest to the least occupied in watching for the most favorable moment for falling upon and pillaging their neighbors; sieges terminated by unspeakable atrocities, and after all this, famine, speedily followed by pestilence to complete the devastation. Then let us picture to ourselves the rich Benedictine abbeys, veritable fortresses set upon the hill-tops."

The strife of the times affected the Church, which was rent by divisions. A contemporary writer speaks of thirty-two heresies rampant in Italy at that time. Chief among these were the powerful Cathari, who renounced marriage and property and advocated suicide. The church might have succumbed had it not been for the "little poor man" of Assisi, who perhaps saved Christianity in the thirteenth century. It was the birth of the mendicant orders which obliged the clergy to take up the practice of preaching and led to the reform of a corrupt church.

It was an iron age of force and of trial by battle. Francis lived in the midst of the seven long Crusades, which represented the Church's resort to violence to achieve her ends. Gibbon records their butchery and bloodshed, their disgraceful orgies of drunkenness and lust. Warfare was frequently followed by epidemics of famine and pestilence. Leprosy was one of the worst scourges of Europe following the Crusades. Devastated by war, the peasants and the poor were often reduced to pathetic destitution. Assisi was at times left as a city of the dead. "There the women, with their children clinging round their necks, were sold in the market-place as slaves, and exposed to the cruellest treatment by their masters. Even tiny children of four and five years old were sold. . . . While the slave market was proceeding, amidst the clanging of bells proclaiming the victory the Priors of Perugia sat in their council hall discussing how they could bring about the total annihilation of Assisi."

It was a time not only of misery for the poor, but of reckless revelry for the young nobles who had money to spend. It was an age of knighthood and chivalry, of traveling troubadors and wandering singers. Into this warring age of materialism and strife, of superstition and ignorance, of contrasted privilege and poverty, of heretics and saints, there was born among the revellers a young man who, with his life transfigured, was to lead the world of his day back to the thought of God. He was to lead the way to the glad springtime of the Renaissance, to be the herald of a religious reformation, to become the great peace-maker in the midst of feudal strife, and finally to challenge and bring freedom from the gross materialism of his day. Such was the materialistic world of strife into which Francis was born.

2. WHAT DID FRANCIS DO?

Francis was born in 1182, the son of the wealthiest cloth merchant of the city, Pietro Bernadone. The father took great pride in his son and his ambitions, and Francis joined him in business and was successful in making money; though he was even more so in spending it. The princely merchants of that day were considered as almost nobles of a second order, and with the young nobles Francis consorted. He was popular both for his lavish expenditure and for his gaiety and love of splendor, which made him a favorite at every feast. He responded readily to the prevalent vices of the time. Celano says, "He was always first among his equals in all vanities, the first instigator of evil, and behind none in foolishness, so that he drew upon himself the attention of the public by vain-glorious extravagance, in which he stood foremost. He was not chary of jokes, ridicule, light sayings, evil-speaking, singing, and in the wearing of soft and fine clothes; being very rich he spent freely, being less desirous of accumulating wealth than of dissipating his substance; clever at trafficking, but too vain to prevent others from spending what was his, withal a man of pleasant manners, facile and courteous even to his own disadvantage; for this reason, therefore, many, through his fault, became evil-doers and promoters of scandal. Thus, surrounded by many worthless companions, triumphantly and scornfully he went upon his way."

Francis had a passion for the chivalry of the age, fed by the songs of the strolling troubadors from France whose language he spoke. With the young nobles he rode to battle against Perugia as a gay young cavalier at the age of twenty-one, and during the year he was held as a prisoner of war with them, he became known for his singing with indomitable good cheer and for his work as a peacemaker among them. "His early years passed away in feasting and singing with an occasional journey to a neighboring town to sell the Bernardone wares, until 1202 when war broke out between Perugia and Assisi, and the big bell of the cathedral called the citizens to arms in the Piazza della Minerva. Men gathered round their captain, while from the windows of every house women gesticulated wildly, almost drowning the clank of armor and the tramp of horses by their shrill screams. Francis, on a magnificent charger, rode out of the city gates abreast with the nobles of Assisi, filling the bourgeois heart of Pietro with delight, that a son of his should be thus honored." John Ruskin says there were "troops of knights, noble in face and form, dazzling in crest and shield; horse and man one labyrinth of quaint color and gleaming light—the purple, and silver, and scarlet fringes flowing over the strong limbs and clashing mail like sea waves over rocks at sunset."

After his release from prison he returned to his former life of dissipation, which was interrupted in his twenty-second year by a severe illness which brought him face to face with death. During his convalescence, as he walked abroad and beheld the beauty of nature, he was seized with contrition as he felt the utter emptiness and loneliness of his wasted life. Hours of anguish followed, in which he could not enjoy the pleasures of his former life. At a final banquet, at which he had been chosen king of the feast, he broke from his companions, determined to repent of his past life and to espouse his "lady Poverty."

In the two years that followed Francis had a passion for solitude, lost in the contemplation of nature or spending hours in meditation and prayer. One day he borrowed the rags of a beggar and, in order to identify himself with the poor, spent the day in fasting and begging. On another occasion as he was riding he met a poor leper. Suddenly overcome with repulsion, he instinctively turned his horse in the opposite direction. But he was so filled with shame at his defeat that he rode back, threw himself on his knees, kissed the leper's hand and gave him all the money he had. This victory marked an era in his life. The young cavalier now visited the leper asylum and began to comfort and serve the inmates, looking upon them as his peculiar charge.

Francis had now lost all interest in business and neither the threats of his father nor the entreaties of his mother could recall him to his old life. As he was praying in the suburbs in the old church of St. Damian, which was now falling into ruins, he believed he saw a vision of Christ who spoke to his inmost soul, calling him to rebuild His church. This command he took literally. He sold some of his father's merchandise, gave it to the priest and began to carry stones and work for the repair of the ruined church. His father, who had been quite willing to have him squander his money with nobles when it furthered his worldly ambition, lost all patience when it was spent upon churches and beggars. As Francis, now pale, emaciated and in rags, passed through the city he was pelted with stones by the children who followed, calling him "madman." His father in a rage dragged him home and kept him bound, until he was finally released by his mother.

Going to St. Damian, his father summoned him as the jest of the whole town to leave the country. Francis gave him back the money he had given to the church, and stripping off the clothing which his father had provided he proclaimed publicly that henceforth he called no man father save "Our Father who art in Heaven." "From this moment forward his life was founded on a disbelief in the efficacy of money to obtain anything of ultimate value, and he insisted with ever-increasing vehemence on the non-ownership of property in any form."

Free at last from the world, owning absolutely nothing of the material things about which the world of his day had almost gone mad, Francis, clad in a coarse borrowed mantle, climbed the mountainside above the town singing with the birds the songs of joy that now filled his heart. Empty-handed, he now lived with the lepers and washed their sores, begging his bread from door to door and repairing the little chapel and other neighboring sanctuaries, including the Portiuncula, which later became the cradle of the Franciscan movement. He was living thus far a life of penitence and meditation rather than of activity. It was a time of testing and of transition.

On February 24, 1209, at the age of twenty-seven, as the gospel was being read in the Portiuncula, or Church of St. Mary of the Angels, Francis heard the words in which Christ seemed to give him the command that was to change his life. "Wherever ye go, preach, saying, 'The kingdom of heaven is at hand. Heal the sick, cleanse the lepers, cast out devils. Freely ye have received, freely give. Provide neither silver nor gold nor brass in your purses, neither scrip nor two coats, nor shoes nor staff, for the laborer is worthy of his meat.'" Francis immediately replied, "From this day forth I shall set myself with all my strength to put it into practice." Laying aside his staff, his purse and shoes, he went out possessing literally nothing until the day he died naked upon the earth on the outskirts of Assisi. He was now free to challenge the materialism of his age. Father Cuthbert says, "From a recluse, Francis had been transformed into an apostle: he was now the leader of a knightly company of holy poverty. The zeal of an apostle was upon him, urging him to carry his good news abroad and win souls to his Lord's allegiance."

The next morning Francis went up to Assisi and began to proclaim his message in the open streets. His simple words of love went straight to the heart of his hearers and pierced the conscience like a sword. He who had so recently been counted a madman was now held as a saint. Among the first to be touched by his preaching was a wealthy merchant, Bernardo di Quintavalle, who distributed all his goods to the poor and cast in his lot with Francis. This created a stir throughout the town. He was soon followed by Pietro, a canon of the cathedral who offered his services to the lepers. Then a laborer named Egidio joined the group when he beheld "how those noble knights of Assisi despised the world so that the whole country stood amazed." These were followed by brother Leo, the apostle of love, whom Francis rejoiced to call "the little lamb of God." Thus began the simple order of the little brothers of the poor, identified with the *minores*, or common people.

Three simple passages became the guide of the early disciples: "Sell that thou hast"; "take nothing for your journey"; "follow me"; but the true rule was Francis himself. The little brothers made for themselves coarse tunics, and went with Francis about the countryside, telling their new-found message of good news. In poverty, in joy, in song; working with the peasants in the fields, sleeping in hay-lofts or leper asylums or porches, these men went forth to the people until out of the sodden materialism of the time all Italy began to turn to them. Up and down the country went these joyful troubadors of God with the glad message of the new springtime of the world. Men began to hear again the good news that had sounded along the shores of Galilee, as these little brothers of the poor came preaching penitence and peace.

Francis and his friends were at first known as the "Penitents of Assisi." Though they had simple huts of branches and twigs around the little Church of St. Mary of the Angels, they had no settled abode, they wandered in pairs over the country, dressed in the ordinary garb of the peasants. The keynote of the movement was the imitation of the life of Christ, especially of His poverty. They sought to make no provision for the morrow, to lay by nothing in store, to have no land, no capital, no money, no churches—literally to possess nothing in this world. The movement was an earnest effort in a corrupt age to repeat the Gospel story in exact literalness.

When the Bishop of Assisi protested against their life of rigorous poverty Francis replied, "My lord, if we possessed property we should have need of arms for its defence, for it is the source of quarrels and lawsuits, and the love of God and of one's neighbor usually finds many obstacles therein; this is why we do not desire temporal goods." There were those who reviled or threw mud upon the brothers, but in the midst of tribulation they only were the more filled with joy.

By 1210, as the number of friars was now daily increasing, simple-hearted Francis endeavored to write a Rule for the Order, concerning poverty, manual labor, etc. A party of twelve humble companions then set out to procure the approval of the Pope. Innocent III, the iron statesman, was averse to a new order but the humble persistence and the loving boldness of Francis finally conquered. The Pope insisted, however, on making Francis the Superior and on placing upon the order the tonsure and the spiritual authority of the Roman Church, which despite the fears and struggles of Francis, growingly encompassed the new movement as an ecclesiastical institution.

The sanction of the Pope made the movement more popular and the little brothers spread over Italy, evangelizing the towns and villages. The crowds were soon so great that the cathedral of Assisi had to be opened for Francis to preach. He became the voice of the people and though he awoke the conscience by challenging the sins of his day, the crowds were filled with delirious enthusiasm over his message. Primitive gospel simplicity had returned to the earth once more. Francis called men to repent of their sins, to renounce avarice and to be reconciled with their enemies. He became the great peacemaker of his century, reconciling the rich *majores* and the weak *minores* of his city, and the warring feudal towns which were at war.

Finding the need of a permanent center, the brethren appealed to the Benedictines, who granted them the use of the little Portiuncula church. As they were bound to own no property, they insisted on paying rent. All about the little chapel they built cells of boughs, thatched with straw, each brother having his name on a portion of the mud floor as his resting-place. Their time was divided between manual labor, preaching and prayer. From the first it was a laboring, rather than a mendicant, order.

When Francis preached in the cathedral a young girl of sixteen, Clare of the noble Scifi family, who was soon to become the celebrated Santa Clara, the head of the Franciscan second order of women, came to him with two companions from her castle by night. She wished to renounce the idle pleasures of the world, take the vow of poverty and enter the order. Francis cut off her beautiful tresses as she knelt at the altar to surrender her all. In the days that followed she resisted all the abuse of her family and stood firm until the new order was installed in the little chapel of St. Damian. The relation between Francis and Clare became one of the most beautiful known to history.

Later a third order was added for those who wished to practice the teachings but who could not leave their ordinary vocations. Every rich man who would work with his hands and was willing to contribute to the common fund all that he did not need for himself, could belong to the order, together with the poor who shared the provision of the communal store which they called the "table of the Lord." On June 25, 1227, Gregory IX, by a new bull, solemnly approved the third order, declaring that its members were not liable to feudal oaths and military service. The movement was no less than a social revolution in the midst of a materialistic age. The first Brothers Minor had all things in common. They owned nothing in person and shared the fruits of their labor and their alms at a common table. They gathered twice a year at a general meeting of their Chapter and then scattered over the land on preaching tours and errands of mercy.

We get an interesting picture of the change Francis wrought throughout Italy and of the enthusiasm he kindled among his followers in a letter of Jacques de Vitry, which, being written by a contemporary, has very great value: "While I was at the pontifical court, I saw many things which grieved me to the heart. Everyone was so preoccupied with secular and temporal things, with matters concerning kings and kingdoms, litigations and lawsuits, that it is almost impossible to talk on religious matters. Yet I found one subject for consolation in those lands: in that many persons of either sex, rich, and living in the great world, leave all for the love of Christ and renounce the world. They are called the Friars Minor, and are held in great respect by the Pope and the Cardinals. They, on their part, care nought for things temporal, and strive hard every day to tear perishing souls from the vanities of this world and to entice them into their ranks. Thanks be to God, their labor has already borne fruit, and they have gained many souls; inasmuch as he who listens to them brings others, and thus one audience creates another. They live according to the rule of the primitive church, of which it is written: 'The multitude of believers were as one heart and one soul.' In the day they go into the cities and the villages to gain over souls and to work; in the night they betake themselves to hermitages and solitary places and give themselves up to contemplation. The women live together near to cities in diverse convents; they accept nought, but live by the labor of their hands. They are much disturbed to find themselves held in greater esteem, both by the clergy and the laity, than they themselves desire. The men of this order meet once a year in some pre-arranged place, to their great profit, and rejoice together in the Lord and eat in company; and then, with the help of good and honest men, they adopt and promulgate holy institutions, approved by the Pope. After this they disperse, going about in Lombardy, Tuscany, and even in Apulia and Sicily, for the rest of the year. . . I think it is to put the prelates to shame, who are like dogs unable to bark, that the Lord wills to save many souls before the end of the world, by means of these poor simple friars."

After evangelizing central Italy, Francis, as an ardent knight "inebriated by the excessive fervor of his spirit," longed to convert the Saracens. He failed in his purpose to reach Syria but journeyed to Spain, where he was taken ill. Six years later he went to Egypt where the Crusaders were fighting. He exposed the moral corruption of the army and prophesied its inevitable defeat. He then went boldly into the camp of the Sultan, armed only with the weapons of love, and delivered to him his ardent message of peace and good-will. He seems to have made a deep impression upon him. An eyewitness thus speaks of his work: "The Order of the Brothers Minor is multiplying rapidly on all sides, because it imitates the primitive Church and follows the life of the Apostles in everything. The master of these Brothers is named Brother Francis; he is so lovable that he is venerated by everyone. Having come into our army, he has not been afraid, in his zeal for the faith, to go to that of our enemies. For days together he announced the word of God to the Saracens, but with little success; then the Sultan, King of Egypt, asked him in secret to entreat God to reveal to him, by some miracle, which is the best religion."

He afterward journeyed through the Holy Land, visiting Bethlehem and Jerusalem. From time to time he sent out his little brothers on similar victorious missions, which finally extended into Germany, Hungary, Spain, France and Britain. His longest epistle and one of his last is addressed to all Christians, as his heart opened ever wider to take in all humanity. He sought nothing less than a brotherhood whose cloister was the world.

Francis's absence in the East, however, marked a turning point in the order. The two vicars he had left in his place began at once to overturn everything, losing the simplicity of poverty, multiplying ritualistic or ascetic observances, and imitating the older orders. When Francis returned in 1220 a shout of joy resounded throughout Italy. He commanded the immediate evacuation or destruction of the comfortable houses that had been built, or given to the brethren. As the order had outgrown the simple plans of Francis, however, the powerful Ugolini, who later became Pope Gregory IX, was entrusted with the oversight of the order. In its rapid multiplication it had passed beyond the control of this gentle-hearted man, and the strong hand of the papacy was now laid upon it. Francis, who was no longer minister-general, became for a time a sad and submissive monk in a Roman order. Father Cuthbert says, "The two years immediately following the General Chapter of 1221 may well be described as the agony of Francis. Like thunderclouds the troubles about the Rule descended upon his spirit, oppressing him with forebodings and weariness and despondency. To this soreness of spirit was added an increasing physical weakness and pain. He had returned from the East, broken in health, and the disease which within a few years was to end his life was already making life a torture. But the physical pain he could have borne blithely enough; it was the mental suffering which brought black night into his soul."

The simple Francis was replaced by the shrewd lover of power, Brother Elias. The last five years of Francis's life were one long protest by word and deed against the bondage and formality, the clerical control and worldly power, which Francis saw gradually stifling his simple brotherhood. Weighted down by the defection of the leaders from his primitive principles, the glad troubador had now become a heartbroken penitent. In 1224 the enfeebled and sorrowing Francis made his way to the forest of Alvernia as his Calvary. Here in days of penitence, as he prayed weeping, distressed over the future of the order, he longed "to suffer or to die." It was here upon his Golgotha, while praying upon the mountainside during the feast of the Exaltation of the Cross, that Francis beheld his ineffable vision of the crucified and risen Christ.

When Francis rose after the long watches of the night, as the day broke he is said to have bo.ne upon his body the marks of the Crucified. It was the testimony of the brothers of his order that to the day of his death, "his hands and feet appeared as though pierced through with nails, the heads being on the inside of the hands and on the upper part of the feet."

From an infection received in Egypt aggravated by much weeping, Francis had now become nearly blind. He was worn by fasts and vigils. He repaired to St. Damian where for fifteen days he was quite blind with weeping. Sister Clare, as his devout friend, built him a cell of reeds and with sympathy, insight and courageous good cheer, helped him win back his own faith and courage. Under her kindly sympathy Francis gradually became himself again. One day at the monastery table while in conversation with Sister

Clare he seemed caught up in ecstasy, and upon coming to himself he sang his famous Canticle of the Sun.

Francis was now his old joyous self, and during the last year of his life, though broken in body, he sent his friars singing up and down the country his Canticle of "Brother Sun." As his strength failed he cried with joy, "Welcome, Sister Death." "He went to meet death singing." "He finally dictated his last spiritual Will, to recall the Order to the simple life once more, though the powerful Pope Ugolini, as Gregory IX, tried to absolve the brothers from obeying it.

Francis's work was now ended. On October 1, 1226, as his last act, he requested that he be stripped of his clothing and laid naked upon the ground. He desired to die in the arms of his Lady Poverty. Turning to the brothers, he said, "I have done my duty; may Christ now teach you to do yours." They again sang to him for the last time the Canticle of the Sun. Bread was brought, and he broke it, and gave to his disciples, celebrating the Lord's Supper without an altar and without a priest, for he had remained until the last, with all his brothers, a layman. One Saturday evening, on October 3d, at the age of forty-four, he breathed his last. "The Brothers were still gazing on his face, hoping yet to catch some sign of life, when innumerable larks alighted, singing, on the thatch of his cell, as if to salute the soul which had just taken flight and give the Little Poor Man the canonization of which he was most worthy."

3. WHAT DID FRANCIS SAY?

Francis said nothing new; he gave no body or doctrine to the world. His greatest gift was himself. Men saw the Life lived again that had been seen by the shores of Galilee. He charged his simple followers to gather neither possessions nor learning, and to convert the world by example rather than by precept. He was never troubled about doctrine, or the scruples of orthodoxy, or the theological heresies of his time. Like Wesley after him, he was consumed with a passion for a practical objective. Faith for him lay not in the intellectual but in the moral sphere. He gave to the world an embodied ideal, a life lived in passionate love, lowly humility, transparent simplicity and utter devotion. His whole teaching and life were but the expansion of the first passage of scripture that possessed him—preach the Kingdom, heal the sick, cleanse the lepers. Provide no silver nor gold in your purses. Freely you have received, freely give. His was the first religious order which, as a community, renounced the holding of property as a protest against the sordid materialism of their day.

Francis's first principle was one of absolute poverty, not as an end in itself but as a means to his end, which was God. The "penitents of Assisi" were to own nothing but the peace of their own heart. The three cornerstones on which the order was built were poverty, chastity and obedience, and at the beginning of both the first and second Rule we read, "The Rule of life and these brothers is this: namely, to live in obedience and chastity, and without property."

The three vows appealed to the three aspects of man's life: obedience to the will, poverty to freedom of the mind, chastity to purity of heart in the emotional life. The whole personality was to be utterly devoted to God and man. Francis says to his missionary brothers, "My sons! God has ordered me to send you to the land of the Saracens to announce and make known there His faith. Copy Christ in poverty, obedience and chastity. For the Lord Jesus Christ was born poor, lived in poverty, taught poverty and died in poverty."

Thus the first step into the new life for his followers was to shake the very dust of materialism from off his feet. The novice on entering the order gave up all his money and possessed absolutely nothing that could absorb his attention or divert his care from God or man. Every gift was for them only God's bounty held in trust. Time and again Francis stripped the clothes from his back to give them to any poor man who needed them more.

The few possessions of the brothers, even to their prayer books, were held in common. As in the early church, no man said that aught of the things he possessed were his own.[1] For to Francis, property meant insistence on separateness. That which was in the world was the gift of God for the common use of all men. Of land and churches the early order had none. They refused any monastery which should shut them from needy men. All the world was their monastery, and all humanity their parish.

They sought no cramping asceticism, but complete liberty —freedom from things, from the cares of treasure laid up for one's petty self, from fear of moth or rust, of thief, or loss. For the little brothers of the poor, voluntary poverty was freedom. "He who is willingly poor is free." When the Lady Poverty desired to be shown their monastery, "the brethren lead her to a hill and show her the whole world lying at their feet, and say, 'This is our monastery, Lady'," Francis says to the brothers, "Poverty . . . is a treasure so surpassing and so Divine that we are not worthy to possess it in our most vile vessels; for this is that celestial virtue whereby all earthly things and transitory are trodden under foot and every barrier is removed which might hinder the soul from freely uniting itself to the eternal God." "Let the brothers," he wrote in his will, "take care not to receive on any account churches, poor dwelling-places, and all other things that are constructed for them, unless they are, as is becoming the holy poverty which we have promised in the Rule, always dwelling there as strangers and pilgrims."

In his Rule, Francis insists that the postulant, if he desires to join the order willingly and can do so honorably, must sell all his goods and distribute them among the poor. But the Friars must ever be on their guard against meddling in any way with these affairs; they must neither receive any money for themselves or for any intermediate person. These brethren were then given two tunics, without hood, girdle, and were put on probation for a year. All the brethren

---

[1]Acts 4:32, 2:44 "There was but one heart and soul among the multitude of the believers; not one of them considered anything his personal property, they shared all they had with one another." Moffatt's translation.

must be clad in poor garments which they can patch with bits of the same or other pieces. For from possession arise difficulties and disputes which in their minds raise all kinds of obstacles to the love of God and of one's neighbor.

When the people of Assisi built a house for the Brothers Minor, Francis would not consent to receive it except as belonging to the Bishop, to be used by the Brethren, and each year they took to the Bishop a basket of small fishes in recognition of his ownership. Money was to him the symbol of all he had denounced when he turned his back on his old life. Francis says, "Blessed is the servant who gives up all his goods to the Lord God, for he who retains anything for himself hides 'his Lord's money,' and that 'which he thinketh he hath shall be taken away from him.' " To put in a claim of ownership was to insist on a division in the things which had been provided for mankind in general; it was to erect a claim to finality in a region where God alone was final. For to Francis property implied the mutual exclusion which is the antithesis of love.

In an age of materialism like that of Francis or our own day, we are struck by his idealization of poverty. Thus Thomas of Celano says, "He longed after poverty with all his heart. Considering that she was the familiar friend of the Son of God, he strove in everlasting charity to espouse her, now that she was cast off by all the world. He would tell his sons that she was the way to perfection, the pledge and earnest of eternal riches. No one was so greedy of gold as he of poverty; no one more careful in guarding a treasure than he in guarding this pearl of the Gospel." Francis tells his brothers, "Poverty is that celestial virtue by which all earthly and transitory things are trodden under foot, and all impediments are lifted away from the soul, so that she can freely unite herself to the Eternal God. And this is the virtue which makes the soul, while still retained on earth, converse with the angels in heaven."

In every poor man Francis seemed to see the representative and the living symbol of the poverty of Christ, as he says, "When you see a poor man you must consider in him

Christ Himself whom he represents, Christ who has assumed our poverty." The spirit of all Francis's teaching is shown in his last Will, from which we may select a few special sentences: "See in what manner God gave it to me, to me, Brother Francis, to begin to do penitence; when I lived in sin, it was very painful to me to see lepers, but God himself led me into their midst, and I remained there a little while . . . When the Lord gave me some brothers no one showed me what I ought to do, but the Most High himself revealed to me that I ought to live according to the model of the holy gospel . . . Those who presented themselves to observe this kind of life distributed all that they might have to the poor. They contented themselves with a tunic, patched within and without, with the cord and breeches, and we desired to have nothing more . . . We loved to live in poor and abandoned churches, and we were ignorant and submissive to all. I worked with my hands and would continue to do, and I will also that all other friars work at some honorable trade. And when they do not give up the price of the work, let us resort to the table of the Lord, begging our bread from door to door . . . I absolutely interdict all the brothers, in whatever place they may be found, from asking any bull from the court of Rome."

Brother Leo, Francis's dearest friend, and for the last six years of his life his sick-nurse, secretary and confessor, wrote within a year of his death in the "Mirror of Perfection" the best record of his teaching. A few sentences from it may show the spirit of the master: "The blessed Francis said, 'I understand that the brethren ought to have nothing save their garments with a cord and hosen . . . and if so be they are compelled by necessity they wear shoes' . . . He taught his brethren to make their dwellings after a sorry sort, and would that their cabins should be of wood. And not only did he hate arrogance in their houses, but he did exceedingly abhor much or choice furnishings thereof; so as all things might point toward poverty and all things chant songs of pilgrimage and exile . . . When he was coming back from Siona he met a poor man and saith to his companion, 'Needs must we render up his mantle to the poor man whose own it is, for we only received the same as a loan until such time as we should find one poorer than ourselves. No mind have I to be a thief, for it would be imputed to us as a theft were we not to give it to one more needy.' Whereupon the pious father gave the mantle as a present to the poor man."

At the foundation of Francis's principle of poverty lay the vow of obedience. For God he had renounced his own will, and obedience to men was one way in which he could show that his obedience was sincere. This did not mean slavish subservience, for he showed strong independence in prevailing over two Popes, in his conviction of the ultimate authority of the Spirit. In utter consecration he welcomed every suffering as a joyous discipline to prove his complete obedience. During his illness, after receiving the stigmata, while rocked by his "sister Pain," when the brother attending him was troubled by his suffering, he threw "himself on the ground and kissed it, and cried: 'I give Thee thanks, O Lord God, for all these my pains, I beseech Thee, my Lord, that, if it please Thee, Thou wilt add unto them an hundredfold; for this will be most acceptable unto me, if laying sorrow upon me Thou dost not spare, since the fulfilling of Thy holy will is unto me an overflowing solace.'" And again, "Above all the graces and all the gifts which the Holy Spirit gives to his friends is the grace to conquer oneself, and willingly to suffer pain, outrages, disgrace, and evil treatment, for the love of Christ."

Concerning war and peace Francis was not so much a teacher as an active *maker* of peace. His only weapons were love and humility. A citizen of Bologna tells us as an eye-witness of his preaching of peace there, "I, Thomas, citizen of Spalato, and archdeacon of the cathedral church of the same city, studying at Bologna in the year 1220, saw St. Francis preach in the square before the little palace, where nearly the whole town was assembled . . . His discourse resembled one of those harangues that are made by popular orators. At the conclusion, he spoke only of the extinction of hatred, and the urgency of concluding treaties of peace and compacts of union. His garments were soiled and torn, his person thin, his face pale, but God gave his words unheard-of power. He converted even men of rank, whose unrestrained fury and cruelty had bathed the country in blood. Many who were enemies were reconciled. Love and veneration for the saint were universal; men and women thronged around him, and happy were those who could so much as touch the hem of his habit."

At this time, when war, party feuds and the lawless seizing of property were impoverishing the land, Francis enrolled his Tertiaries under solemn vows to be reconciled to their enemies, to restore their ill-gotten gains, and to abstain from all offensive war. This dealt a severe blow to the feudal system of Italy and roused the opposition of the militaristic barons of his day. In his own city Francis was the peacemaker between the lords and the rich *majores* and the weak *minores*. A treaty of peace which was signed in Assisi November 9, 1210, has been preserved to this day. " 'This is the statute and perpetual agreement between the *Majori* and *Minori* of Assisi: Without common consent there shall never be any sort of alliance either with the pope and his nuncios or legates, or with the emperor, or with the king . . . except with a common accord they shall do all which there may be to do for the honor, safety, and advantage of the commune of Assisi.' The lords, in consideration of a small periodical payment, renounced all their feudal rights; the inhabitants of the villages subject to Assisi were put on a par with those of the city, foreigners were protected, the assessment of taxes were fixed . . . Love had triumphed, and for several years there were at Assisi neither victors nor vanquished." On another occasion he reconciled the Bishop with High Bailiff of Assisi, writing a special verse for the occasion, "Praised be Thou, O My Lord, of them that do show forgiveness for love of Thee."

Coupled with Francis's teaching of poverty, chastity, obedience and peace, was that of the joyous love of nature. During the middle ages, men had lived enveloped in a cowl.

They had been too morbidly introspective; too absorbed in concern for a future heaven and hell, to see the beauties of nature all about them, as the living garment of God. In Francis's joyful appreciation of nature we see the beginning of the modernism of the Renaissance. In the Rule Francis wrote, "and the friars must take care not to be sad and dull like hypocrites, but let them show themselves joyful in the Lord with a cheerful face and be filled with engaging amiability." His followers record in the "Mirror of Perfection" that "drunken with the love and passion of Christ the Blessed Francis would at time . . . pick up a stick from the ground and setting it upon his left shoulder, would draw another stick after the manner of a bow with his right hand athwart a viol or instrument, and making befitting gestures, would sing in French of one Lord Jesus Christ." The followers of Francis so imitated him that Franciscan cheerfulness soon became proverbial.

He was aglow with the recognition of the unity of the world and of all his fellow-men. He saw the universality which underlay all division and all difference. He saw God everywhere in nature and in man. From his brother the sun to his sister the earthworm, all were dear to him. All nature was to him a sacrament, a symbol, a parable that spoke of the underlying reality of the one Father in Heaven. Father Cuthbert tells us that "he would never allow the brethren to uproot a tree or to cut it down in such wise that it could not grow again; nor would he allow them so to enclose a garden that the flowers and growing things could not spread out in their natural freedom. He would take up the worms and slow-moving insects from the road where they might be crushed under foot and put them in safety. In a hard frost he was known to put honey near the bees that they might not die of hunger. All life to him was sacred, because it came from the Hand of God."

Like one before him who had loved the lilies and the sparrows, Francis was passionately fond of the birds. "My little brethren birds," he said, after saluting them as was his custom, "ye ought greatly to praise and love the Lord who created you, for He provideth all that is necessary, giving unto you feathers for raiment and wings to fly with. The Most High God has placed you among His creatures, and given you the pure air for your abode; ye do not sow neither do ye reap, but He keeps and feeds you." As he left Mount Alvernia after the experience of the stigmata, he cried, "Farewell, sacred mount. Farewell, mount Alvernia. Farewell, mount of the angels. Farewell, beloved Brother Falcon, I thank thee for the charity thou didst show me, farewell. Farewell, oh rock which didst receive me within thine heart . . . never more shall we behold one another." With special joy he gazed upon all that was lightsome, beautiful and bright, the light and fire, the pure running water, "our brothers the flowers" and "our brothers the robins." In Siena he built nests for the doves. Every being was for Francis a direct word from God, and everywhere he saw his Father's face.

His feeling for nature is best shown perhaps in the tender grace of his Canticle of the Son. It was after the union of his entire being with the Crucified One, and after long days of blindness that the joy of life and the light of nature broke again upon his inmost soul. The following is Matthew Arnold's English translation, though cold English cannot reproduce the liquid Italian of Francis.

> O most high, almighty, good Lord God, to thee belong praise, glory, honor and all blessing!
>
> Praised be my Lord God with all his creatures and specially our brother the sun, who brings us the day and who brings us the light; fair is he and shines with a very great splendor: O Lord, he signifies to us thee!
>
> Praised be my Lord for our sister the moon, and for the stars, the which he has set clear and lovely in heaven.
>
> Praised be my Lord for our brother the wind, and for air and cloud, calms and all weather by the which thou upholdest life in all creatures.
>
> Praised be my Lord for our sister water, who is very serviceable unto us and humble and precious and clean.
>
> Praised be my Lord for our brother fire, through whom thou givest us light in the darkness; and he is bright and pleasant and very mighty and strong.

Praised be my Lord for our mother the earth, the which doth sustain us and keep us, and bringeth forth divers fruits and flowers of many colors, and grass.

Praised be my Lord for all those who pardon one another for his love's sake, and who endure weakness and tribulation; blessed are they who peaceably shall endure, for thou, O most Highest, shall give them a crown.

Praised be my Lord for our sister, the death of the body, from which no man escapeth. Woe to him who dieth in mortal sin! Blessed are they who are found walking by thy most holy will, for the second death shall have no power to do them harm.

Praise ye and bless the Lord, and give thanks unto him and serve him with great humility.

4. WHAT KIND OF A MAN WAS FRANCIS?

Francis's character, though many-sided, was transparent and simple. He was a man of utter humility, abounding love, overflowing joy and poetic insight, of boundless devotion, of strong independence and usually of balanced sanity. Perhaps his basic characteristic was his deep humility, showing itself in his passion for reality, the frank confession of his every fault, his eagerness to take the lowest place as the servant of all, and his obstinate resistance to all the encroachments of wealth and rank and power.

When brother Masseo complained that he had neither beauty, learning nor noble family, yet all men were eager to follow him, Francis replied, "Because the eyes of the Most High . . . have not found among sinners any smaller man, nor any more insufficient and more sinful, therefore he has chosen me." When, in order to protect him from the cold, a brother sewed a piece of fox skin under his coarse mantle. Francis insisted on placing a piece on the outside as well that there might be no false pretence of austerity which he was not really practicing. On another occasion when he had been persuaded to eat some chicken as he was recovering from fever he had himself led naked by a rope as he confessed the fact to all the people. Brother Leo writes, "When he was led naked before the people, he said, 'You and all that by my example do leave the world behind and enter into the religion and life of the brethren, ye do all believe that I am a holy man, yet do I confess unto God and unto you that in this sickness of mine I have eaten of flesh meats and broths sodden of meat.' And all as it were did begin to weep over him for exceeding pity and compassion, especially as it was the winter time and the cold was exceeding sore, and he was not yet free of the fever."

No less remarkable than his humility was the abounding love of Francis. It is probably not too much to say that Francis of Assisi was the most lovable man that has ever lived since the time of Jesus. His tender care for the lepers lasted all his life. He beheld in every poor man the representative of Christ. He triumphantly loved his enemies and particularly those who abused him or pelted him with stones or slander. His love took in all men and all nature, from the shining sun above, to the birds, the flowers and the helpless earthworm at his feet, and even the rock upon which he lay at night. Everywhere he saw God, and all things seemed to him transfigured in his radiant love. Love, for him, meant the absorption of himself and his fulfillment by God, as when he prayed, "I beseech Thee, O Lord, that the fiery and sweet strength of Thy love may absorb my soul from all things that are under heaven, that I may die for love of Thy love as Thou didst deign to die for love of my love."

Joy, and his esthetic and poetic love of all beauty, were closely related in his life. Daily his life seemed a new discovery of happiness. He went to meet life singing:

"Let me go where e'er I will,
I hear a sky-born music still.
E'en in the meanest, darkest things,
There always something, something sings."

Joy was one of the precepts of his Rule, and it was the word most often on the pen of the early Franciscan writers. They believed that "a joyous army is a victorious army." Upon sending out the lay friars to preach and sing the canticle of the sun he said, "Is it not in fact true that the servants of God are really like jugglers, intended to revive the hearts of men and lead them into spiritual joy?" "Like a ray of brilliant sunshine St. Francis dispersed the gloom of the middle ages, teaching men that the qualities of mercy and love were to be looked for from God instead of the inflexible justice that had overshadowed a religion intended to be all light. He walked the earth with joyous steps, inviting all to come with him and see how beautiful was the world; he looked upwards, praising God in bursts of eloquent song for the rain that fed the flowers, the birds that sang to him in the woods, and the blueness of his Umbrian sky."

As the last act of his life, with the brothers about him, Francis sang with strong voice the one hundred and forty-first Psalm. "Francis of Assisi had closed his lips forever; he went into eternity singing." Above his cell the larks were twittering. "It was Francis's good friends, the larks, who said the last farewell."

Francis's life was marked by utter devotion. His confessor, his companions, his biographers, not only passionately loved him, but seemed to stand in awe of him. Eighteen centuries have scarcely produced a man more constantly God-conscious. This was the central, unifying fact of his life. He moved about in the world but he lived in God. Francis seemed to see God as the substance of all things. Where others saw a shadow world of appearance he saw God. Like Jesus before him he seemed to see all life in parables which voiced the presence and beauty of the Divine. Renan maintained that the movement of St. Francis to restore primitive Christianity was the most powerful since the time of the Apostles.

Although at times a God-intoxicated man with his transports of joy, Francis normally maintained a rugged sanity and poise, an intuitive common sense that could often read the human soul and see to the heart of things with piercing glance. His sane view of the simple life he maintained with patient yet persistent independence against the constant pressure of the encroachments of formalism, asceticism, ecclesiasticism and materialism. Popes, cardinals, priests or populace, the voice of the *majores* or of the popular majorities could not move him from the direct inspiration of the Spirit, or loyalty to his earlier vision of the simple life. With all his deep reverence for the Church and its priesthood, the voice of God and his own soul was ultimate. He compares the hospitality of a cardinal to imprisonment for his spirit. "The cardinal desired to be kind to me, and I have truly great need of repose, but the Brothers who are out in the world, suffering hunger and a thousand tribulations, and also those others who are in hermitages or in miserable houses, when they hear of my sojourn with a cardinal will be moved to repine . . . They think me a holy man and see, it needed demons to cast me out of prison."

Francis's limitations were transparent, for he was the child of his age. He lived in a mediaeval world of demons and angels, of superstitions and credulous miracles. In the midst of it his sanity is the more remarkable. The tradition of his life, which grew apace both before and after his death, found expression in the lovely "Little Flowers of St. Francis." Though wonders and miracles are on every page, the fragrance of his life and the tender humility of his spirit are faithfully preserved. The taming of his brother wolf, the silencing of the chattering swallows while he preached, the conversion of robbers and murderers, the playing and singing of the angels at his request as he lay ill in his lowly cell—there were always miracles for those who expected them.

One of his limitations was his aversion to learning. He did not possess a speculative mind. He said everything in concrete images. He had an aversion to the pride of abstract knowledge. Father Cuthbert says, "Francis did not anathematize academic study and book-learning as an evil in itself, but he valued as a supreme treasure of his vocations that heart-knowledge which is gained in the battle of life when men are wholly intent upon the achievement of the cause to which they are consecrated. Any learning other than this was to him a mere mental luxury and a distraction from the real business of life, and tended to self-conceit more than to the service of God." Learning was indeed abused by some of the monks of the older orders. Men were pulling down their barns to build greater storehouses, both of earthly treasure and of proud learning divorced from human needs. He would say, "Get your books into your heart of hearts; whoever heard of Christ opening books save when he opened the book in the synagogue, then closed it and went forth to teach the world forever." With all his limitations and self-confessed sins, Francis remains, as we have said, probably the most lovable man that the last eighteen centuries have produced, with the unstained spirit of a little child, the world's younger brother.

5. WHAT WERE THE RESULTS OF FRANCIS'S LIFE?

What happened to Francis himself can soon be told. Reviled and disinherited by his father, jeered and pelted with stones as a madman by the children of his city, opposed by many of the cardinals and priests to whose comfortable lives he was a silent rebuke, thwarted by his successor Elias and other leaders, circumvented by the ubiquitous control of clericalism which settled like a pall upon his simple order, and at times baffled by the worldliness which crept into his fellowship even during his lifetime, he simply repeated and literally reproduced the life of his Master before him. He was persecuted, bound and crucified in the flesh, yet the spirit of love that was reincarnated in this little poor man rose triumphant in his order and in thousands who are still affected by his life, whose influence seems undiminished after seven centuries.

In the words of Matthew Arnold: "He brought religion to the people. He founded the most popular body of ministers of religion that has ever existed in the church. He transformed monachism by uprooting the stationary monk, delivering him from the bondage of property, and sending him, as a mendicant friar, to be a stranger and sojourner; not in the wilderness, but in the most crowded haunts of men, to console them, and to do them good."

Least among the lasting results of his life were the more immediate material effects. The people of jealous Perugia lay in wait by the road as Francis was borne in his last illness to carry him off by force so that he might die there and bless their city. Soldiers were sent to escort him by another road that he might die on the ground by his beloved church, the Portiuncula; for Francis was now their "saint." Within two years, his friend Pope Gregory IX canonized and placed among the greatest of the saints the poor man of Assisi. Here was built the first Gothic church in Italy in the dawn of the Renaissance. Here first Cimabue, the father of Italian art, in 1240, "born in the city of Florence to give the first light to the art of painting," decorated parts of the great basilicas. In the lower church, Giotto, the friend of Dante, and himself a member of Francis's third order, in whom the "Italian genius first attained to self-expression," produced his greater masterpieces. Perhaps it was fitting that in the beauty of his church the Renaissance of Italian painting was born, yet Sabatier thus concludes his life of Francis, "This marvellous basilica is also one of the documents of this history. . . . Go and look upon it, proud, rich, powerful, then go down to Portiuncula, pass over to St. Damain, hasten to the Carceri, and you will understand the abyss that separates the ideal of Francis from that of the pontiff who canonized him."

Dante, who was also a Tertiary in the Franciscan order, tells the story of Francis in the eleventh canto of his "Paradise," in the Divine Comedy. He speaks of him who "rose upon the world a sun." For him for more than eleven hundred years the lady Poverty had "waited without a suitor till he came."

> "On the rude rock 'twixt Tiber and the Arno, from Christ did he receive the final seal, which during two whole years his members bore.
> When he who chose him unto so much good, was pleased to draw him up to the reward that he had merited by being lowly,
> Unto his friars, as to the rightful heirs, his most dear Lady did he recommend, and bade that they should love her faithfully,
> And from her bosom the illustrious soul wished to depart, returning to its realm, and for its body wished no other bier."

The movement at first was a group of twelve friends gathering about Francis as a leader. Before the time of his death some five thousand had joined the order. They included all classes of men "rich and poor, prudent and simple, clerics and laymen." When Francis died in 1226 Brother Elias had already been minister-general of the order for five years, backed by Pope Gregory IX. He built the great church and monastery at Assisi in opposition to all Francis' ideas, he organized and extended the order throughout the world, as the Franciscans entered the universities in Oxford, Paris and other parts of Europe as teachers of theology and law. The rule of Elias, however, was despotic and tyrannical and it produced a violent reaction which deposed him in 1239.

The order was now divided into three parties. There was a minority of Zealots, or Spirituals, who stood for the literal observance of the strict rule of Francis. At the other extreme was a party of relaxation. Between were the majority of moderates who stood for the simple life, somewhat modified, coupled with a position of influence in the universities in theology and the sciences. This moderate party included most of the friars of England, France and Germany.

At the time of the Reformation in 1517 Pope Leo X divided the order into two distinct bodies. The Conventuals followed the papal dispensations and were allowed to possess property. The more strict Observants were bound to the observance of Francis' rule. The latter have ever since been the more numerous and influential body.

No other order has so closely clung, throughout its whole history, to the humble ministry of the poor. They have maintained missions to the Mohammedans in North Africa and the Near East; as well as to non-Christians in China, Japan, India, North and South America. The Franciscans entered England in 1224 and settled in Canterbury, London and Oxford. Here they excelled in intellectual achievement. Francis numbers among his sons the great friar Roger Bacon, the father of modern scientific investigation; Dons

Scotus, Occam and a galaxy of notable scholars. There were four Franciscan Popes.

The Franciscan body has always been by far the most numerous of all the religious orders. At the time of the Reformation the Friars Minor numbered nearly a hundred thousand. Today there are about 26,000 of Francis' little brothers scattered abroad in the world, many of whom have preserved much of his spirit. His influence is undiminished in the world after seven centuries and the number of those influenced directly or indirectly by his life is a great multitude which no man can number.

CHAPTER 4

FREEDOM FROM ECCLESIASTICAL BONDAGE

Martin Luther

1. WHAT KIND OF A WORLD DID LUTHER LIVE IN?

Few men have ever lived during whose lifetime such momentous changes occurred as those which took place during the days of Martin Luther. One great revolution is sufficient to make notable the century of its occurrence. Yet during the lifetime of Luther, (1483-1546) three stupendous revolutions are recorded: the conclusion of the Renaissance, the beginning of the Reformation, and the rise of Capitalism. Rapid strides were also made in the direction of Individualism and Nationalism.

Only four decades before Luther's birth came the notable invention of printing by Gutenberg, thus making possible the spread of popular education and the rise of modern democracy. During this period new universities and institutions of higher learning were springing up throughout Europe. Many notable men of science and art were laying the foundations of the new learning. Copernicus and Servetus, Machiavelli and Reuchlin, Erasmus and Hutten, Leonardo da Vinci and Titian, Holbein and Durer, Raphael and Michelangelo, all were Luther's contemporaries. Luther was a boy of nine when Columbus discovered America, and before he died Vasco da Gama and Magellan had completed their voyages of circumnavigation, thus opening up a whole new world.

Profound economic changes took place during the fifteenth and sixteenth centuries. During the Middle Ages production had been carried on by cooperative effort through the guilds. The land belonged to the village and was allotted for given periods or held for common use. Gradually, however, the "natural economy" system, in which payments were made in the form of service or barter, gave way to "money economy," in which gold and silver became the medium of exchange. The guild system of production was supplanted by production with private capital. Communism yielded to individualism. Money became king. Increasing power fell into the hands of bankers and traders. Commercial men began to buy up the estates of the nobles.

Great areas of communal had passed into private ownership. The gradual breakdown of feudalism and the freedom of the serfs created a landless proletariat who drifted into the towns and cities. The cost of living advanced rapidly and the rank and file of workers lived in a state of almost indescribable misery. Strikers and riots became increasingly frequent and serious. The notables and middle class merchants and bankers were for the most part callous to the sufferings of the poor.

With the rise of the commercial classes came a demand for strong and stable government. It was natural, therefore, that under such circumstances the power of kings should be increased. Thus nationalism received a great stimulus. The unfolding of nationalism began in France, during the twelfth and thirteenth centuries. By the middle of the fourteenth century the German nobles were almost independent of the emperor and declared that he derived his title from them and not from the pope. The Hapsburgs came into power in 1438 and furnished emperors to Germany for the next three hundred years. From the beginning of the sixteenth century the opposition within Germany to Roman rule began to assume formidable proportions. Without the continuous support of powerful German nobles, Luther could never have achieved his work.

By far the most significant fact about Europe at the time when Luther began his work was the enormous power wielded by the Catholic Church. The absolute domination of every realm of life by the Church seems almost incredible to persons reared in modern America. No longer was Christianity a despised and persecuted religion, numbering only the meek and lowly among its adherents. The leaders of the Church now sat in the seats of the mighty and ruled a vast continent with an iron hand. To understand the significance of Luther's life and work one must keep in mind the essential Catholic doctrines and the actual effects of ecclesiastical domination on the life of Europe.

The mediaeval conception of society was very simple. The whole of Christendom was regarded as a unity. Church and state were not sharply divided but were looked upon as two phases of one society. Spiritual and temporal were opposite sides of the same shield. The emperor of the Holy Roman Empire was temporal sovereign of most of Europe, while the pope was spiritual lord of Christendom. As the spiritual side of life is vastly more important than the temporal, so the pope was regarded as superior to the emperor, the supreme authority of Christendom, the successor of Peter and Jesus. By the twelfth century the popes were actually exercising absolute sovereignty in matters of state throughout most of the continent. They made and unmade kings and emperors, they exercised a minute supervision over thought and deed in every part of the land. The church levied taxes and fees for the support of the innumerable army of its hierarchy. Even the humblest priest was inviolable. No matter what crime he might commit he was beyond reach of the secular arm and only the Church had jurisdiction over him.

The Church controlled the education, the amusement, and the worship of people everywhere. Spiritual and temporal blessings in this world and salvation in the world to come had their sole origin in the Church. Baptism at the hands of a representative of the Church was the only means of gaining salvation. Those persons, including infants, who had not been baptised, at the time of death, were consigned to the flames of hell throughout eternity. The Church alone could join in marriage or give honorable burial, and its courts alone administered the bequests of the deceased. The

Church alone could interpret the Scriptures and all truth was in its infallible keeping. It spoke with absolute authority and insisted upon implicit obedience to every doctrine and command. Dissent was heresy and was punished with the utmost rigor.

The Inquisition

In the thirteenth century a special institution known as the Inquisition was inaugurated to hunt out and restrain heretics. Since heretics were regarded as lost souls who would burn endlessly in hell if they died unrepentant, extreme bodily and mental torture was inflicted by the Church in the endeavor to restore the guilty one to orthodoxy and salvation. The most violent punishment at the hands of the Church was regarded as an act of mercy to a vile sinner. Far better than the body should suffer than that the soul should be damned. Especially so since the guilty one, if left unrestrained, would drag many of the faithful with him into the depths of perdition.

No sooner had Christianity conquered the Roman emperor than force was resorted to in dealing with dissenters. Before his death Constantine had inflicted confiscation of property, torture and the death penalty in seeking to suppress the dissenters. Then the Church was torn with bitterness and violence over the Arian controversy. Not until the fifth century and the beginning of the Dark Ages was heresy effectively stamped out. For nearly five hundred years thereafter human intelligence was so dormant that heresy ceased to be a force. Early in the eleventh century, however, thirteen heretics were burned at the stake in France. Then followed a period of five centuries when the Church availed itself of every conceivable weapon of torture in seeking to restrain the rising tide of dissent and heresy. Excommunication, banishment, confiscation, imprisonment, bribery, whipping, branding, loss of the tongue, torture with the rack, the pulleys, hot irons, and other devices, (the prisoner, whether man or woman, being stripped nude), starvation, hanging and burning at the stake. The death penalty was not actually administered by the Church. The condemned man was turned over to the secular arm for this purpose. The Church, however, not only sanctioned the death penalty, it insisted that the State must enforce it in the case of extreme offenders condemned by the Inquisition, and threatened the excommunication of any delinquent official of the State. The inquisitors were given a special immunity not only from interference at the hands of secular officials but also from the supervision and control of bishops and other ecclesiastics.

To grasp the real significance of the limitless power wielded by the Inquisition, it is necessary to remember that it was regarded as heresy to deny the truth of any doctrine of the Church or to refuse in any way to obey the ecclesiastical authorities, whether the doctrine dealt with astronomy or physics, geography or geology, medicine or chemistry, education or government. For extent, duration and intensity the reign of terror which everywhere accompanied the Inquisition is unparalleled in human history.[1] Germany, however, escaped its worst horrors. It never did take root there as in Italy, Spain, France and elsewhere. While it still maintained a nominal existence in Germany at the time of Luther's revolt, it retained so little actual power that it was helpless to silence or destroy even such an arch-heretic as Luther. And thus the course of history was changed.

The Degeneracy of the Church

It is extremely painful to call attention to the condition of Christendom at the time Luther began his work. The Church had fallen on evil days. Graft and corruption were widespread. High ecclesiastical offices were openly purchased. Simony, the buying and selling of the things of God, was almost universal. Every function of the priest became a source of revenue. "Marriage and funeral cere-

[1]Concerning the total number of victims of the Inquisition no reliable figures are available. Llorente calculated that the number condemned was 219,653 of whom 14,344 were burned at the stake. Most authorities believe that these figures are far too high. Father Gams puts the number burned alive at 4,000. See H. C. Lea, History of the Inquisition. Vol. 3, pp. 517, 518.

monies were refused unless the fees demanded were paid in advance, and the Eucharist was withheld from the communicant unless he offered an oblation." A chief source of ecclesiastical revenue was the sale of indulgences, or the remission of temporal penalties of sin, including penance in this life and the pains of purgatory. Indulgences were first granted as rewards to warriors who fell fighting the infidel. The Church not only claimed power to free the living from the future pains of purgatory but also to remove the dead from purgatory. Thus, for the payment of a fee, the faithful could relieve the agonies of their deceased loved ones. Indulgences of this sort became one of the most fruitful sources of revenue for the Church. At the time of Luther's activity, the sale of indulgences had become a "thoroughly commercialized business of selling grace and remission of the penalties of sin." The sale of indulgences was not confined to the clergy; laymen were enlisted as well. The rich banker, James Fugger, sold indulgences on a commission basis of 33 1-3 per cent.

Heavy fees and tithes were assessed for building and maintaining huge cathedrals. Beard tells us that at the beginning of the sixteenth century one-fourth, perhaps one-third of the land of Germany, was in the hands of the Church. Vast wealth was squandered by ecclesiastics in the effort to maintain the protection and patronage of powerful princes and nobles. Many priests, bishops and higher officials lived in riotous luxury.

The gross immorality of many ecclesiastics, high and low, had long been notorious. In the early church the clergy were permitted to marry but at the beginning of the fourth century a movement was launched which sought to enforce celibacy upon the priesthood. In 384 the pope issued a decree imposing celibacy upon all ministers of the altar but this command was for centuries flagrantly violated. At the beginning of the eleventh century the ancient prohibitions were still theoretically in force, but "they were practically obsolete everywhere. Legitimate marriage or promiscuous profligacy was almost universal, in some places unconcealed, in others covered with a thin veil of hypocrisy." At the middle of the eleventh century "marriage was a universal privilege of the Milanese clergy." In 1215, however, the Fourth Council of Lateran insisted upon strict celibacy for priests. Thereafter open marriages among ecclesiastics ceased. But illicit relations and open concubinage were widely practiced. Mr. Lea has summarized a vast volume of evidence in these words: "Unfortunately, there can be no denial of the fact that notorious and undisguised illicit unions, or still more debasing secret licentiousness, was a universal and pervading vice of the Church throughout Christendom. Its traces amid all the ecclesiastical legislation of the thirteenth, fourteenth, and fifteenth centuries, are too broad and deep to be called into question, and if no evidence remained except the constant and unavailing efforts to repress it, that alone would be sufficient. National and local synods, pastoral epistles, statutes of churches, all the records of ecclesiastical discipline are full of it."

"In Germany," says Beard, "at the end of the fifteenth century, it seemed as if the contest against invincible propensities of human nature had been given up in despair; from such a prelate, for instance, as Albert of Mainz, no one would have expected chastity, and on one thought the worse of him for not practicing it; while parish priests everywhere openly kept women in their houses, who were wives in all but the name, and the mothers of children whose recognition involved no shame."

The eminent Catholic historian, Father Grisar, quotes with approval the following statement: "The numerous regulations of bishops and synods leave no doubt about the fact that a large portion of the German clergy transgressed the law of celibacy in the most flagrant manner."

That conditions were becoming intolerable was manifest to a growing number of devout men within the Church. There were many forerunners of the Reformation. The Albigenses and Waldenses had revolted against rigid ecclesiasticism and carnal mindedness within the church and had received the reward of heretics. Eckhart, Tauler, Thomas á

Kempis, Wyclif, Huss and Savonarola had raised their voices in eloquent protest and had not lived in vain. But only the merest beginning had been made in removing even the grossest abuses within the Church. Notwithstanding the prevalence of appalling corruption and unspeakable immorality in all ranks of the hierarchy, the Church still ruled with an iron hand and all of Christendom must obey without question or be subjected to unrelenting persecution in this life and eternal damnation in the world to come. In most realms of thought and activity the human spirit was shackled and bound. Human progress was conditioned upon bursting asunder the chains of ecclesiastical tyranny. It was into such a world and at such an hour that Martin Luther was born.

2. *What Did Luther Do?*

Few great men of history began life under such obscure and humble circumstances as did Martin Luther. He was born on November 10, 1483, in the village of Eisleben in central Germany. His father was a peasant miner, with only meager natural gifts and with no advantages. His mother was a quiet, austere woman, a most rigid disciplinarian. Martin was the oldest child. Shortly after his birth the family moved to the mining town of Mansfield, where they lived in abject poverty. In the village school Latin was the chief subject and the pupils were required not only to read it but to speak it as well. Ignorance and brutality were marked characteristics of the teachers of those days. In referring to his painful experiences in school Luther later said: "The examination was like a trial for murder." The teacher once beat him fifteen times in a single morning.

At the age of thirteen, Martin was sent away to a religious school at Marburg, where he earned his way by begging on the streets. The following year he was transferred to Eisenbach. Here he was taken into the home of a very devout and wealthy family named Cottas. In 1501 his father, by great effort and privation, sent him to the famous old University of Erfurt. The studies which he pursued while here would seem unbearably dry and barren to a modern student. The next year he received the bachelor of arts degree, and three years later he was awarded the master's degree.

In accordance with the wishes of his father he then began to study law, one of the easiest roads to fame and fortune. Within two months he abruptly abandoned the law and entered a monastery. Various explanations have been advanced for this precipitous action. It seems that he became disgusted with the study of law and went home to secure his father's permission to change his course. On his way back to the university he was overtaken by a terrible thunderstorm and in his fright vowed to St. Anna to be a monk if his life was spared. People of that day were exceedingly superstitious and regarded storms as the direst interposition of the devil. Moreover, there is every reason to believe that Martin, deeply religious as he was, had frequently contemplated the abandonment of the world and may have partially decided upon this step. At any rate, in a blinding storm he reached the decision which was destined to change the course of history.

On July 17, 1505, at the age of twenty-two, he entered the Augustinian Convent at Erfurt as a noviciate. Here the brilliant university scholar began to scrub floors and to beg upon the streets. Shortly afterward, through the efforts of the Vicar John von Staupitz, he was relieved of his servile labours and sent back to his studies. He now began to specialize in the study of the Bible and to read speculative theology. On May 2, 1507, Luther was admitted to the priesthood and continued as inmate of the Convent at Erfurt until the end of 1508. During these years he devoted himself with great zeal to the monastic method of reaching perfection, praying industriously night and day, practicing long fastings and sleepless vigils. But he found little spiritual satisfaction. Later he wrote: "When I was the most devout, I went a doubter to the altar, a doubter I came away from it; if I had confessed my penitence, I still doubted; had I not, I was in despair." Staupitz seemed to understand him and finally helped him to overcome his doubts and to regain his faith.

In 1508 he accepted an invitation to become a teacher in the University of Wittenberg, which had recently been founded by Frederick the Wise, Elector of Saxony. And so he began his work in the town in which he was to spend the rest of his days. Not very much is known of his work at Wittenberg between 1508 and 1512, when he took his doctor's degree. The most important event was the trip to Rome in 1511. A pilgrimage to the Holy City was the deepest longing of a pious monk, and Luther eagerly embraced the opportunity to become the travelling companion of John von Mecheln, who was making the trip for the purpose of transacting certain business for the Augustinian order. The long journey was made on foot. The first sight of the ancient city deeply stirred the devout heart of Luther, and he fell on his face and cried: "Hail, Holy Rome! Thrice holy thou in whom the blood of the martyrs has been poured out!" While in the city he spent most of his time visiting various holy places and institutions of mercy. The most significant thing about his visit, however, was the terrible shock he received upon observing the moral corruption and spiritual destitution of clergy and laity alike. This sad experience did not for the moment destroy his faith in the Church, nor break his loyalty to the pope, but it was the beginning of the complete breach which came ten years later.

From 1512 to 1517 Luther was a professor at the University of Wittenberg, of which his old friend Staupitz had become dean. He now began to lecture on the Bible, a practice which he never abandoned throughout his lifetime. At this period Luther's growing revolt against Scholasticism came to a climax. In September, 1517, a month before he issued his renowned ninety-five theses, he published ninety-seven theses denying the value of Aristotle's works as text-books. In his lectures he poured contempt on the methods of Aristotle. He was so successful in his protests that a complete reform of the university curriculum was carried through. Luther devoted himself to the Bible and to the Fathers, especially to Augustine. He was not yet prepared to make the Bible his ultimate authority, but he was moving rapidly in that direction.

In addition to his duties at the university, Luther was preaching constantly and soon developed into a most powerful orator, with "vivid imagination, picturesqueness of style, fluency of speech, personal magnetism, passionate earnestness, and an uncommon knowledge of the religious emotions born of his own heart-searching experiences." He also had many additional duties, as may be seen from the following summary from his own pen: "I am lecturer in the cloister and reader at meals; I am daily asked to preach in the parish church; I am director of studies; I am vicar, which means being prior eleven times over; inspector of fish-ponds at Leitzpan; advocate of the Herzberger's cause at Torgan; I am lecturing on Paul, and gathering material on the Psalms—all this besides my letter-writing."

On October 31, 1517, came the turning point in Luther's career. On that day he nailed his ninety-five theses concerning indulgences on the door of the church in Wittenberg. This was in accord with the custom of the day in announcing theological debates on important questions. In this dramatic manner Luther announced his intention of discussing the vital question of indulgences. The situation at once became electric, because Pope Leo X, in his efforts to secure funds for the rebuilding of St. Peter's Church at Rome, had only a short time before proclaimed a plenary indulgence, "offering to believing purchasers all sorts of benefits, including remission of sins, freedom from the necessity of penance, and the release of their deceased friends from purgatory." The Archbishop of Mayence was appointed to superintend the traffic in a part of Germany, and he in turn engaged as his chief agent a Dominican monk named John Tetzel. When Luther's parishioners flocked to an adjoining town to buy indulgences from Tetzel, he became enraged and refused to accept Tetzel's papers in lieu of confession. For some months, however, he refrained from launching a public attack against the traffic. After a long and intensive study of the whole subject he chose the method of announcing a debate as the best means of making public his convictions. And so he drew up the propositions which he proposed to defend and nailed them to the church door. In his theses he not only attacked the idea of indulgences, but repudiated the principles upon which the whole penitential system of the church was based. The effect was instantaneous and stupendous. The fact that Luther at once became the target of a terrific volley of abuse from the hierarchy was not so significant as was the tremendous enthusiasm with which his action was received by the rank and file of people throughout Germany. The widespread resentment against ecclesiastical abuses which had only been smouldering burst into a flame, and instantly Luther became a national figure, and his action became a subject of controversy throughout Christendom. His own sovereign, the Elector of Saxony, and several powerful nobles rallied to his support. The Humanists welcomed him as an ally, and the populace looked upon him as a national hero and deliverer. His theses were translated into German and spread like wildfire throughout the country.

At first the Pope dismissed the matter of the theses by saying: "A drunken German wrote them. When he is sober he will think differently." It was soon discovered, however, that the sale of indulgences was falling off rapidly. After threatening excommunication, the Archbishop referred the case to Rome. The Pope then requested the head of the Augustinian order to silence his rebellious monk. Luther was so popular with Staupitz and other Augustinians in Germany that headquarters did not deem it wise to press the case.

Luther then published a commentary on the theses, in which the conflict was widened to include an attack on the idea of papal authority, although Luther still regarded himself as a loyal subject of the Pope and was still unwilling to attack the papacy itself. In anticipation of possible excommunication, he preached a sermon in which he declared that exclusion from the Church could harm no one provided he retained the Christian virtues. This sermon fanned the flames of fury within ecclesiastical circles and also alienated some secular supporters, who regarded it as undermining law and order.

On August 7, 1518, Luther received an imperative summons to appear in Rome within sixty days and answer the charge of heresy. Without waiting for the expiration of this time, the Pope called upon the Elector of Saxony to turn Luther over to Cardinal Cajetan, the papal legate at the Diet of Augsburg. Luther's life depended upon the Elector's decision. Had his sovereign faltered in his support, the history of Christendom would have been utterly different. While Frederick disavowed sympathy with heresy, he urged that the case be transferred to Germany. The political situation was such that the Pope did not dare risk alienating so powerful a figure, and so it was agreed that Luther should appear for trial at Augsburg. Upon his arrival, Luther was given a reception by leading men of the town. His interviews with the Cardinal proved to be unsatisfactory, and finally he was dismissed with the command not to appear again until he was prepared to recant. He was smuggled out of town by friends and returned to Wittenberg. The Cardinal then demanded of Frederick that he turn Luther over to Rome or expel him from Saxony. After consultation with Luther, the elector refused to follow either course and suggested that Luther be brought to trial before an impartial tribunal to see if any of his teachings were really heretical.

During 1519 occurred two events of great importance—the election of Emperor Charles and the famous Leipzig debate. The election of the new emperor gave a tremendous impetus to nationalism in Germany and had an important bearing upon the progress of the Reformation. Dr. John Eck, of the University of Ingolstadt, one of the ablest Catholic theologians of the day, challenged Carlstadt and Luther to a debate. The challenge was accepted and the great debate began on June 27th. In the course of his argument, Luther challenged the absolutism and infallibility of the Pope. "He did not deny the supremacy of the Pope.

He claimed only that he ruled by human, not divine, right, and a Christian might therefore be saved even if he refused to submit to his authority." When Eck rejoined that this was in accord with the heretical doctrine of John Huss, Luther replied: "It is certain that among the articles of John Huss and the Bohemians are many most Christian and evangelical, and these the universal church cannot condemn." This was the climax of the debate and made inevitable the final break with Rome. Luther's friends were horrified and felt sure he had signed his own death warrant. Rome proceeded with great caution. The ecclesiastical authorities knew that Luther was a heretic, but they also knew that he was supported by the most important prince in Germany and that the aroused public sentiment in his favor could not lightly be disregarded. After several months' delay, the papal bull Exurge Domine, published on June 15, 1520, condemned forty-one propositions from Luther's writings, forbade the reading of his books and called upon Christians to burn them, suspended him from the ministry, announced his excommunication if he did not recant within sixty days, and threatened with the ban anybody who should support or protect him. On December 10th Luther took the final step by publicly burning the bull and the canon law in Wittenberg.

It was now the emperor's move. The Pope had done his worst when he issued the ban of excommunication. Elector Frederick had sufficient influence with the emperor to prevent Luther's condemnation without a hearing. And so an imperial summons was issued requiring Luther to appear before the Diet of Worms and guaranteeing him safe conduct both in going and returning. Luther's journey to Worms "was nothing less than a triumphal procession."

When he appeared before the diet he was shown a pile of some twenty of his own books and asked whether he would retract the whole or any part of their contents. He asked for a delay in answering and was given twenty-four hours in which to reach a decision. The next day he replied that he would retract if it should be proved that his teachings were not in accord with the Bible. When reproved for evasion and commanded to give a direct answer whether or not he would recant, he replied in the following memorable words: "Since your Majesty and your Lordships asks for a plain answer, I will give you one without either horns or teeth. Unless I am convicted by Scripture or by right reason —for I trust neither in popes nor in councils, since they have often erred and contradicted themselves—unless I am thus convinced, I am bound by the texts of the Bible, my conscience is captive to the Word of God, I neither can nor will recant anything, since it is neither right nor safe to act against conscience. God help me. Amen."[2] Carlyle speaks of this occasion as "the greatest scene in modern European history; the point, indeed, from which the whole subsequent history of civilization takes its rise."

On April 26th Luther left Worms with an imperial safe conduct good for twenty days. Shortly after his departure an imperial edict of condemnation was issued. He was to be seized wherever found and sent to the emperor. All his books were ordered burned, and to befriend or hold communication with him was to commit the crime of lese-majesty. From that hour until death Luther lived as an outlaw and a fugitive from justice.

Elector Frederick was still prepared to support Luther, although he did not care to do so publicly, and decided to seclude him for a while. Accordingly, while Luther and two friends were riding through the great forest near Möhra, masked men appeared and took Luther captive to the Elector's castle at Wartburg. In this beautiful spot he remained hidden for nearly a year.

During Luther's absence, his friends at Wittenberg proceeded to put his principles into immediate practice. Carl-

---

[2]Preserved Smith, Life and Letters of Luther, p. 118. See also A. C. McGiffert, Martin Luther, p. 203 for a similar version. In this connection Hartmann Grisar says: "The celebrated exclamation put into Luther's mouth: 'Here I stand. I cannot do otherwise. God help me, Amen!' usually quoted....is a legend which has not even the credit of being incorporated in Luther's Latin account of his speech." (Luther, Vol. 2, p. 75.)

stadt publicly attacked clerical celibacy and a number of priests married. Many innovations were made in the religious services. Soon certain fanatical spirits from Zuickan appeared in Wittenberg, claiming supernatural illumination, and proceeded to stir up the populace. Riots broke out, and when the situation got beyond the control of Melanchthon, the town council sent an urgent request to Luther, imploring him to return. Against the wishes of Frederick, Luther responded to this appeal and soon appeared at Wittenberg. He risked his life by appearing publicly and preaching on eight successive days. He exhorted the people to refrain from violence and to exercise moderation. After pacifying Wittenberg, he visited Weimar, Erfurt, and other neighboring places, preaching with great success against violence and sedition.

The revolt against Rome was now spreading rapidly. Town after town took charge of its own religious affairs and made many changes in the form of worship. The Reformation was beginning to assume large proportions. From this time on Luther was constantly appealed to for advice and became more and more of an overseer or bishop of the churches which broke away from Rome.

In the summer of 1522, Franz von Sickingen, who formerly had valiantly supported Luther, sought to enlist his aid and that of his followers in an attack upon the Archbishop of Treves. He hoped by this means to restore the rapidly waning power of the nobles. Luther refused to become involved in this civil war and Sickingen's campaign was a complete failure. This experience strengthened Luther's determination not to use violence in promoting his cause.

In 1525 occurred the famous Peasants' Revolt, which had very serious consequences for the Reformation. The peasants were normally a harmless and peaceable people, but were goaded into revolt by terrible exploitation. The first attempts at rebellion were put down ruthlessly. This only tended to arouse the peasants and make them more violent. Revolutionary and communistic ideas spread rapidly. Riots broke out in many sections and serious civil war was imminent. The peasants everywhere expected the aid of Luther and quoted his words as their charter of freedom. But to their dismay, he took sides against them. He proclaimed the doctrine of the divine right of kings and said that only the constituted authorities had the right to use the sword. He published two pamphlets which had wide influence and helped to defeat the peasants, the second of these being entitled, "Against the Murderous and Thieving Mobs of Peasants." The princes soon got together and the rebellion was ruthlessly crushed. The effects on Luther and the Reformation were stupendous. Thousands of supporters fell away to the radical Anabaptists. No longer was Luther the popular hero of Germany. He himself became hardened and embittered. His position was made even more dangerous and difficult by his unfortunate quarrel with Erasmus and subsequent break with the humanists. To have lost the support of the peasants and the intellectuals within a single year was a tragedy from which the Reformation never fully recovered.

Tremendous excitement was created by Luther's marriage with Katharine von Bora on June 13, 1525. He had long since attacked the idea of clerical celibacy and had often thought of marrying, as an example to his followers. Katharine was a former nun who, with eight others, had left the convent and come to Wittenberg. The marriage proved to be very successful. Katharine survived her husband by six years.

Until his death in 1525, Elector Frederick protected Luther and quietly supported his work. When his brother, John, succeeded him the situation changed. The latter became an open and aggressive supporter of the Reformation. From this time forward Luther spent much time in visiting the churches throughout Saxony. The imperial Diet of Spires in 1526 gave a tacit approval to the Reformation. In 1530 the Protestant princes formed the League of Schmalkalden for mutual protection and advantage. Within ten years this league was one of the great powers of Europe.

Gradually a new Church was emerging. For a time it looked as if the whole of Germany might be swept into a national Church, but hostility among the princes made this impossible. At the time of Luther's death northern Germany was officially Protestant, while southern Germany was predominantly Catholic.

From the very beginning of his work, Luther was an extraordinarily prolific writer. A steady stream of books and pamphlets poured from his pen. His greatest monument, says one of his biographers, is the German Bible. The New Testament was completed during the year he was in seclusion in the Wartburg in 1521. The Old Testament appeared in sections, the last part being published in 1532. It seems almost incredible that this man, in addition to his regular work of preaching, teaching, and visitation of the churches, should have produced 420 separate works, many of them of great length.

3. WHAT DID LUTHER SAY?

Three of Luther's writings, known in Germany as the "Three Great Reformation Treatises," contain the heart of his message. They are: "The Liberty of a Christian Man," "To the Christian Nobility of the German Nation," and "On the Babylonian Captivity of the Church." They were all published in 1520, when Luther was thirty-seven years old. Of the first Luther later said: "A very small book so far as the paper is concerned, but one containing the whole sum of the Christian life." Its main thesis is *the priesthood of all believers as a consequence of justification by faith.* If a man has faith, he has all; if he has not faith, he has nothing. Religious ceremonies may be helpful, but they are not essential. At best they are merely means to an end; if they prove to be a hindrance they ought to be swept away. Upon this idea the Reformation was founded. Its implications were far-reaching. It undermined the whole doctrine of exclusive salvation at the hands of the Church and broke the bonds of ecclesiastical authority. Few ideas in history have produced greater changes in human society than this one, which now appears so obvious to millions of Christians.

In the "Babylonian Captivity of the Church," Luther dealt with the sacramental system and severely denounced many current attitudes and practices of the Church. Without faith no sacrament is efficacious, with faith no sacrament is essential.

His appeal "To the Christian Nobility of the German Nation" was a call to all Germans to unite against alien Rome. He set himself the task of demolishing the three great ideas which had held Europe in awed submission for so many centuries. First, the doctrine of spiritual power, which was regarded as superior to the temporal power of kings and princes; second, the conception that no one can interpret Scripture but the Pope; third, the idea that no one can summon a General Council but the Bishop of Rome. Over against the first of these he set the idea of the priesthood of all believers; against the second, the idea that any true believer who possesses the mind of Christ can interpret the Word of God; against the third, the lack of Scriptural authority and the precedent of the early Church, when emperors called General Councils.

In his ninety-five theses on indulgences he attacked the ceremonial system and declared that the Christian who has truly repented has already been forgiven by God and has no need of an indulgence. Christ demands only true repentance and no intermediary is required in asking pardon from God.

While Luther was severe in his denunciation of ecclesiastical abuses, it was with great reluctance that he broke with Rome, and even after the final breach he had no intention of founding a new church. President McGiffert says: "From the beginning it was reformation, not revolution, Luther wished—the old church brought into conformity with the word of God, not a new church independent of the old." The ban against him became a dead letter because of the refusal of the secular offices to enforce it, and he continued his work as teacher and preacher at Wittenberg until his death.

For the infallible authority of the Church, Luther substituted the authority of the Bible, as interpreted by the enlightened conscience of the Christian individual. He believed that in the Scripture God spoke to him in the same way that He had spoken to the Apostles. The Bible was, therefore, a means of direct access to God. It is a mistake, however, to think that Luther regarded the Bible as infallible in its entirety. He believed that some parts were more inspired than others, for example, the Gospel and First Epistle of John, the letters to the Romans, to the Galatians and to the Ephesians, and the First Epistle of St. Peter, and the Psalms. On the other hand, he rejected the Epistle of James as an Epistle of straw. "He denied the Mosaic authorship of part of the Pentateuch; he declared Job to be an allegory; Jonah was so childish that he was almost inclined to laugh at it; the book of Kings were 'a thousand paces ahead of Chronicles and more to be believed.' 'Ecclesiastes has neither boots nor spurs, but rides in socks as I did when I was in the cloister!' . . 'In comparison with them (St. Paul's epistles), James is a right straw epistle, for it has no evangelic manner about it.'" On another occasion he said: "Many sweat to reconcile St. Paul and St. James, as does Melanchthon in his Apology, but in vain. 'Faith justifies' and 'faith does not justify' contradict each other flatly."

On the other hand, it should be pointed out that Luther by no means accepted the modern view of Biblical criticism. He constantly used the proof-text method of dealing with his opponents and as a means of buttressing practices in which he believed, such as polygamy and witchcraft. Following his death the idea of an infallible and inerrant Bible became an even greater stumbling block to scientific and even moral progress.

Until the year 1531 Luther consistently refused to sanction the use of armed resistance to the emperor, "not because he disapproved of war as such, for as a German patriot he warmly advocated war against the Turks, but because he believed in submission to lawful rulers in all circumstances and whatever their character." But following the formation of the League of Schmalkalden he made use of "flimsy arguments" to justify armed resistance.

Luther did not believe in democracy, as we moderns understand the word. He failed to grasp the real significance of the peasants' revolt and met their cry for justice with the hoary doctrine of the divine right of kings. He had a profound distrust of the masses and often spoke of them in contemptuous tones, as, for example: "accursed, thievish, murderous peasants." At the time of the revolt he wrote: "It is better that all the peasants be killed than that the princes and magistrates perish, because the rustics took the sword without divine authority. The only possible consequence of their Satanic wickedness would be the diabolic devastation of the kingdom of God." As a consequence of this attitude, he failed to win the permanent support of the masses. His movement thereafter drew its main strength from the upper middle class, and to this day Lutheranism has only a feeble hold upon the rank and file of workers in Germany.

Luther's conception of woman and her place in society falls far short of present-day ideas. He accepted many of the current attitudes which assumed the inferiority of women. Her place is in the home, where she must be industrious, faithful and obedient. Her chief function is to bear children. Luther believed that chastity was impossible and urged everyone to get married. After the break with Rome, he had brothels closed in the reformed cities. Concerning his attitude toward immorality, Father Grisar, a prominent Catholic historian, says: "Luther never sanctioned sexual commerce outside matrimony."

Luther was strongly opposed to divorce and thought polygamy was preferable. One of the most serious blots on his record was his attitude toward the bigamy of Philip of Hesse, one of the most powerful princes of Germany and a mainstay of Protestantism. Philip, who was a notorious debauchee, secured written permission from his first wife to marry seventeen-year-old Margaret von der Saal, and then approached Luther for his approval. On the ground that bigamy is better than adultery or divorce, Luther consented, on condition that the affair be kept secret. He even went so far as to advise Philip to deny the marriage and, if necessary, "tell a good, strong lie for the sake and good of the Christian Church." On the other hand, it should be pointed out that Luther had a very high conception of the home and did much to elevate the whole idea of marriage. He rendered no small service to humanity by ascribing to married life a sacredness far above the celibacy of a monk or nun.

One of the significant phases of Luther's teaching was his denunciation of mendicancy and begging and his glorification of honest toil. In a world filled with religious beggars who lived on alms and where asceticism was widely prevalent, to dignify labor above idleness was a service of incalculable value. Among Luther's sayings in this connection are the following: "God has no use for the lazy, unfaithful idler . . . Work is divine; it is God's command; we cannot be too diligent; work belongs to human nature; as a bird to fly so is a man born to work—there he finds his divine destination. . . To cultivate the earth is a divine work. . . If you do not work so that you may support yourself and have to give to the needy, you are no Christian, but a thief and a robber."

4. WHAT HAPPENED TO LUTHER?

It is exceedingly difficult for modern Protestants to understand the intensity with which Luther was hated by the ecclesiastical leaders of his day. From their point of view he was not only a vile heretic doomed to eternal damnation, but was also an open rebel who was doing his utmost to destroy the holy Church. Thousands of men and women had been burned at the stake for heresies which were inconsequential as compared with that of Luther. That he was not immediately reduced to ashes following his excommunication by the Pope was due entirely to the protection he received from German princes. His life would have been snuffed out before his work was well started if it had not been for the rise of nationalism in Germany and the growing resentment against the domination of Rome. During the last twenty-six years of his life he was an outlaw and fugitive from justice. It was only the refusal of the German princes to carry out the edict of Worms that enabled him to avoid execution. Few men have ever been subjected to such severe abuse as was heaped upon Luther.

5. WHAT KIND OF A MAN WAS LUTHER?

Concerning almost no other man in history are there such violently divergent estimates of his character as there are of Luther. To millions of persons he is the worst hated man who has lived for many centuries, while to other millions he is given a place above any man since the days of Jesus and Paul. Two diametrically opposite points of view regarding Luther are possible because of the contradictory elements in his character.

He has often been criticized because of the harshness and coarseness of his language. In this respect he was a child of his age, although it must be admitted that at times he was worse than other leaders of his day. In his monumental biography of Luther, Father Grisar, an eminent Catholic historian, has gathered together numerous illustrations of Luther's loose talk. By way of summary, he says: "It is true, that what he said was improper rather than obscene, coarse rather than lascivious. Nor, owing to the rough and uncouth character of the age and the plainness of speech then habitual, were his expressions, taken as a whole, so offensive to his contemporaries as to us. . . Even Catholic preachers in Germany, following the manners of the time, show but scant consideration for the delicacy of their hearers when speaking of sexual matters or of the inferior functions of the human body."

In his attacks upon the ecclesiastical authorities, Luther used extreme language: "I maintain that all public houses of ill-fame, strictly forbidden by God though they be, yea, manslaughter, thieving, murder and adultery are not so wicked and pernicious as this abomination of the Popish Mass. . . that the procurer should daily make prostitutes of virgins, honest wives and cloistered nuns, is indeed frightful to hear of; still, his case is not so bad as that of the Popish preacher. . . Discalced Friars are lice placed by the devil on God Almighty's fur coat, and Friars-preacher are the fleas of His shirt." He once referred to Henry VIII as "Henry, by God's disgust, King of England." He used strong language deliberately and often defended it. On one occasion he said: "Our Lord God must begin with a pelting thunder-storm, afterward it rains gently and so soaks into the ground. A willow or hazel twig you can cut with a bread-knife, but for a hard oak you must have an ax and then can hardly fell it and split it." One of his biographers says: "As well apologize for the fury of the wind as for the vehemence of Martin Luther."

Luther was generally intolerant of those who differed with him. "His treatment of opponents," says President McGiffert, "grew more bitter with the passing years." He quarrelled not only with the Catholics, but also with other Protestant leaders and with the humanists, notably with Zwingli and Erasmus. In his later years he was eager to use force in driving out Catholics and in compelling attendance at Lutheran services. In 1525 he insisted that the Catholic mass should be prohibited in Saxony. During the next year he said: "In each locality there must be but one kind of preaching." In fairness to Luther, however, it should be pointed out that his intolerance was not of the same brand as that of the Catholic Church. To him "unbelief and heresy were not crimes deserving punishment. Only the public teaching of them was to be forbidden. Consistently therewith, he always refused to approve the traditional death penalty for heresy."

He liked his glass of beer or wine, "but that he became intoxicated is never recorded." In spite of many rumors which were circulated by his enemies, Luther's own moral life was above reproach. Father Grisar cannot be accused of partiality toward Luther, and yet he says: "No detailed accusation was ever brought against Luther of having had relations with any woman other than his wife." In reply to the question, Did Luther indulge in the "worst orgies" with the escaped nuns in the Black Monastery of Wittenberg? Father Grisar says: "To give an affirmative reply to this would call for very strong proofs, which, in point of fact, are not forthcoming." President McGiffert says: "Pure he was in life, too. Attacks, of course, were made upon his moral character by his enemies, and all sorts of unsavory stories were told about him. But for none of them can a shred of evidence be found, although he lived for twenty-five years in a blaze of publicity, observed of all the world and spied upon by countless critics." It is necessary to record this because vile slander against Luther has been repeated so often that there is a widespread belief that he was grossly immoral.

Luther had his faults, some of which were so serious as to lead to disastrous consequences. He also had his virtues, and in sufficient variety and abundance to make him one of the great characters of history. The most significant part of Luther's life was his religion. To him God was the great reality of life. He believed himself to be called of God to remove the abuses of the Church and never wavered in this conviction. The individual's relation to God was the central theme of his formal writings, his letters and his table-talk. He was deeply mystical. It is true that he was also very superstitious. While the apocryphal tale of his throwing an inkstand at the devil has no historical foundation, he did have an intense belief in a personal devil. He also believed in demons and in witchcraft.[3]

A notable characteristic of Luther's was his absolute sincerity. He hated hypocrisy and could be depended upon to say exactly what he thought, regardless of consequences.

[3] Concerning witches, Luther said: "Show them no mercy! . . . I would burn them myself, as we read in the Law that the priests led the way to stoning the evil-doer." (Grisar, Vol. 5, p. 294.)

His courage has rarely been surpassed. His reply to a friend who warned him against going to the Diet of Worms is characteristic of his whole life: "Even if they kindled a fire as high as heaven from Wittenberg to Worms, I would appear in the name of the Lord . . . and confess Christ." Few events in history have so moved succeeding generations as his courageous refusal, in the presence of the assembled prelates and nobles of Europe, to retract his words or forsake the way of life which he had chosen for himself. An eminent Catholic historian writes: "A defiance so utterly overwhelming as Luther's the world had never seen before."

Luther was a most kindly and human individual. He was generous to a fault. "He was very free with what he had, giving away his last gulden without hesitation, and when there was no more money, tableware and household ornaments, presented to Käthe or himself by admiring friends, would often go to relieve the wants of the needy." He was famous for his humor. His capacity for work was stupendous. Few of the mighty men of the earth have ever equalled his record of 420 books and pamphlets, in addition to continuous preaching, heavy administrative work and constant visitation of the churches. His record becomes all the more marvelous when we recall that he constantly suffered ill health. At various times he was afflicted with serious kidney and liver trouble, gall stones, gout, rheumatism, sciatica, ulcers, abscesses in the ears, toothache, headaches, dizziness and palpitation of the heart. He suffered many things from many physicians. For many years prior to 1546 he was in constant expectation of death and was often irritable and melancholy.

"He was very human, this hero of ours," says President McGiffert, "fiery-tempered, passionate, imperious, lovable withal, warm-hearted, and generous to a fault. Full of contradictions, he had the frankness and carelessness of genius, and what he was he showed, and what he thought he said, without concealment or diplomacy. Like a Cromwell or a Napoleon in his masterful will, he was like our own Lincoln in his human sympathies, his simplicity of character, his transparent honesty."

Dr. Preserved Smith says: "Luther's character combined traits not usually found in the same nature. He was both a dreamy mystic and a practical man of affairs; he saw visions and he knew how to make them realities; he was a God-intoxicated prophet and a cool calculator and hard worker for results. His faith was as simple and passionate as his dogmatic distinctions were often sophistical and arid. He could attack his foes with berserker fury, and he could be as gentle with a child as only a woman can. His hymns soar to heaven and his coarse jests trail in the mire. He was touched with profound melancholy and yet he had a wholesome, ready laugh. His words are now brutal invectives and again blossom with the most exquisite flowers of the soul—poetry, music, idyllic humor, tenderness. He was subtle and simple; superstitious and wise; limited in his cultural sympathies, and very great in what he achieved."

6. WHAT WERE THE RESULTS OF LUTHER'S LIFE?

Upon this question there is very sharp difference of opinion. To many Luther seems the most destructive individual who has appeared on the pages of history for many centuries, while to others he appears to be one of the great saviours of mankind. There is, however, general agreement upon one point: Luther, more than any other one man, broke the bond of ecclesiastical tyranny which was strangling the life out of Europe. Whatever faults he may have had and whatever harmful results flowed from his life, the fact that he was the chief instrument in delivering the world from an intolerant and corrupt ecclesiasticism would forever insure him a place among the great makers of freedom.

The claim of the Catholic Church to dominate every phase of the individual's life had to be broken before science and democracy could begin their work of liberation. Contemporary religion was adding burdens instead of removing them. The whole spirit of mediæval theology was opposed to the scientific method and the democratic process. So long as an ecclesiastical hierarchy, headed by an infallible pope and based upon a dogmatic theology, continued to exercise supreme sovereignty in all matters of state and church, real freedom for the individual was impossible. The complete submission and absolute obedience demanded by the hierarchy entombed the human spirit within an intellectual dungeon. It was Luther's chief glory that he battered down these prison walls and led much of Christendom out into the freshness and brightness of a new world where character and salvation depended, not upon rites and ceremony, nor upon the intervention of an intermediary, but upon loyalty to the will of God as revealed through individual interpretation of the Scriptures and by direct revelation to the individual heart.

Luther made the Bible a new and living book to millions of Christians. His German translation of the Bible was immediately received with great enthusiasm and exercised a tremendous influence everywhere it was read. President McGiffert says that "his version remains one of the great classics of the world. . . . The result of his efforts was a Bible translation which, after the lapse of four centuries, still stands unapproached in its vital and compelling power." Luther's numerous hymns also have had a profound influence throughout Christendom. Coleridge said that "Luther did as much for the Reformation by his hymns as by the Translation of the Bible; the children learned them in the cottage, and martyrs sang them on the scaffold." To this day "Ein' feste Burg" is one of our noblest and most moving hymns. "Luther's influence," says Dr. Preserved Smith, "exerted chiefly through this work, has been so enormous on the literature of his people that it is sometimes said that he created the modern written language." Luther also made a great contribution to popular education. Some writers go so far as to call him the father of German education. It must also be recorded that an indirect result of his work was to stimulate a counter reformation within the Catholic Church.

It is obvious that Luther did not complete the work of

liberation which he began. He fell into bondage to the letter of the text and his followers to an even greater extent became victims of bibliolatry. The proof-text method was used to refute scientific discoveries to justify the persecution of witches and the waging of religious wars.[4] The theory of an inerrant Bible became a stumbling-block in the path of intellectual and moral advance and is even now being overthrown with great difficulty. Luther had only the faintest conception of democracy, and his attitude toward the peasants' revolt had disastrous consequences for the downtrodden masses of Europe. His emphasis upon the right of individual judgment was a major cause of the excesses of capitalism, although Calvin's influence in this direction was much greater than Luther's.[5] His advocacy of the divine right of kings and his teaching regarding the duty of absolute loyalty to the state had an important bearing on the spread of virulent nationalism in Germany and elsewhere. His supreme emphasis upon justification by faith led to a pietistic type of religion which has often been divorced from the great social and international problems of the modern world. As a result of his work Christendom has been divided into many sects and denominations. Much of his theology has been outgrown or rejected by Protestantism.

On the other hand, after a full list of his limitations is drawn up and a catalog made of the evil influences which were released by his work, the fact remains that he rendered a four-fold contribution to humanity which has proved to be of incalculable value. He broke the bonds of ecclesiastical tyranny and threw off the yoke of papal domination; by his insistence upon the right of private judgment he laid the foundations of religious intellectual and civil liberty, and made possible the rise of modern democracy and the spread of the scientific method; he dignified honest toil and en-

[4]Luther was strongly opposed to the Copernican theory and said: "I believe the Holy Scriptures, which say that Joshua commanded the sun, and not the earth, to stand still." (Smith, The Age of the Reformation, p. 621.)

[5]See an interesting article by Dr. P. T. Forsyth, "Calvinism and Capitalism." The Contemporary Review, Vol. 97, p. 728.

nobled the humble duties and ordinary relations of life, and thereby helped to break down the wall between the sacred and the secular; he made the Bible live again in the hearts of common people, and helped to restore much of the vitality of early Christianity.

"His career," says Dr. Smith, "marks the beginning of the present epoch, for it is safe to say that every man in Western Europe and in America is leading a different life today from what he would have led, and is another person altogether from what he would have been had Martin Luther not lived." Professor Walker says: "He is one of the few men of whom it may unhesitatingly be said that he made the world other than it would have been had he not done his work." Such a man deserves to be ranked as one of the greatest makers of freedom.

CHAPTER 5.

FREEDOM FROM MORAL AND SPIRITUAL INSENSIBILITY

John Wesley

1. WHAT KIND OF A WORLD DID WESLEY LIVE IN?

The life of John Wesley almost spanned the eighteenth century. He was born in 1703 and died in 1791. It was an age of moral corruption and spiritual destitution throughout the British Isles. Of George II it was said that he "united the morals of a rake with the tastes of a boor." Thackeray tells of the king's many mistresses in an age of "infidelity endemic, and corruption in the air." Walpole as Prime Minister set an example of shameless profligacy. Judges swore in court, and chaplains cursed their inattentive congregations of soldiers and sailors. The upper classes for the most part were unblushingly immoral and the impoverished masses were brutalized. The historian Green informs us that purity and fidelity were sneered out of fashion. Bullbaiting, cock-fighting, prize fights and public executions were the favorite brutal sports. There was a mania for gambling, and state lotteries were common. Stakes ran high at the king's palace. Lord Ilchester lost thirteen thousand pounds at a sitting. The statesman Fox was reduced to poverty. The populace were demoralized by lotteries and horseracing. It was an age of drunkenness so gross that Mr. Lecky considers the passion for gin-drinking the most serious fact of the century, "incomparably more so than any event in the purely political or military annals of the century." Every sixth shop in London was a public house. Signs invited the poor to get drunk for a penny, or dead drunk for twopence, while straw was provided free for them to sleep off their debauch. The famous Dr. Johnson speaks of the time "when all the decent people of Lichfield got drunk every night and were not the worse thought of.[1]

Within the city of London, footpads by night, and even assaults and robberies by day, were not uncommon, while just outside the city walls coaches were frequently held up and the passengers plundered by the celebrated highwaymen of the day, such as Dick Turpin. Ruthless legislation hardened but did not restrain the criminal classes. The following "crimes" were punishable by death: stealing a sheep or a horse, stealing an article worth five shillings from a shop, picking a man's pocket for more than twelve pence, cutting down a tree in an orchard, breaking the dam of a fishpond so that the fish might escape. Blackstone has listed a total of 160 offences that were punishable by death.[2] The prisons were indescribably filthy and many of the prisoners who escaped the gallows died of slow torture or came out emaciated and diseased. " 'Tis reckoned there are about sixty thousand miserable debtors perishing in the prisons of England and Wales, where hundreds die weekly of want and infectious diseases."

By the agrarian and industrial revolutions, England was changed in one eventful century from a country of farming into a land of smoky cities and factories. The Enclosure Acts, which dispossessed the workers, could, up to 1774, be passed by the limited franchise of the favored few, without the people concerned even hearing that their eviction from the land was contemplated. Legislation was enacted chiefly

---

[1]Mark Pattison, in his Essays, describes the age as "one of decay of religion, licentiousness of morals, public corruption, profaneness of language . . . an age destitute of depth and earnestness; an age whose poetry was without romance, whose philosophy was without insight, and whose public men were without character; an age of 'light without love, whose very merits were of the earth, earthly'." Essays, Vol. ii, p. 42.

[2] Not until 1790 was the law repealed by which women were burned at the stake for murdering their husbands.

by the property-holding classes and naturally in their own interests. The masses without the vote were politically powerless. The enclosure of the common land had left many of them in abject poverty. Village laborers were receiving only from sixty to ninety cents a week in wages. Hunger and want drove many of them to poaching in the rich game preserves for food. Cobbett tells of a young man working at breaking stones who when asked how he could live on sixty-two cents a week replied: "I don't live upon it. I poach; it is better to be hanged than to be starved to death."

While the outstanding feature of the age was its *moral insensibility*, it was also deeply irreligious. The Deism of the eighteenth century which had banished God from a mechanical world, had driven the prevailingly formal and lifeless religion of the day to a hard, rationalistic apologetic that largely eliminated the supernatural. A cold morality, barely touched with emotion, or visited by an absentee God, was the religious fashion of the day. "God was an idol compounded of fragments of tradition and frozen metaphysics." Montesquieu on his visit to England could say of the higher classes of society that "every one laughs if one talks of religion." The clergy of England were considered the most lifeless in Europe and "the most remiss of their labors." They were prevailingly formal and conventional. The clergy of all branches of the church were "convinced that the immediate, direct action of the living God upon the spirits of men was practically impossible in reality and well-nigh blasphemous in conception." Immorality was condoned as common, but any sign of enthusiasm or zeal was quickly branded as bad form or madness. Two texts were worn threadbare by the preachers of that day: "Let your moderation be known to all men," and "Be not righteous overmuch,"[3] "Cold, selfish, and unspiritual" are the words used by Mr. Lecky in describing the religion of that day,

[3] In 1739 the Rev. Joseph Trapp, D.D., published a pamphlet of 69 pages entitled "The Nature, Folly, Sin and Danger of being Righteous over-much; with a particular view to the doctrines and practices of certain Modern Enthusiasts."

and he goes on to say: "The old religion seemed everywhere loosening round the minds of men." There had been a widespread decay of faith.

One of the great intellects of the time, Bishop Butler, writes: "The deplorable distinction of our age is an avowed scorn of religion, and a growing disregard of it." He says in his great "Analogy", "It has somehow come to be taken for granted that Christianity is not so much a subject of inquiry, but that it is now at length discovered to be fictitious. . . Men treat it as if in the present age this were an agreed point amongst all people of discernment, and nothing remained but to set it up as a principal subject to mirth and ridicule."

Concerning this period of English life, the Cambridge Modern History says: "The masses were ignorant and brutalized. Government insulted humanity by the brutal ferocity of the criminal code. A governing class intent only on pleasure or politics, a church occupied chiefly with patronage and controversy. . . ." Carlyle sums up this eighteenth century of ill repute with the words, "Soul extinct; stomach well alive." This was symbolic of an age which had confessed, "Our light looks like the evening of the world."

2. WHAT DID WESLEY DO?

Into this world John Wesley was born in the rectory of Epworth, a little country town of some two thousand ignorant and degraded peasants. He was the fifteenth of nineteen strong children. By inheritance and training he owed most to his Spartan mother, Susanna Wesley, who was the twenty-fifth child of the great Dr. Annesley. Lacking in humor, but strong in mental vigor and moral earnestness, she reared her family in "plain living and high thinking." Of her son John she wrote in her meditations, "I do intend to be more particularly careful of the soul of this child . . . that I may instill into his mind the principles of true religion and virtue." Such was the mother who was training the child destined to change his century.

His father, struggling to live on a meager stipend, was at one time imprisoned for debt, but on his deathbed spoke these prophetic words to his boy John: "The inward witness, son, the inward witness—this is the proof, the strongest proof of Christianity." Though he did not understand the words at the time, the boy was later to share his inward experience with an irreligious age.

From the austerity of the Epworth parsonage, John was sent at the age of eleven to the Charterhouse School. Here every morning a lean little boy might be seen methodically running three times round the grounds, building up that tireless constitution which was to traverse England for over half a century. After six years of hard work and self-discipline in the school, at the age of seventeen, John entered Christ Church College at Oxford on a scholarship of forty pounds a year.

In the Oxford of that day, averse to "enthusiasm" in scholarship, morals or athletics, lax professors drew salaries for lectures that were never given, and students, occupied with drinking and gambling, bought dispensation for absence from classes which were never studied. Wesley's terrible indictment of the system in his sermon a few years later in the college chapel is a revelation of the corruption of the age. At Oxford Wesley was a hard student. He was described at that time by a friend as "a very sensible active collegian, baffling every man by the subtleties of his logic . . . a young fellow of the finest classical tastes, of the most liberal and manly sentiments, gay and sprightly, with a turn to wit and humor." Wesley read widely in the classics, but what was far more important, he now mastered his own mind and learned to think.

He had as yet little concern for religion, and writes of himself at that time, "I still said my prayers, both in public and private, and read with the Scripture several other books of religion, especially comments on the New Testament. Yet I had not all this while so much as a notion of inward holiness; nay, went on habitually, and for the most part very conceitedly, in some one or other known sin."

At the age of twenty-two, as he anxiously faced the question of his life work, a change took place in his experience. As he read Thomas á Kempis's "Imitation of Christ" and Jeremy Taylor's "Holy Living and Dying", he says, "I began to alter the whole form of my conversation and to set out in earnest upon a new life. I set apart an hour or two a day for religious retirement; I communed every week; I watched against all sin, whether in word or deed."

Two years later, owing to a combination of his scholarship, character and social gifts, he was elected Fellow of Lincoln College. Here, he writes, "Leisure and I have parted company"; for the remaining fifty-five years of his life they never met again. He was now appointed Greek lecturer and Moderator of the classes, which gave him the invaluable training of presiding at the daily debates and criticizing their arguments. Referring to this period he afterward wrote, "Entering now upon a new world, I resolved to have no acquaintance by chance, but by choice, and to choose such only as I have reason to believe could help me."

At twenty-four he took a small parish near his home, but during these early years he says, "I preached much but saw no fruit of my labor." At this time in life, just after leaving college, he seemed to himself, as a stern Puritan, almost a complete failure. Unsatisfied in this work, he returned to Oxford at the age of twenty-six and remained there until he was thirty-two. In November, 1729, he began to meet with three other friends, including his brother Charles, "to spend three or four evenings a week together. Our design was to read over the Classics . . . and on Sunday some book on divinity." They took the communion every Sunday and fasted twice a week. They methodically divided their time, undertaking to live by rule, and passed all their life in review. They also began to visit the sick and work among the prisoners in the jails. George Whitefield, a poor boy who had for a year and a half acted as bartender at his father's tavern in Gloucester, soon joined the band. The group was small and was instantly and continuously reviled and persecuted, never numbering at the most over twenty-nine members at Oxford.[4]

The Holy Club was just such a group as young Saul of Tarsus might have formed; but it was not like that which the young Carpenter of Nazareth drew about him. It still lacked the note of sanity, balance and joy. But with all their shortcomings they could say they were "always gaining ground." They were seekers, desperately in earnest. They had not yet found the message that was to transform them and give freedom from the moral insensibility of eighteenth-century England.

Somewhat Pharisaical and stiff high churchman though he then was, Wesley finally grew tired of this methodical spiritual treadmill of self-righteous good works. While thus dissatisfied, he was called by General Oglethorpe, the founder of the new colony of Georgia in America, to go as a clergyman, to preach to the settlers and Indians of the community. When her permission was asked, his mother replied, "Had I twenty sons, I should rejoice that they were all so employed, though I should never see them more." The young ascetic Oxford scholar of thirty-two writes as he starts for Georgia, "My chief motive is the hope of saving my own soul. I hope to learn the true sense of the gospel of Christianity by preaching it to the heathen. . . I am assured if I be once converted

---

[4] The group included John Wesley, England's greatest religious worker; Charles Wesley who, with Isaac Watts, was her greatest hymn writer; George Whitefield, her greatest preacher; and Robert Kirkham, William Morgan, James Harvey and Charles Kinchin of saintly life.

The practical tests by which each member was to try himself were:

1. Have I embraced every probable opportunity of doing good, and of preventing, removing or lessening evil?
2. Have I thought anything too dear to part with, to serve my neighbor?
3. Have I spent an hour at least every day in speaking to some one or other?
4. Have I in speaking to a stranger explained what religion is not—not negative, not external—and what it is, the recovery of the image of God; searched at what step in it he stops, and what makes him stop?
5. Have I persuaded all I could to attend public prayers, sermons and sacraments? Journal, Vol. i.

myself, God will then employ me." He is still looking on his "own soul" rather than on all the world as his parish. While practicing renewed austerities on the voyage he came in contact with the simple Moravian missionaries, whose triumphant faith, joyful assurance and fearlessness in the ocean storms, convinced him that he lacked what they had.

One may still read the worn copy of the little diary kept by Wesley in America, accounting for every hour of the busy day of work and devotion. But after a fruitless mission, he writes, "I went to America to convert the Indians; but O! who shall convert me? . . . It is now two years and four months since I left my native country. . . I who went to convert others was never myself converted to God."

After his return from Georgia to England, his journals reveal his terrific struggle to escape from the round of Pharisaic self-righteous good works which he engaged in to earn his own salvation by merit. Yet he was unable or unwilling to enter by simple childlike trust into a filial relation to God. His narrative reads like Paul's seventh chapter of Romans or the early confessions of St. Augustine, Martin Luther or John Bunyan. His contact, however, with Peter Bohler and other Moravians in London finally helped him to see that he lacked only one simple act of trust to enter a new relationship of childlike dependence upon God. The memorable step was taken on the evening of Wednesday, May 24, 1738, at the age of thirty-five, long delayed, as in the case of Luther, by the erroneous teaching of the time and by the proud struggles of his own stubborn will. He writes, "In the evening I went very unwillingly to a society in Aldersgate Street, where one was reading Luther's preface to the Epistle to the Romans. About a quarter before nine, while he was describing the change which God works in the heart through faith in Christ, I felt my heart strangely warmed. I felt I did trust in Christ, Christ alone, for salvation; and an assurance was given me, that he had taken away *my* sins, even *mine,* and saved *me* from the law of sin and death. I began to pray with all my might for those who had in a more especial manner despitefully used me and persecuted me.

I then testified openly to all there what I now felt in my heart."

Of the significance of this event, Mr. Lecky says, "It is scarcely an exaggeration to say that the scene which took place at that humble meeting in Aldersgate Street, forms an epoch in English history." Three weeks later he went for a short time to Germany to confirm his new experience by a study of the colony of the Moravian Brethren, who had so influenced him, both in Georgia and in England. He interviewed the zealous Count Zinzendorf, Christian David, and the simple folk of Hernhut. He was confirmed in his new-found personal experience, but he was not blind to the quietism, the exclusiveness, and other limitations of the Moravians of that time.

Upon his return to England Wesley began preaching with tremendous zeal and new power in the churches of London. Owing, however, to his "enthusiasm" and his searching evangelical teaching, one by one the churches were closed against him, until by the end of the year only three or four were still open to him. It is a terrible indictment of the moral insensibility of the age that even the churches would not tolerate the one challenging and disquieting message of the time. As he was now almost an ecclesiastical outcast, he turned from the churches to the prisoners in the jails. But a more important work was awaiting him. The two Wesleys and Whitefield overflowing with their new experience, had gathered in London and with a few others were spending occasionally whole nights in prayer. Wesley had seen the value of small groups of like-minded persons meeting for fellowship while at Oxford, in Georgia and among the Moravians in Germany. He now began to organize such groups of "bands" of five or ten to meet twice each week and to unite them each Wednesday evening for prayer, and once a month in a "love-feast." These were composed at first chiefly of Moravians and met in a room in Fetter Lane, which then became the center of Wesley's work in London.

George Whitefield, who was only twenty-five years of age, was at this time attracting much wider attention than Wesley.

Throngs were crowding the London churches to hear him and sometimes larger numbers were forced to wait outside who could not get in. This, Whitefield said, "put me first upon thinking of preaching without doors. I mentioned it to some friends, who looked upon it as a mad notion." By the end of January, 1739, all the London churches were closed to Whitefield, the Bishop objecting that his teaching was "tinctured with enthusiasm"! At Kingswood, near Bristol, after the churches there also closed their doors and the chancellor of the diocese had threatened to excommunicate him, one Saturday afternoon, February 17, 1739, he took his stand on a little hill outside the city and preached to some two hundred people. Though ecclesiastical propriety was scandalized, he was reminded of One, "who had a mountain for his pulpit and the heavens for a sounding-board." Whitefield's first audience of 200 rose at the second meeting to 3000, then 5000, and soon extended to 20,000. An outcast like his Master, he had suddenly stepped from the stifling atmosphere of a dead church into the open sunshine of a throbbing world of living men. A new power was loosed in England.

Six weeks later when Whitefield was summoned to Georgia, he called for Wesley to carry on the work begun among the degraded colliers of Kingswood. "Ignorant, lewd, profane and brutal, they were the terror of the law and the despair of philanthropy." Wesley thus records his entrance upon this outdoor work which so shocked him at first, "All my life till very lately, I have been so tenacious of every point relating to decency and order that I should have thought the saving of souls almost a sin if it had not been done in a church."[5] Scenes were now witnessed among these

[5] "I reached Bristol and met Mr. Whitefield there. I could scarce reconcile myself at first to this strange way of preaching in the fields, of which he set me an example on Sunday. . . . At four in the afternoon, I submitted to be more vile, and proclaimed in the highways the glad tidings of salvation, speaking from a little eminence in a ground adjoining to the city to about three thousand people, (among them) . . . the colliers of Kingswood . . . neither fearing God nor regarding man: so ignorant of the things of God, that they seemed but one remove from the beasts." Journal, Vol. i, pp. 184, 250.

throngs in the open air that recall those of the early Acts of the Apostles. The conviction of the miners was seen by the tears that left "white gutters on their blackened cheeks."

John and Charles Wesley and Whitefield now became the messengers of the revival that began to sweep England, Wales and, later, Scotland and Ireland. For the first two years Wesley divided his time chiefly between Bristol and London, preaching to vast throngs in the open air and meeting his little inner groups and Christian societies indoors to foster permanent centers of life. Whitefield was reaching the fashionable circles and the gentry of Blackheath, as well as the masses of the poor in the slums of London, where the audiences reached as high as 60,000.

Opposition to their work was increased by the strange phenomena that began to appear in the meetings of men falling fainting to the earth under terrible conviction, or crying out in agony of mind. Such manifestations were a source of perplexity and anxiety to both Wesley and Whitefield. It was the more strange because Wesley was in no sense an emotional preacher, but appealed to the mind and conscience of his hearers. Each listener seemed to feel he was speaking directly to him.

When serious doctrinal differences arose, Wesley and a score of followers withdrew from the Fetter Lane society, so that the Methodist movement was now separate and free from the quietism and division which characterized the Moravians. The first Methodist Society was formed in London with a dozen humble folk in 1729. In two years there were than a thousand members in this first branch. Similar societies were organized in Bristol, Kingswood and Bath, and later throughout the British Isles. Thus began the vast network of an organization that was finally to spread all over the world. To raise a penny per member from the band in Bristol the society was divided into groups of twelve, with a collector or' class "leader" for each. The weekly meeting of these groups gradually developed into the Methodist "Class Meeting," where each leader met his group for prayer and conference regarding their personal spiritual experience.

Wesley here sees a new development of great possibilities. He writes, "You must find companions or make them. The Bible knows nothing of a solitary religion." He always gave to his personal religion a social form. While Wesley's followers were rapidly multiplying by the thousand, he and his brother and Whitefield, as the only ordained clergymen, were utterly unable to meet the needs of these multitudes. He was alarmed when an untutored clergyman, Thomas Maxfield, began preaching. Wesley hastened to London to forbid him, but after hearing him exclaimed, "It is the Lord's doing; let Him do what seemeth good. What am I that I should withstand God?" Thus commenced the work of the famous local preachers who soon began to take the masses of England by storm.

Within five years of his first field preaching, England was being stirred and converts were multiplying by thousands. But problems were multiplying with them. To face the problems, Wesley called a group of ten men to "confer" with him in 1744, consisting of six ministers and four laymen. From this humble beginning in order better to organize, standardize and unify the work, there was gradually evolved the "annual conference" of preachers and workers over which Wesley presided for forty-seven years. Thus there was gradually perfected one of the most highly effective, centralized and yet personal ecclesiastical systems ever devised. It was at once a cabinet, parliament and court; executive, legislative and judicial. In choosing what he calls "a handful of raw young men, without name, learning, or eminent sense," Wesley was going back to an earlier precedent of a Galilean Carpenter who, in calling a similar group of simple fishermen, declared, "Blessed are ye poor." Yet of those humble followers of Jesus of Nazareth it was complained in a few years, "These that have turned the world upside down are come hither." So it was with Wesley's followers. While the bishops and clergy were closing all respectable doors against him, Wesley was appealing straight to the hearts of the people. They responded in the mighty uprising of the Evangelical Revival of the eighteenth century.

In the matter of physical endurance, Wesley has been seldom equaled. For more than fifty years he traveled as an itinerant preacher, chiefly on horseback, over the bad roads of that day, some four thousand five hundred miles a year, or a total of 250,000 miles. It was a common occurrence for him to walk twenty-five miles in a day. He discovered that "for ten miles of the journey it was practicable to read without inconvenience." For fifty-two years he delivered from two to five sermons a day, preaching on an average of fifteen times a week, or a total of over forty thousand sermons. Whitefield spoke from forty to sixty hours a week to audiences ranging often from five to over fifty thousand. Whitefield was, however, a broken wreck at the age of fifty.

Wesley himself kept chiefly to the great industrial cities, as he followed the path of the industrial revolution, leaving his itinerant and local preachers to carry the message to the country districts. Beginning in London and Bristol, his work spread to the north of England and beyond. He made twenty-one tours through Scotland, where his work was attended with wonderful results. He crossed St. George's channel forty-two times and worked with signal success in Ireland, among both Protestant and Catholics, who thronged his great meetings. Gladstone was exhausted after his great Midlothian campaign of more than a score of speeches in a fortnight, but Wesley campaigned for more than fifty years in three kingdoms and came out fresh and serene from the mobs and multitudes he subdued. John Morley is amazed at Mr. Gladstone's great speech of two hours to 20,000 people at Gravesend when he was sixty-two, but such an event was all in an ordinary day's work with Wesley.

The story of a single typical day is the story of the whole fifty years. Wesley rose at four o'clock, read his devotional books until five, preached in the open air to the colliers or other workers who had to go to their tasks at half-past six. After breakfast at seven, he mounted his horse, and drew rein for a few minutes from time to time to read a page in some book that he was analyzing. After twenty or thirty miles' ride, he preached in a public square or some church-yard at noon; dismissed his hearers at one o'clock that they might return to their work; then rode rapidly, often twenty miles, to his next appointment, where he preached at five. After supper, when the evening twilight fell, he preached again, holding a service that often lasted until nine or ten o'clock.

This little man who had suffered from hemorrhage in early life and who never weighed over a hundred and twenty pounds, was preaching to thirty thousand people in the open air at the age of seventy. On one occasion as he paces off the distance he notes that the crowd could hear him even a hundred and forty yards away.[6] In his Journal are frequent entries like this: "Wet from morning till night; but I found no manner of inconvenience." Toward the close of his life we read in his Journal, "This day I enter into my eighty-eighth year. For above eighty-six years, I found none of the infirmities of old age, my eyes did not wax dim, neither was my natural strength abated."

This man who was an introspective ascetic in poor health at twenty-three, was now free from himself for the rest of his life to draw on the illimitable resources of a divine dynamic for all his needs, and to look on all the world as his parish. Throughout his life, Wesley carried on prodigious literary activities. Not "a man of one book," he was one of the best-read men of his day. On every road in England might be seen the familiar figure of this tireless worker with the reins thrown over his horse's neck, as he rode fifty or

[6] "It is no exaggeration to say that Wesley preached more sermons, rode more miles, worked more hours, printed more books, and influenced more lives than any Englishman of his age, or perhaps of any age. And the performance did not even tire him! In 1776 he writes 'I am seventy-three years old, and far abler to preach than I was at twenty-three.' Ten years later this amazing old man writes, 'I have entered upon the eighty-third year of my age. I am a wonder to myself. I am never tired, either with preaching, writing or traveling.'" Wesley and His Century, W. H. Fichett, p. 201.

sixty miles a day, reading the latest publication. Not only a wide reader, he was also a tireless author. The twenty-six volumes of his Journal, 700,000 words in length, now condensed in extracts that cover four volumes, are one of the outstanding documents of that century. On the first page of each volume he wrote, "I resolve to devote one hour morning and evening to private prayer, no pretense or excuse whatever." By issuing cheap books for his local preachers and followers, he helped to democratize learning, printing over four hundred and fifty different publications. He himself wrote a grammar, a logic, histories of England and of the Church, and published a Christian Library. He established one of the first popular magazines in 1778, and wrote popular handbooks on medicine, chemistry, physics, politics, poetry, and various books on religion.

In his overcrowded life he found time to engage in the study and practice of medicine for the neglected multitudes. He started the first free dispensary, and founded widows' homes. He devoted much time to the relief of the poor. He organized schools for poor children and promoted popular education in an age of illiteracy. He devised a loan fund a century and a half before modern methods of co-operative credit. He was a pioneer in many forms of social service. Great movements like that of the Salvation Army sprang indirectly from his work. One of Wesley's correspondents, Miss Ball, started the first Sunday School fourteen years before Robert Raikes began his work, which was warmly seconded by Wesley. He was one of the earliest temperance advocates and rendered heroic service in the cause.

3. WHAT DID WESLEY SAY?

Wesley's teaching, which seemed such a daring innovation to his own dead century, was simply the rediscovery of the essentials of primitive, fundamental Christianity. It was the outgrowth of his own experience, and he would have been in entire accord with the later statement of Huxley, "Experience first, inference second. This is the order of science."

The whole emphasis of his life and teaching was fortunately placed, not upon theological dogma, but in the sure realm of practical experience, capable of repeated verification in every age. The result is that the millions of his followers to this day are more occupied in making a better world by means of love to God and man, than in excommunicating one another in barren and fruitless theological dissension between fundamentalists and modernists over dogmas, many of which can never be proved or disproved. Out of the rich experience of his own conversion, Wesley, like Luther, found in real life the great truth of "justification by faith." In an age of dead formalism, barren sacerdotalism and frigid self-righteousness, Wesley turned in the spirit of a little child in quiet trust to a loving Father. All his life and teaching are but the natural unfolding of the growing fulness of this filial relationship.

Wesley says himself, "Our main doctrines which include all the rest, are repentance, faith and holiness. The first of these we account, as it were, the porch of religion; the next, the door; the third, religion itself." And again, "My doctrines are simply the common fundamental principles of Christianity." He merely shifted the emphasis from non-essentials to essentials, and rediscovered long-forgotten truths.

Emerson says, "The hero is the man who is immovably centered." All his life Wesley strove to avoid fruitless controversy and to maintain a position immovably centered in the experience of God in Christ. For admission to the society of Methodists, he says, "They do not impose in order to their admission any opinions of whatever. . . . *They think and let think.* One condition and only one, is required—a real desire to save the soul. They lay stress upon nothing else." "They have no such overgrown fondness for any opinion as to think that these alone will make them Christians, or to confine their affection and esteem to those who agree with them therein." And again, "I will not quarrel with you about any opinion. Only see that your heart be right toward God, that you know and love the Lord Jesus Christ; that you love your neighbor, and walk as your Master walked; and I desire no more. I am sick of opinions. I am weary to bear them. My soul loathes this frothy food. Give me solid and substantial religion; give me an humble, quiet love of God and man."

For his essentials, Wesley believed in God as Father Almighty, and in the freedom of the human will. Man is, "not a clod of earth, a lump of clay without sense or understanding, but a spirit like his Creator; a spirit endowed with a free will, the power of choosing good or evil." He believed in man's responsibility, in his sinfulness and in the atoning work of Jesus Christ. Man is justified by vital faith or childlike trust in Christ as his personal Savior. By faith he experiences an inward change of nature, called "regeneration," and an outward change in his relationship, called "justification," a new standing in the moral universe through the act of forgiveness. He has entered "the straight way of the religion of love, even by faith." "By this faith we are saved from all uneasiness of mind, from the anguish of a wounded spirit, from discontent, from fear and sorrow of heart, and from that inexpressible listlessness and weariness, both of the world and ourselves, which we had so helplesly labored under for many years; especially when we were out of the hurry of the world and sunk in calm reflection. In this we find that love of God and of all mankind which we had elsewhere sought in vain." This results in "assurance" or the glad sense of sonship, releasing a man from the spirit of the servant or slave who is seeking to work out his salvation by his own merit, and setting him free as a son, at leisure from himself, for a joyous life of service for God and his fellowmen.

This life of faith in glad sonship results in personal holiness, striving to live in the moral "perfection" of a life well-rounded and mature. Wesley never claimed sinless perfection for himself or his followers, but was in deadly earnest about the pragmatic test of daily living. He defined it simply as "loving God with all the heart and soul and mind and strength." "Sanctification" was the growth of the new man into maturity. In his insistence upon experimental religion in heart and life Wesley moved in the sphere of the great truths of grace, faith, assurance and perfect love.

Nowhere is the practical nature of his teaching more manifest than in his emphasis upon the means of spiritual growth in the reading of the Bible and prayer. He says, "I want to know one thing . . . God himself has condescended to teach the way; for this end he came down from heaven. He hath written it down in a book. O give me that book! At any price give me that book of God. I have it: here is knowledge for me. Let me be *homo unius libri* (a man of one book) . . . Here then I am, far from the busy ways of men. I sit down alone; only God is here. In his presence I open, I read the book."

Yet he will not dogmatize concerning inerrant, verbal inspiration. On critical questions he said, "We think and let think." He freely acknowledges, for instance, the error in Matt. 27 : 9, "The word 'Jeremy' evidently is a mistake: for he who spoke what Matthew here writes was not Jeremy but Zechariah."

Wesley refuses to dispute about eternal divine decrees and predestination, but proclaims, "*Now* is the day of salvation." He spoke straight to the individual heart and conscience in the language of his own day. He concerned himself with facts, and for the most part, let theories take care of themselves. By his fruits and the moral change he wrought in the life of his time, his teachings may be judged. Avoiding metaphysical theology, the revival of the eighteenth century was grounded in vital evangelical truths which "changed the whole tone of English society." It was not by metaphysics or abstract theology, but by a personal, practical and vital emphasis that he secured freedom from the moral insensibility of his age.

Wesley's practical mind dwells upon the moral and social issues of his day. While Whitefield, as an ardent Calvinist, was contending for predestination, he also bought slaves for his orphanage in America, includes them with the cattle in his stock, and thanks God for their increase. Wesley flamed out in moral indignation against slavery and war, and wrote his last letter with trembling hand to Wilberforce, "Go on in the name of God and the power of his might, till even American slavery, the vilest that ever saw the sun, shall vanish away before it."

In a later section we shall call attention to the stupendous social changes in English national life which resulted from Wesley's work. Yet it is a fact that in one sense Wesley was no social reformer. He showed very little interest in fundamental changes in the social system of his day. He warned the rich against the perils of wealth, he sought to relieve the miseries of the poor, yet he did not challenge the economic order which produced riotous luxury on the one hand and dire want on the others. He was opposed to any relaxation of the barbarous penal code of that day.

On the other hand, Wesley was surprisingly modern in some of his views. For example, he accepted the idea of evolution. Many decades before Darwin produced his Origin of Species, Wesley wrote: "All is metamorphosis in the physical world. Forms are continually changing. The quantity of matter alone is invariable. The same substance passes successively into the three kingdoms . . . By what degree does nature raise herself up to man? How will she rectify this head that is always inclined toward the earth? How change these paws into flexible arms? What method will she make use of to transform these crooked feet into supple and skillful hands? Or how will she widen and extend this contracted stomach? In what manner will she place the breasts and give them a roundness suitable to them? The ape is this rough draught of man; this rude sketch, an imperfect representation, which nevertheless bears a resemblance to him, and is the last creature that serves to display the admirable progression of the works of God."

4. WHAT HAPPENED TO WESLEY?

History repeated itself in the opposition which broke upon Wesley. The glad gospel of the early Galilean springtime, in the life of Jesus of Nazareth, recorded in the first chapter of Mark, has in the second chapter already given place to the fierce opposition of the religious leaders of his day. Within a year he is a religious outcast, shut out of the synagogues, without a place to lay his head. The early disciples in the Acts of the Apostles are beaten, stoned and persecuted. The noble army of martyrs are persecuted from age to age as each new reformer hurls himself against the moral insensibility of his time. For men are proverbially blind to the deepest ills of their own day.

Opposition burst upon Wesley the moment he found a life and a message that were vital and that challenged the moral insensibility of his time. It came from two quarters, the religious leaders of the day and the vulgar mob. The "Holy Club" had been instantly persecuted at Oxford, and later the newly-converted minister was driven from churches. Within a year no church in London would hear him. For personal abuse, he cared nothing, but when the work was hindered he replied to the bishops who attacked him. By 1762 three hundred and thirty-two anti-Methodist books and pamphlets had been published. Many of these were cruelly unjust and bitter, accusing Wesley of almost every sin. Toplady, author of "Rock of Ages," called Wesley "the most rancorous hater of the Gospel system that has ever appeared in this land," and spoke of Wesley's "Satanic guilt" and "Satanic shamelessness," Rowland Hill referred to Wesley as a "designing wolf," "as unprincipled as a rock and as silly as a jackdaw," "a venial profligate," an "apostate miscreant." In the Edinburgh Review, Sydney Smith wrote of "the nasty and numerous vermin of Methodism."

Everywhere churches were closed to him and his followers In Bristol, Bishop Butler said to him: "You have no business here; you are not commissioned to preach in this diocese. Therefore I advise you to go hence." The Bishop of London complained that "they have had the boldness to preach in the fields and other open places, and by public advertisement to invite the rabble to be their hearers."

For a decade he faced the violence of mobs and for twenty years the opposition of the churches. "A thousand wild scandals broke on Wesley himself. His friends fell from him, his comrades often proved faithless. He was pelted by the crowds, sneered at by the educated, frowned on by the clergy; and not seldom the very men who were plucked from sin and death turned against him . . . The one steadfast, unshakable soul who never doubted, never faltered, never grew discouraged, was Wesley."

The savage mob of his day found as much pleasure in persecuting a poor preacher as in baiting a bear or watching a prize fight. In the north of England the war against the Methodists was carried on with more zeal than against the Spaniards. In one place in Wednesbury which was given over to mob rule for some months, after advice given them from the pulpit and the bishop's chair, 1743 houses and shops were plundered and the members of the society were in daily peril.

Wesley always faced a mob in person and feared not the face of man. "Again and again he preached," says Lecky, "like the other leaders of the movement, in the midst of showers of stones or tiles or rotten eggs . . . Drums were beaten, horns blown, guns let off, and blacksmiths hired to ply their noisy trade in order to drown the voices of the preachers . . . On other occasions packs of hounds were brought with the same object, and once, in order to excite the dogs to fury, a live cat in a cage was placed in their midst. Fire engines poured streams of fetid water upon the congregation. Stones fell so thickly that the faces of many grew crimson with blood. At Hoxton the mob drove an ox into the midst of the congregation. At Pensford the rabble, who had been baiting a bull, concluded their sport by driving the torn and tired animal full against the table on which Wesley was preaching. At Plymouth and Bolton "howling fanatics, dancing with rage such as had never been seen before in creatures called men, hunted the preacher like a pack of wolves."

Repeatedly one finds in Wesley's Journal entries like the following at Falmouth: "The house was beset on all sides by an innumerable multitude . . . Away went all the things at once and the door fell back into the room. I stepped forward at once into the midst of them and said, 'here I am; which of you has anything to say to me?' . . . I came bareheaded as I was into the middle of the street, and then raising my voice, said, 'Neighbors, countrymen, do you desire to hear me speak?' They cried vehemently, 'Yes, yes. He shall speak. He shall' . . . At Walsall . . . I received some blows, lost part of my clothes, and was covered with dirt. Here, although the hands of perhaps some hundreds of people seemed lifted up to strike or throw, yet they were one and all stopped in some way so that no man touched me."

A few further extracts from his Journal show his frequent experience with mobs: "April, 1740. Not only the court and the alleys, but all the street, upwards and downwards, was filled with people, shouting, cursing and swearing, and ready to swallow the ground with fierceness and rage . . . October, 1743. Two years ago a piece of brick grazed my shoulders. It was a year after that the stone struck me between the eyes. Last month I received one blow, and this evening two; one before we came into the town and one after we were gone out. But both were as nothing; for though one man struck me on the breast with all his might, and the other on the mouth with such a force that the blood gushed out immediately, I felt no more pain from either of the blows, than if they had touched me with a straw. . . . October, 1749. We came to Bolton about five in the evening. . . . Such rage and bitterness I scarcely ever saw before, in any creatures that bore the form of men. They followed us in full cry . . . My heart was filled with love, my eyes with tears, and my mouth with arguments. They were amazed, they were ashamed, they were melted down, they devoured every word. What a turn was this!"

On another occasion he had this experience: "While I was speaking, a gentleman rode up very drunk; and, after many unseemly and bitter words, laboured much to ride over some of the people. I was surprised to hear he was a neighboring clergyman. And this, too, is a man zealous for the Church! Ah, poor Church, if it stood in need of such defenders."

5. WHAT KIND OF A MAN WAS WESLEY?

The secret of Wesley's marvelous work lay in his own life and character. Yet we may frankly acknowledge his limitations, for in some measure he shared the contradictions of his time. Many of these are unconsciously recorded in the twenty-six volumes of his Journal. He was a political Tory. Even he has some of the eighteenth century's exaggerated reliance upon reason in his passion for logic. At times he even shares its distrust of enthusiasm. He had, however, a sense of criticism far beyond the spirit of his age.

He shared in part the superstitions of his day. He believed in ghosts, in devil-possession and in witchcraft. At a time when witches were being burned in England and persecuted on Boston Common, he felt that to surrender that belief would be to renounce the authority of the Bible. With most childlike simplicity, he was often credulous of particular Providence that looked for miracle in most natural events.[7] His credulity and fond trust in men sometimes lent itself to his being imposed upon. His rapid and intense life led him at time to hasty, superficial or dogmatic judgments. His ascetic enthusiasm led him to attach at times an exaggerated importance to such things as tea-drinking and meat-eating, but he was far in advance of his age as a sane critic. His lack of imagination, his absence of a sense of humor, and his failure to understand women and children, brought him into difficulties, as in his own unhappy home life, and in his school

[7] He preached a sermon on "The Causes and Cure of Earthquakes," in which he said: "Sin is the moral cause of earthquakes, whatever their natural cause may be . . . . (earthquakes are) the effect of that curse which was brought upon the earth by the original transgression." In another sermon he declared that earthquakes are "God's strange works of judgment, the proper effect and punishment of sin." Quoted by White, Vol. i, pp. 220, 221.

at Kingswood. At times there was an element of harshness about him.[8] He did not show good judgment in his relations with women, although he was always highminded and absolutely upright. S. Parks Cadman speaks of Wesley's "witless susceptibility to feminine society." While in Georgia he fell in love with Miss Sophy Hopkey, "a beautiful, modest and affectionate girl of eighteen." When one of his friends seriously objected to this marriage because of the probable detrimental effects upon Wesley's religious work, they proceeded to cast lots about the matter. When the paper was drawn on which were written the words, "Think no more of it," Wesley at once "accepted this as a divine injunction against the marriage . . . The credulity he displayed in arriving at his decision by lot . . . was always latent in Wesley."

After returning to England he fell in love with Mrs. Grace Murray, who had nursed him in a period of illness, but this match was prevented by the vigorous action of his brother Charles. At the age of 48, he married Mrs. Vazeille, widow of a London merchant, "an essentially vulgar woman with a tendency to hysteria." The marriage was an exceedingly unhappy one. Wesley was undoubtedly inconsiderate of his wife and she in turn was wholly unfitted to be the wife of an itinerant preacher. She was abnormally jealous and suspicious. Southey says "she deserves to be classed as a triad with Xantippe and the wife of Job as one of the three bad wives." On the other hand, some of Wesley's actions toward her were inexcusable. For example, he once wrote to her: "Of what importance is your character to mankind? If you were buried just now, or if you had never lived, what loss would it be to the cause of God?" In a tract on marriage Wesley says the duties of a wife may

[8] "When he started a school at Kingswood, he resolved that no children of 'tender parents' should be received, but only of those who would consent to give their children entirely to the school, without taking them away 'even for a day.' The children themselves were to rise at four winter and summer, and fast until three on Fridays; there were to be no playtimes and no holidays." H. R. Gamble, Nineteenth Century, April 1920, p. 672.

be reduced to two: she must recognize herself as the inferior of her husband; and she must behave as such.

With all his faults, his many-sided character towers above his century like a vast Himalayan peak. He was rational, logical, warm-hearted, forgiving, humble, yet a man of iron will and a born leader of men. He ended every meeting with his Societies with the words, "Little children, love one another." He was fearless and courageous, calmly facing raging mobs. He was sane, tranquil and well-poised, a man of quiet dignity. In the presence of bitter persecution he maintained remarkable self-control and forbearance. Even in the strenuous theological controversies which raged between the Arminians and the Calvinists he never descended into the gutters of slander and abuse as did so many of the participants. So well versed was he in the classics that from the year 1731 it became his life-long habit to correspond in Latin with his brother Charles. He was swift, yet never hurried, energetic yet tranquil, with deep emotion yet controlled, gentle yet authoritative, ambitious yet selfless, a mystic yet rational, a scholar and a gentleman yet a leader of the masses and a friend of the poor. He was generous in the extreme. The royalties on his numerous publications are said to have yielded him $150,000, a vast sum of money in those days. Yet he never hoarded it or wasted it on himself. Like Cromwell, he was a "practical mystic." He was transparently honest and frank. He was a man of deep moral earnestness. He seemed an embodied conscience to his age. He had a passion for order and a statesman's capacity for organization. His mind was wide and tolerant and he was quick to receive suggestions and to profit by criticism. Added to all this was the drive and dynamic of a boundless devotion and sacrifice, coupled with a tireless patience. It was the balance of these qualities that made him the great preacher, writer, organizer, statesman, reformer, educator, physician, social servant, evangelist and dominant leader of the Evangelical Revival of the eighteenth century. He was the director of a religious crusade which changed England, awakened his century and helped to uplift mankind. It would be a different world today had he not lived. As Augustine Birrell says, "No man lived nearer the center than John Wesley . . . You cannot cut him out of our national life. No single figure influenced so many minds, no single voice touched so many hearts. No other man did such a life's work for England."

He was not unlike Milton, both in character and in appearance. We can picture him before us today, as he was described by a contemporary, "A clear, smooth forehead; an aquiline nose; an eye, the brightest and most piercing that can be conceived; and a freshness of complexion scarcely ever to be found at his years, and impressive of the most perfect health . . . In his countenance and demeanor, there was a cheerfulness mingled with gravity; a sprightliness, which was the natural result of an unusual flow of spirits, and yet was accompanied with every mark of the most serene tranquillity. His aspects, particularly in profile, had a character of acuteness and penetration . . . a head as white as snow gave an idea of something primitive and apostolic; while an air of neatness and cleanliness was diffused over his whole person."

He declared that "he had not felt lowness of spirits one quarter of an hour in his life. Ten thousand cares were no more weight to his mind than ten thousand hairs to his head. His Journal shows, however, that his memory late in life was sometimes colored by the gladness of the moment. His passion for order led him to become the great organizer. Everything and every moment had its place, every man his work in his program. He writes with trembling hand, "For upwards of eighty-six years I have kept my accounts exactly; I will not attempt it any longer."[9] Macaulay says he had "a genius for government not inferior to that of Richelieu;" while Matthew Arnold speaks of his "genius for godliness."

[9] His passion for system and order and economy is revealed by the following entry in his Journal: "Healthy men require above six hours sleep; healthy women, a little above seven, in four and twenty. If any one desires to know exactly what quantity of sleep his own constitution requires, he may very easily make the experiment, which I made about sixty years ago. I then waked every night about twelve

6. WHAT WERE THE RESULTS OF WESLEY'S LIFE?

Few men have ever lived who made so great a change in the moral and spiritual life of their day as did John Wesley. Whitefield preached to vaster throngs than Wesley, and as the greater orator, emotionally moved them more deeply. He had neither the time nor talent to tarry and organize, or to deal adequately with individuals or small groups. One visible remnant of his wonderful work is left in the chapel that bears his name in London. Wesley not only preached to the multitudes, but paused, patiently and painfully, with infinite care, to deal with individuals in personal work and organize his little groups of obscure followers. As a result, more than thirty million Methodists and Wesleyans are carrying forward his work today in more than fifty lands, and unnumbered multitudes besides have felt the effect of his work. In his combined gifts as preacher, organizer and tireless worker, Wesley was unsurpassed.

The Evangelical Revival that shook Great Britain in the eighteenth century was destined to spread from the group of four students at Oxford around the world. Wesley writes, "The first rise of Methodism was in November, 1729, when four of us met together in Oxford; the second was at Savannah in April, 1736, when twenty or thirty persons met at my home; the last was at London, when forty or fifty of us agreed to meet together every Wednesday evening, in order to free conversation, begun and ended with singing and prayer."

One of Wesley's German converts in Ireland, Philip Embury, emigrated to America in 1764, and built the first or one

---

or one, and lay awake for some time. I readily concluded, that this arose from my being in bed longer than nature required. To be satisfied, I procured an alarm, which waked me the next morning at seven, (nearly an hour earlier than I rose the day before) yet I lay awake again at night. The second morning I rose at six; but notwithstanding this, I lay awake the second night. The third morning I rose at five; but, nevertheless, I lay awake the third night. The fourth morning I rose at four, as, by the grace of God, I have done ever since; and I lay awake no more." Journal, Vol. iv., p. 536.

of the first Methodist churches there four years later. In answer to urgent appeals from the colonies, Boardman and Pilmoor were sent as workers and the wise and saintly Francis Asbury followed in 1771. When Wesley sent George Shadford in 1773, he wrote, "I let you loose, George, on the great continent of America. Publish your message in the open face of the sun." A little later Wesley ordained Coke as "superintendent" or Bishop. Over eight million Methodists in America, and their multiplying missions in many lands, are the result of this first venture into the wide world that was now the parish of this man, who was shut out of the churches in his own country and mobbed in many a town. He had a whole Christ for his salvation, a whole Bible for his staff, a whole Church for his fellowship, a whole world for his parish.

Under the new intellectual stimulus given to laboring men and adult education, the workers began to read, to speak, to preach, to form unions for self-government, and to agitate to improve their wretched conditions. It might almost be said that the British Labor Movement was born in the chapels of primitive Methodism. One result has been that instead of the materialistic, Marxian, and often anti-religious attitude of organized labor in Central, Eastern and Southern Europe, the British Labor Movement has probably been the most religious, the most deeply imbued with high idealism and the most determined to use education and constitutional methods of any labor movement in the world. Such deeply religious men as Keir Hardie, Ramsay MacDonald and Arthur Henderson, were one social result of Wesley's work.

Woodrow Wilson well said: "The Church was dead and Wesley awakened it; the poor were neglected and Wesley sought them out; the gospel was shrunken into formulas and Wesley flung it fresh upon the air once more in the speech of common men; the air was stagnant and fetid; he cleared and purified it by speaking always and everywhere the word of God; and men's spirits responded, leaped at the message and were made wholesome as they comprehended."

Sir Leslie Stephen referring to the century of Marlborough, Pitt, Clive, Warren, Hastings, Frederick the Great and George Washington, said of Wesley, "No such leader of men appeared in the eighteenth century." George Dawson points out that he stands among the great Johns of English history; John Wycliffe, the reformer; John Milton, the poet; John Bunyan, the seer; John Locke, the philosopher. But his total spiritual influence was perhaps greater than all combined. It was felt upon the established Church of England, of which he strove so earnestly to remain a part. "Wesley, preaching on his father's tombstone outside the Epworth Church, made impossible the drunken vicar inside. The spectacle of the vast open-air crowds that hung on Wesley's lips made the empty churches forever intolerable." If English Deism helped to produce the French revolution, the Evangelical Revival averted it in England. "England escaped a political revolution because she had undergone a spiritual revolution." William Boyd Carpenter said that the religious influence of Wesley was "greater than that exercised by any Christian during the last three hundred years."

The British Weekly said of him: "The grand and solitary figure of Wesley seemed always in the front of what ever was making for righteousness. He breathed upon the evils of his time with a fiery breath of purification." S. Parks Cadman, in referring to the results of Wesley's works, speaks of the "almost unparalleled transformation of the English national character." Newel Dwight Hillis says that "the two bright names of the eighteenth century are seen to be the names of Washington and Wesley." Canon Moore Ele, in his Hulsean Lecture, said: "The man who did the most to reform the social life of England in the last century was John Wesley." The historian Lecky gives this estimate of Wesley: "It is no exaggeration to say that he has had a wider constructive influence in the sphere of practical religion than any other man who has appeared since the sixteenth century . . . (his preaching was) of greater historic importance than all the splendid victories by land and sea won under Pitt."

On March 9, 1791, Wesley's worn body was carried to its grave by six poor men, "leaving behind him nothing but a good library of books, a well-worn clergyman's gown, a much-abused reputation, and—the Methodist Church." For some time his strength had been failing. Four months before, while preaching, he had to be sustained in the pulpit by two ministers and his feeble voice was barely audible. As he preached his last sermon in the open air, "the tears of the people flowed in torrents." He now penned his final letter to the young Wilberforce to encourage him in his fight against the slave trade. On Friday he asked to be left alone in his last half-hour with God. As his last moment drew near, with friends gathered about him, he cried with all his failing strength, *"The best of all is, God is with us."* Such was the life that helped to free men from moral and spiritual insensibility in a darkened age.

Chapter 6

FREEDOM FROM SOCIAL INJUSTICE

J. Keir Hardie

1. WHAT KIND OF A WORLD DID HARDIE LIVE IN?

Keir Hardie was the father of the British Labour Party He was born in 1856 and died in 1915. The significance of his life and work cannot be understood apart from a knowledge of the social conditions which prevailed throughout the British Isles during his lifetime.

Fortunately, there is an abundance of evidence available. The monumental survey of London made by Mr. Charles Booth and his associates during the years 1886 to 1888, gives us a vivid picture of the life of the masses in a great city, while the survey of York made in 1899, by Mr. B. Seebohm Rowntree, head of a great business, gives us similar information concerning conditions in a typical provincial city. From other sources we are also able to secure facts concerning agricultural workers.

Four volumes of the Booth survey dealt with poverty. Of the 4,309,000 residents of London, 1,292,737 persons, or 30 per cent of the total population, were living in poverty. In Mr. Rowntree's investigations, the minimum expenditure upon which a family of father, mother, and three children could maintain physical efficiency was set at 21s. 8d ($5.41) per week. Families that fell below this income were defined as living in "primary" poverty, while those that just approximated this amount were classified as living in "secondary" poverty. Mr. Rowntree summarized his findings as follows:

		Proportion of total population of York
Persons in "primary" poverty	7,230	9.91 per cent
Persons in "secondary" poverty	13,072	17.93 per cent
Total number of persons living in poverty	20,302	27.84 per cent

After a detailed examination of prevailing wage schedules, Mr. Rowntree says: "It is thus seen that the wages paid for unskilled labour in York are insufficient to provide food, shelter, and clothing adequate to maintain a family of moderate size in a state of bare physical efficiency. It will be remembered that the above estimates of necessary minimum expenditure are based upon the assumption that the diet is even less generous than that allowed to able-bodied paupers in the York workhouse, and that no allowance is made for any expenditure other than that absolutely required for the maintenance of merely physical efficiency."

One of the worst features of poverty was the matter of housing. Conditions in the slums of London were terrible beyond description. Tens of thousands of families were herded together in apartments of only one and two rooms, and compelled to live in the utmost of squalor and filth. Lord Shaftesbury once described an experience in the slums in these words: "I can assure you that some of those places in which large families reside, are so filthy, that I have found it impossible to go into some of them. The stench, the closeness of the air, pressed so strongly upon the senses, that I was unable to do so; and, in spite of all the resolutions I made at the entrances of some passages, I never could succeed in penetrating to the bottom of them. And I am not singular in that; for when I went on an inspection last year with an eminent physician, he told me that, habituated as he was to enter places of that description, he was frequently obliged to write his prescriptions outside the door. These houses are never cleaned or ventilated; they literally swarm with vermin. It is almost impossible to breathe. Missionaries are seized with vomiting or fainting upon entering them. 'I have felt,' said another, 'the vermin dropping on my hat like peas. In some of the rooms I dare not sit, or I should be at once covered.' "

Out of long experience in the slums of London, General William Booth, founder of the Salvation Army, wrote: "I sorrowfully admit that it would be Utopian in our present social arrangements to dream of attaining for every honest Englishman a gaol (jail) standard of all the necessities of life. Some time, perhaps, we may venture to hope that every honest worker on English soil will always be as warmly clad, as healthily housed, and as regularly fed as our criminal convicts—but that is not yet. Neither is it possible to hope for many years to come that human beings generally will be as well cared for as horses."

If we are to get an accurate picture of social conditions in the British Isles during the days of Keir Hardie, we must supplement this story of the abysmal poverty of the masses with an account of the riches and luxury of a small class at the top.

In 1873 an official "New Domesday Book" showing the ownership of the soil was published. The contents of this official report were carefully analyzed by Mr. John Bateman and published in a large volume under the title "The Great Landowners of Great Britain and Ireland." Mr. Bateman found that 2,512 persons each owned 3,000 acres or more, divided into the following classes:

	No. of Holders
Owning 100,000 acres and upwards	42
Owning between 50,000 and 100,000 acres	72
Owning between 20,000 and 50,000 acres	283
Owning between 10,000 and 20,000 acres	490
Owning between 6,000 and 10,000 acres	611
Owning between 3,000 and 6,000 acres	1,014
	2,512

Some of the largest individual holdings included in the above were:

The Duke of Sutherland	1,358,546 acres
The Duke of Buccleuch	458,739 acres
The Earl of Breadalbane	438,358 acres
Sir James Matheson	424,560 acres
The Earl of Seafield	305,930 acres
The Duke of Richmond	286,411 acres
The Earl of Fife	259,003 acres
Alexander Matheson	220,663 acres
	3,752,210 acres

That is to say, a single individual owned considerably more than a million acres, while the average for the eight was nearly half a million acres each.

No recent official figures are available concerning land ownership. We are able, however, to gain an insight into the extent of great wealth from the official income tax and death duties records. Sir Leo Chiozza Money's "Riches and Poverty" is an exhaustive study of these records. He found that in 1908 the two upper groups, comprising about 12 per cent of the population, receive about half of the national income, while the upper group, comprising one-thirtieth of the population receive one-third of the income. The average for each individual in the upper group is nearly twenty times the average for the lower group.

This vast inequality of wealth and privilege existed throughout the lifetime of Keir Hardie. And yet very few of the middle or upper classes showed any real concern over it. For the most part, they accepted it, rationalized it, and forgot it. Here and there an individual reformer raised his voice and exerted his influence against conspicuous evils. Chief among these was Lord Shaftesbury with his Factory Acts. In 1833, two decades before Hardie was born, Lord Shaftesbury began his activities which twenty years later resulted in a series of legislative reforms. The difficulties he encountered were almost insuperable. The facts as to glaring evils were easily ascertained. It was a simple matter for him to point out that children from the almshouses were turned over to overseers for work in the mills where they were worked unmercifully and treated with great brutality. "Day and night the machinery was kept going; one gang of children working it by day, and another set by night, while, in times of pressure, the same children were kept working day and night by remorseless task-masters." And yet it required many years of continued activity before even the worst of the abuses were remedied.

Another obvious evil was found in the work required of chimney sweeps. Very young children were used in this dangerous service. "Little children, from four to eight years of age, the majority of them orphans, the rest bartered or sold by brutal parents, were trained to force their way up the long, narrow, winding passages of chimneys to clear away the soot. . . . They began the day's work at four, three, or even two, in the morning; they were half stifled by the hot sulphurous air in the flues; often they would get stuck in a chimney, and faint from the effects of terror, exhaustion, and foul air, and then, if the usual remedy of lighted straw failed to "bring them round," they were often half-killed, and sometimes killed outright, by the very means used to extricate them." And yet many years of activity were required before adequate legislation was secured.

Another reform to which Lord Shaftesbury devoted many years had to do with the work of women and children in mines. A vivid summary of prevailing conditions in the mines has been given as follows: " 'Hurrying'—that is, loading small wagons, called corves, with coals, and pushing them along a passage—was an utterly barbarous labour performed by women as well as by children. They had to crawl on hands and knees, and draw enormous weights along shafts as narrow and as wet as common sewers, and women remained at this work until the last hour of pregnancy. When the passages were very narrow, and not more than eighteen to twenty-four inches in height, boys and girls performed the work by 'girdle and chain'; that is to say, a girdle was put round the naked waist, to which a chain from the carriage was hooked and passed between the legs, and crawling on hands and knees, they drew the carriages after them."

It now seems almost incredible that there should have been such terrible social blindness and such a volume of opposition to even the mildest of reforms. Lord John Russell once said that Lord Shaftesbury "is under a delusion which he has created for himself, if he supposes that a great many children are suffering under the infliction of grievances." A certain manufacturer of Darlington by the name of Pease declared that "if the hours of labour were abridged, he must, unless he submitted to torture and over-drive the children, inevitably close his manufactory." The excuse given for all the revolting cruelty practiced upon children in the mines was that "without the employment of child-labour, the pits could not possibly be worked with profit; that after a certain age the vertebrae of the back do not conform to the required positions, and therefore the children must begin early, and that unless early inured to the work and its terrors no child would ever make a good collier."

Lord Shaftesbury once complained: "The love of many waxeth cold;—not a newspaper will re-echo the appeal, and I have mourned like a dismal bird of the night, frightening many and fascinating none." Concerning the attitude of the churches, Lord Shaftesbury wrote at various times: "I find that Evangelical religionists are not those on whom I can rely." "To whom should I have naturally looked for the chief aid! Why, undoubtedly, to the clergy, and especially those of the trading districts. Quite the reverse; from them I have received no support, or next to none. And this, throughout my whole career." "In very few instances did any mill-owner appear on the platform with me; in still fewer the ministers of any religious denomination." "I have had more aid from the medical than the divine profession." "Prepared as I am, I am oftentimes distressed and puzzled by the strange contrasts I find: support from infidels or non-professors; opposition or coldness from religionists or declaimers!"

In writing of the middle decades of last century, Harold Begbie said: "It was an age in which only science held a taper into universal darkness. Everywhere else that one looked this darkness reigned and deepened. . . . One looks in vain, even from the giants of that age, for any recognition of this universal darkness. . . . . It is difficult for a modern mind to conceive truly of the England of that period. Nearly every suggestion for bettering the condition of the poor was regarded as blasphemous republicanism and treated with a wrathful disdain. Tory and Whig desired office for the sake of patronage, and there was no difference in the blindness of the one and the other, no difference in the deadness of their imaginations to the evils of the time. Religion, politics, art, even literature, struck no blow for justice and advance."

Abysmal poverty, excessive luxury, barbarous cruelty, callous indifference! What a world in which to be born!

2. WHAT DID HARDIE DO ABOUT IT?

If by agitator we mean a person who stirs up other people, Keir Hardie must be described as a supremely great labor agitator. He was born in a one-roomed house in Lanarkshire, Scotland, on August 15, 1856. His parents were exceedingly poor people. His first job was that of messenger boy for the Anchor Line. After a brief period in a brass-finishing shop, he obtained work in a lithographer's for which he received seventy cents per week. He then worked in a baker's shop and in a shipyard, at the rate of $1.12 per week, during which times his wages were the sole income of the family, as his father was unemployed for six months due to a lock-out by the shipowners. In sheer despair his father went off to sea and the family moved to Newarthill.

Here, at the age of ten, Hardie began his life in the mines.

He was employed as a trapper. His job was to open and close a door. For ten hours a day he sat in underground darkness alone. Later he became a pit pony driver, then went to coal hewing and by the age of twenty he was a skilled miner. Shortly after he began work as a trapper he started to night school, and was fortunate in finding an unusually intelligent and sympathetic teacher. Later he studied shorthand and became quite proficient at it.

He was discharged from the mines because he served with a deputation of miners who protested to the managers against certain abuses in the mines. At this time the miners were receiving 1s. 9d. ($.43) per day. At a huge meeting of the miners at Hamilton, on July 3, 1879, Hardie was appointed Corresponding Secretary. Later he was appointed Miners' Agent. At a national conference at Dunfermline Hardie was made National Secretary, although the national organization existed only on paper. In 1879 he was married to Miss Lillie Wilson and moved to Cummock in Ayrshire. Here he served as the Ayrshire Miners' Secretary, although as yet there was no Ayrshire miners' union. He also began to write regularly for the Cummock News. In 1886 the Ayrshire Miners' Union was formed, and he was appointed Organizing Secretary, with a salary or allowance of £75 ($375) per year. During this same year he was appointed Secretary of the Scottish Miners' Federation. In January, 1887, Hardie became editor of a new paper, "The Miner."

In 1882 Hardie joined the Liberal Party and became an active worker. Gladstone was then at the height of his power and was generally trusted by the workers. The Franchise Act of 1884, which extended household franchise to the counties, gave the vote to practically all adult miners. Shortly after this event, Hardie and some of his associates began the discussion of a new political party especially devoted to the interests of the workers. In May, 1887, at a meeting of Ayrshire miners, the following resolution was adopted: "That, in the opinion of this meeting, the time has come for the formation of a Labour Party in the House of Commons, and we hereby agree to assist in returning one or more members to represent the miners of Scotland at the first available opportunity."

Hardie was then adopted as the miners' candidate for North Ayrshire. His first recorded political utterance is an account of a speech delivered at Irvine in October, 1887, from which the following is taken: "The Liberals and Conservatives have, through their organizations, selected candidates. They are both, as far as I know, good men. The point I wish to emphasise, however, is this: that these men have been selected without the mass of the people being consulted. Your betters have chosen the men, and they now send them down to you to have them returned. What would you think if the Miners' Executive Council were to meet in Kilmarnock and appoint a secretary to the miners of Ayrshire in that way? Your candidate ought to be selected by the voice and vote of the mass of the people. . . . I am not specially anxious to go to Parliament, but I am anxious and determined that the wants and wishes of the working classes shall be made known and attended to there."

That the year 1887 was an exceedingly busy one for Hardie is indicated in the following quotation from his annual report: "There is scarcely a district in Scotland where my voice has not been heard, with what effect it is for others to say. I find, leaving out the deputations to London and the big conferences, that I have attended on behalf of the Federation 77 meetings, 37 of which have been public, and 40 Executive and conference meetings, involving 6,000 miles of railway travelling. I have sent out over 1,500 letters and circulars, and over 60,000 printed leaflets."

In 1888 the representative in Parliament from Mid-Lanark resigned. Since this was pre-eminently a mining constituency, an effort, which proved to be unsuccessful, was made to get the Liberal Association to adopt Hardie or some other miner as its candidate. Hardie thereupon decided to stand as an Independent Labour Candidate, the first of the kind in British history. His election address was interesting and significant: "I adopt in its entirety the Liberal programme agreed to at Nottingham, which includes Adult Suffrage; Reform of Registration Laws; Allotments for Labourers; County Government; London Municipal Government; Free Education; Disestablishment. On questions of general politics I would vote with the Liberal Party, to which I have all my life belonged."

An important incident of the campaign was described by Hardie in these words: "The following day, Mr. C. A. V. Conybeare, then M. P. for the Camborne Division of Cornwall, induced me to pay a visit to Sir George Trevelyan, also at the George Hotel. Sir George was very polite, and explained the unwisdom of Liberals and Labour fighting each other. They wanted more working men in Parliament, and if only I would stand down in Mid-Lanark he would give men an assurance that at the General Election I would be adopted somewhere, the party paying my expenses, and guaranteeing me a yearly salary—three hundred pounds was the sum hinted at—as they were doing for others (he gave me names). I explained as well as I could why his proposal was offensive, and, though he was obviously surprised, he was too much of a gentleman to be anything but courteous. And so the fight went on."

The result of the election in 1888 was as follows:

J. W. Phillips (Liberal)	3,847
W. R. Bousfield (Conservative)	2,917
J. Keir Hardie (Labour)	617

In May a group of twenty-seven men met in Glasgow for the purpose of forming a Labour Party. A committee was appointed, of which Hardie was a member, to arrange for a larger conference without delay. On August 25th this conference was held and the Scottish Parliamentary Labour Party was formed, with Hardie as Secretary. At this time Hardie was also serving as Secretary of the Ayrshire Miners' Union and of the Scottish Miners' Federation, and Editor of "The Miner."

In 1892 Hardie accepted an invitation to stand as an independent labour candidate in West Ham, with the following result:

J. Keir Hardie (Independent Labour) 5,268
Major G. E. Banes (Conservative) .. 4,036

At this election John Burns, another labour candidate, was also successful. Hardie and Burns were thus the first independent labour members of the House of Commons.

In the interval between Hardie's election and the assembling of Parliament an event of tremendous significance occurred. The Independent Labour Party, now familiarly known throughout the world as the I. L. P., was formed. Following the formation of the Scottish Parliamentary Labour Party in 1888, similar organizations had been started in various districts of England. The Social Democratic Federation was also operating, chiefly in London. On January 13th and 14th, 1893, a conference was held at Bradford, which resulted in the formation of the I. L. P., with Hardie as Chairman. Among the delegates present at this historic conference were Bernard Shaw, Robert Smillie, Ben Tillett and Robert Blatchford.

On February 7, 1893, Hardie made his first speech in the House of Commons in moving the following amendment to the Address: "To add, 'And further, we humbly desire to express our regret that Your Majesty has not been advised when dealing with agricultural depression to refer also to the industrial depression now prevailing and the widespread misery due to large numbers of the working class being unable to find employment, and direct Parliament to legislate promptly and effectively in the interests of the unemployed.' "

The most effective means of gaining publicity for his ideas was by asking questions of the different members of the Government. Thus we find him at various times making inquiries concerning the number of unemployed, the prosecution of strikers, the dismissal of certain postal employees, the graduated income tax, the pay of policemen, factory inspection, the use of soldiers in industrial disputes, and so on, almost interminably. His biographer says: "A mere list of the questions which he asked during his first Parliamentary session almost forms an index to the social conditions of the country at that time." So persistent was he in demanding action with regard to the problem of unemployment that he earned the title, Member of the Unemployed.

At the first annual conference of the Independent Labour Party in 1894, Hardie was elected chairman. During that year the Labour Leader was changed from a monthly to a weekly, with Hardie as editor and business manager. He now severed all official connections with the trade union movement, although he continued to speak and write incessantly on behalf of organized labour.

Hardie was defeated in the General Election of 1895, and consequently was free to accept an invitation from the Chicago Labor Congress. He spent fifteen weeks in America, going as far west as the Pacific coast. In July, 1896, he was defeated as the Labour candidate in the East Bradford by-election.

Hardie and the I. L. P. made strenuous efforts to prevent the South African War. In a manifesto issued five weeks before war broke out, the I. L. P. said: "The policy of the Government can be explained only on the supposition that their intention has been to provoke a war of conquest to secure complete control in the interests of unscrupulous exploiters. A war of aggression is, under any circumstances, an outrage on the moral sense of a civilised community and in the present instance particularly so, considering the sordid character of the real objects aimed at." After war was declared Hardie joined vigorously in a Stop-the-War movement, frequently facing howling mobs of super-patriots who regarded him as pro-Boer.

In 1900, Hardie was an active participant in the Labour Conferences at Glasgow and London, out of which came the Labour Representation Committee, forerunner of the present Labour Party. The Glasgow Conference passed the following resolution: "Recognising that no real progress has been made with those important measures of social and industrial reform that are necessary for the comfort and well-being of the working classes, and further recognising that neither of the two parties can or will effect these reforms, this Conference is of the opinion that the only means by which such reforms can be obtained is by having direct independent working-class representation in the House of Commons and on local administrative bodies, and hereby pledges itself to secure that end as a logical sequence to the possession of political power by the working classes." Hardie was elected a member of the first executive committee of the L. R. C. After seven years as chairman of the I. L. P., Hardie resigned in 1900. At the General Election during that year he was a candidate in two constituencies, being successful at Merthyr. He was now back in the House of Commons for a period in office which lasted until his death in 1915.

In 1903 Hardie gave up the editorship of the Labor Leader, the paper being transferred to the I. L. P. The following year he participated in the International Socialist Congress at Amsterdam. At the General Election in 1906 twenty-nine Labour members were elected to the House of Commons, including MacDonald, Snowden and Jowett. Prior to this, Hardie, Arthur Henderson and Will Crooks were the only independent labor members, although other working-class representatives were serving in the Liberal Party. An independent Parliamentary Labour Party was now formed, with Hardie as chairman. For the first time it was now possible for Hardie to go beyond agitation into the realm of political achievement. During the next few years the Labour Party was instrumental in securing the following results: "The passing of the Trade Disputes Act; the final and definite legalising of the right of combination; the struggle for the feeding of school children, resulting, at least, in the feeding of those who were necessitous; the determined and continuous pressing for the right to work, ultimately compelling the Liberal Party to look for a way out through Unemployment Insurance; the forcing of Old Age Pensions —these and many other seemingly commonplace achievements, yet all tending to raise the status of the workers and increase their sense of self-respect and of power as a class."

In 1907, as a result of over-work, Hardie broke down in health and was compelled to take a long rest. He then determined to make a tour around the world, in the course of which he visited Canada, India, Australia, New Zealand and South Africa. Upon his return to England, Hardie vigorously denounced the proposed military and naval agreements with Russia. In 1910 he retained his seat at both General Elections. He was now a leading figure in international labor circles and exerted himself to the limit on behalf of the movement for a general strike as a means of preventing war. From 1910 to 1914 he participated in international gatherings at Copenhagen, Lille, Basle, Budapast, Zurich, Jena and Brussels.

In December, 1913, Hardie presided at a great mass meeting in Albert Hall, London, called for the purpose of "strengthening the solidarity of Labor in all countries against war," and attended by eminent representatives from the continent. Sixteen months before war broke out, upon failing to secure desired information from Sir Edward Grey, Hardie said in a satirical way: "I suppose we shall be allowed to say a word or two before war begins." During the early weeks of 1914 the I. L. P. waged a vigorous campaign against conscription. In April, 1914, Hardie presided over the twenty-first annual conference of the I. L. P. Astounding as it now seems, his presidential address made no reference to the possibility of war, striking evidence of the blindness of even the most alert leaders to the approaching catastrophe.

When it began to look as if Great Britain might become involved in the war, "on Sunday, August 2nd, in every city, town and village where there was a branch or group of the Independent Labour Party, a public protest against the nation being dragged into the war was made, and a demand that whatever might happen to Europe, this country should stand neutral and play the part of peacemaker." Hardie was one of the speakers at a mass demonstration against war at Trafalgar Square, and was one of the signers of a manifesto issued by the British Section of the International Socialist Bureau. The manifesto was addressed to the British Working Class, and was, in part, as follows: "Hold vast demonstrations in London and in every industrial centre. Compel those of the governing class and their press, who are eager to commit you to co-operate with Russian despotism, to keep silence and respect the decision of the overwhelming majority of the people, who will have neither part nor lot in such infamy. The success of Russia at the present day would be a curse to the world. There is no time to lose. Already, by secret agreements and understandings of which the democracies of the civilised world know only by rumour, steps are being taken which may fling us all into the fray. Workers, stand together therefore for peace. Combine and conquer the militarist enemy and the self-seeking Imperialists to-day once and for all."

The efforts of Hardie, MacDonald and other Labour members in the House of Commons to prevent Britain from declaring war were, of course, unsuccessful. The chief result was that those who opposed the conflict became the victims of a war-intoxicated populace. When Hardie tried to speak to his constituents in Aberdare he was howled down and the meeting ended in general pandemonium. Abuse and vilification were showered upon him. Lifelong friends spoke bitter words that pierced his heart like dagger thrusts. He was utterly crushed at the thought of the workers of the various countries shedding each others' blood in a war from which they had so little to gain and concerning the real causes of which they knew so little. The experiences of these months dealt him a mortal blow, and on September 26, 1915, he passed away, a casualty of the Great War.

3. WHAT DID HARDIE SAY ABOUT IT?

From the beginning to the end, Hardie was a champion of the unfortunate and the dispossessed. He was constantly engaged in the task of exposing and denouncing exploitation and injustice. Perhaps no man of his day was more conscious of the poverty and misery of the masses than was this miner's son. Because he felt so deeply the needs of his people, his voice was never silent. From the public platform and in the House of Commons, in the public press and in numerous pamphlets and books, he thundered out his protests against the existing state of affairs and uttered his demand for a new social order.

Hardie became convinced that drastic changes in the economic system were necessary before the workers could be assured of justice. He once said: "Ours is no old-fashioned sixpence-a-day agitation. We aim at the complete emancipation of the worker from the thraldom of wagedom." Early in his career he proclaimed himself a socialist, but his brand of socialism was a source of amazement to many Marxians and communists on the continent. Mr. J. Bruce Glasier says: "I doubt if he ever read Marx or any scientific exposition of Socialist theory. He certainly had not done so before he avowed himself a Socialist. So far as he was influenced toward Socialism by the ideas of others, it was, as he himself stated, by the Bible, the songs of Burns, the writings of Carlyle, Ruskin and Mill."

He repudiated with vigor the doctrine of the class war. "Socialism," he once said, "makes war upon a system, not upon a class. . . . The working class is not a class. It is a nation. It is a degradation of the Socialist movement to drag it down to the level of a mere struggle for supremacy between two contending factions." When asked to define Socialism, he replied: "It means, on its economic side, that land and industrial capital shall be held as common property to be administered by the community in the interests of the whole of its members; and that industry shall be organized on the basis of Production for Use instead of the present-day method of Production for Profit."

Hardie was in no sense a doctrinaire socialist and showed little interest in the dogmas of continental radicals. Max Beer once said that Hardie was guided by "a practically unerring proletarian instinct," rather than "by theorising and speculating about revolution." Hardie always contended that socialism could be ushered in without violent and bloody revolution. He repudiated violence in the industrial struggle, as well as between nations. "No revolution," he once said, "can succeed which has not public opinion behind it, and when that opinion ripens, it, as we have seen over and over again, breaks down even the walls of self-interest."

What Hardie meant by socialism is indicated in the following quotation from a resolution which he introduced in the House of Commons in 1901: "That considering the increasing burden which the private ownership of land and capital is imposing upon the industrious and useful classes of the community, the poverty and destitution and general moral and physical deterioration resulting from a competitive system of wealth production which aims primarily at profit-making, the alarming growth of trusts and syndicates, able by reason of their great wealth to influence governments and plunge peaceful nations into war to serve their own interests, this House is of the opinion that such a state of matters is a menace to the well-being of the Realm and calls for legislation designed to remedy the same by inaugurating a Socialist Commonwealth founded upon the common ownership of land and capital, production for use and not for profit, and equality of opportunity for every citizen."

The closing words of his speech in support of the foregoing resolution were as follows: "Socialism, by placing the land and the instruments of production in the hands of the community, will eliminate only the idle and useless classes at both ends of the scale. The millions of toilers and of business men do not benefit from the present system. We are called upon to decide the question propounded in the Sermon on the Mount, as to whether we will worship God or Mammon. The last has not been heard of this movement either in the House or in the country, for, as surely as Radicalism democratised the system of government politically in the last century, so will Socialism democratise the industrialism of the country in the coming century."

As early as 1894, in advocating the nationalization of the mines, he wrote: "Here are the people of Scotland—over four million of them, wanting coal to burn, and willing to pay for it. Here are you, the miners of Scotland, seventy thousand of you, willing to dig the coal in exchange for a living wage. But between you and the public stand the landlords and the mine-owners, who say: 'The coal is ours, and we won't allow the miners to work nor the public to be supplied unless on our terms.' So long as the landlords and the mine-owners own the mines they are within their rights when they act as they have been doing, and the cure lies not in cursing the mine-owners, nor in striking, *but in making the mines public property*."

4. WHAT HAPPENED TO HARDIE?

Persons who seek to make drastic changes in the status quo always find themselves the victims of abuse, vilification, persecution and often of violence. So tireless an agitator as Keir Hardie could not expect to escape this common fate. In the beginning of his activities, he found not only that the mine-owners were against him, but also that the great mass of the workers were hostile to his proposal for an independent labor party. For years he was confronted with vigorous opposition from trade union leaders. He was frequently the object of bitter attacks by Marxian socialists. Blatchford, Hyndman and Grayson once refused to appear on the same platform with him. In the House of Commons he stood alone again and again . The reception accorded one of his speeches was described by an eye-witness in these words: "I've been in a wild beast show at feeding time. I've been at a football match when a referee gave a wrong decision. I've been at rowdy meetings of the Shoreditch vestry and the West Ham Corporation, but in all my natural life I have never witnessed a scene like this. They howled and yelled and screamed, but he stood his ground."

Hardie once had the experience of being "hooted and mobbed" by students at Cambridge University. On the occasion of his visit to India a vicious attack was launched upon him in the London press, concerning which one observer wrote: "The Yellow Press was seized with a violent eruption. It vomited forth volumes of smoke and flame and mud, and roared at Keir Hardie like a thousand bellowing Bulls of Bashan. . . . For a full fortnight Hardie was the most violently detested man throughout the English-speaking world."

Hardie's experiences in South Africa are described by his biographer as follows: "The opposition manifested itself in calculated and unbridled rowdyism, unchecked by the authorities, except at Johannesburg, where murder was feared. At Ladysmith, the windows of the hotel in which he stayed were smashed by the paid rowdies, 'no one, not even the hotel-keeper, trying to restrain them.' At Johannesburg a gang had been organised, and a detachment was sent to Pretoria, where the crowd, after the meeting, was the most turbulent of any, and smashed the carriage in which he drove back to the hotel with stones and other missiles." Throughout his whole career, his words and actions were grossly distorted. Downright falsehoods concerning him received wide circulation. On one occasion a political opponent circulated the lie that Hardie had sold his paper to I. L. P. for $100,000.

5. WHAT KIND OF A MAN WAS HARDIE?

The most impressive thing about Keir Hardie was his love for working people. He was tender and sympathetic to a very marked degree. Human suffering moved him to the depths of his being. His entire life was devoted to the relief and prevention of suffering and misery. Few men have ever manifested a finer quality of unselfish devotion to the cause of humanity than did this miner and statesman. "Not until my life's work found me," he said on one occasion, "stripped me bare of the past and absorbed me into itself did life take on any real meaning for me. Now I know the main secret. He who would find his life must lose it in others." The key to his life is found in this idea of losing himself in the great cause of abolishing exploitation and poverty.

During his early years in Parliament the members received no salary, and so he was compelled to earn his own living and support his family with outside activities. Again and again he refused gifts of money, which he thought would put him in a compromising position. Throughout his later years, when money could have been secured easily if he had desired it, he continued to live in the utmost simplicity.

He was a man of prodigious energy. The volume of work he was able to do was a constant source of wonder to his associates. After enumerating his activities for a fortnight, his biographer says: "How he managed to accomplish this work it is difficult to say. He had long ago acquired the faculty of being able to think and write under almost any circumstances, and much of his journalistic work was done in third-class railway compartments. . . . His correspondence itself was enormous, and he had no private secretary. His advice was sought by all sections of the Labour movement. Every day brought its committees, deputations, interviews and visitors from far and near; while every week-end found him on the propaganda platform in some part of the country. . . . Not infrequently he spent his two hours beyond midnight, after the House had risen, assisting at one or other of the Salvation Army shelters."

Hardie had great ability both as speaker and writer. The Leeds Mercury once referred to him as "one of the most cultured speakers the present House of Commons can boast." Mr. F. W. Jowett says: "His power over a crowd, indoor or outdoor, was amazing. In what did it lie? Not in eloquence, nor voice, nor gesture, for his voice was harsh with much speaking and his gestures were few—an outstretched hand and a pointing finger and little else. Nor was he eloquent after the manner of orators. It was his sincerity and simplicity of statement that carried his audience, and his invariable habit of associating himself with the poor man." He possessed unbounded physical and moral courage. He did not fear to stand alone. Neither friend nor foe could swerve him from a given course, once his mind was made up. An associate describes his first impressions of Hardie in these words: "There was always something in his uncompromising directness and complete indifference to the approval of the majority which attracted me."

One of Hardie's most notable characteristics was his deep religious faith. He was often accused of being an agnostic or infidel, but nothing was further from the truth. He did attack conventional religion and barren ecclesiasticism with great vigor. On Christmas, 1897, he wrote in his paper: "When I think of the white-livered poltroons who will take the Christ's name in vain, and yet not see His image being crucified in every child, I cannot think of peace. . . . If the spiritually-proud and pride-blinded professors of Christianity could only be made to feel and see that the Christ is here present with us, and that they are laying on the stripes and binding the brow afresh with thorns, and making Him shed tears of blood in a million homes, surely the world would be made more fit for His Kingdom." On another occasion he wrote: "The world today is sick and weary at heart. Even our clergy are for the most part dumb dogs who dare not bark. . . . We need today a return to the principles of that Gospel which, by proclaiming all men sons of God and brethren one with another, makes it impossible for one, Shylock-like, to insist on his rights at the expense of another."

On still another occasion he wrote: "The Archbishop of Canterbury, writing the other day (June, 1905), said he had to devote seventeen hours a day to his work, and had no time left in which to form opinions on how to solve the unemployed problem. The religion which demands seventeen hours a day for organization, and leaves no time for a single thought about starving and despairing men, women, and children, has no message for this age."

Hardie was a profound mystic in his own religious life. His intimate friends have often spoken of the quality of his religion. His biographer writes: "This inherent spiritual emotionalism—if it may be so called—was continually manifesting itself in various ways all through life, whether, as in the early Ayrshire days, in evangelising on the Ayrshire highways and byways, or, as in later days, preaching in Methodist pulpits or on Brotherhood platforms." Mr. Herbert Stead says: "Keir Hardie was essentially Labor evangelist, not politician. . . . he made the Parliamentary Labor Party more of a Church than a mere political body. The meeting in Queen's Hall to celebrate the return of the first Labour Party to Parliament was the only political meeting I have ever attended in which the divine Nazarene would have been an entirely sympathetic spectator."

He once declared: "The impetus which drove me first of all into the Labor Movement, and the inspiration which has carried me on in it, has been derived more from the teachings of Jesus of Nazareth than from all other sources combined. . . . Behind nature there is a Power, unseen but felt. Beyond death there is a Something, else were life on earth a mere wastage."

On May 5, 1913, in Browning Hall, Hardie said: "My friends and comrades, I often feel very sick at heart with politics and all that pertains thereto. If I were a thirty years younger man, with the experience I have gained during the past thirty-five years, I would, methinks, abandon house and home and wife and child, if needs be, to go forth among the people to proclaim afresh and anew the full message of the Gospel of Jesus of Nazareth. . . . Brothers, preach anew the Kingdom of God upon earth. . . . I know of no ideal so simple, so inspiring, so noble, as the Gospel of Jesus Christ of Nazareth."

Keir Hardie had many faults, some of them serious. He was inordinately stubborn and found it difficult to give in even when in the wrong. He was sometimes aggressively pugnacious in controversy. A close friend says: "He was often blunderingly tactless and rough." In his political and social philosophy, he was often superficial. He was given to over-simplification in his analysis of a social situation and many of the remedies he advocated were utterly inadequate. But in spite of obvious shortcomings, he was one of the most lovable and attractive men of his day, and had few equals in the degree of his sympathy for the oppressed, and no superiors in the quality of his devotion to the great cause of preventing exploitation and misery.

6. WHAT WERE THE RESULTS OF HARDIE'S LIFE?

In one sense Hardie's life was a dismal failure. The primary objective of his life was not achieved, for the British Isles are still the home of exploitation, unemployment, poverty and misery. Hardie struggled to prevent the World War and failed. The war dealt British industry a staggering blow from which it has not recovered. For five years consecutively more than a million workers at a time have been unable to find work and therefore compelled to accept unemployment doles. It is highly improbable that British industry will ever regain the dominant position it occupied in world trade in pre-war days and the prospects for the next decade are most gloomy.

It is yet too soon to say to what extent Hardie's life was successful. Europe is now confronted with two grave dangers; on the one hand, dictatorship of the proletariat, and on the other, dictatorship of the reactionary nationalists and capitalists. Russia and Italy represent the two contending forces. If any country in Europe has a chance to escape wholesale violence and bloodshed during the decades ahead, that country is Great Britain. In the temper and philosophy of Hardie, MacDonald and other moderate leaders of the British Labour Party lies the hope of avoiding a cataclysm in Europe. During the short time the Labor Party was in power it achieved notable successes in the pacification of Europe. Now Hardie, more than any other one person, was responsible for the formation of the Labour Party and was its head for many years. To his vision and tireless leadership its early successes were primarily due. He was everywhere acknowledged as one of the greatest labor leaders of his day.

Among the many tributes to the greatness of Keir Hardie is this one from Thomas Johnston, a member of Parliament: "Though dead, James Keir Hardie yet speaketh. No man has exercised a more potent influence in the moulding and direction of the British Labour Party. . . . The broad tolerance of doctrine in the British Labour Party, the absence of cloudy metaphysics in its creed, the strong dash of Puritanism in its programme and policy, are surely the attributes of the founder of the Labour Party, the poor Lanarkshire boy who became the prophet, priest, and patron saint of his class."

Many of Keir Hardie's most ardent desires were not realized, some of his theories and methods are being discarded, but he has left as an enduring monument the British Labour Party, perhaps the most idealistic and constructive political party in the world.

Chapter 7

FREEDOM FROM MAN'S DOMINATION

Susan B. Anthony

1. WHAT KIND OF WORLD DID MISS ANTHONY LIVE IN?

When Susan B. Anthony was born, in 1820, women all over the world were under the domination of men. Indeed, with rare exceptions, women have always been subjected to male control. Some of the exceptions, of course, are notable ones. There was a period in the history of ancient Egypt when women enjoyed almost as many rights and privileges as were exercised by men. Under Roman law women were accorded many significant personal and property rights. In the reign of Queen Elizabeth, England was referred to as the Paradise of Women. From 1776 to 1807 the women of New Jersey exercised the right to vote. The list of rights possessed by women in different countries at various periods could be greatly extended, but when completed it would appear almost insignificant in contrast with the disabilities and indignities to which women have ever been subjected.

Throughout history, until recently, vast numbers of women in many lands have lived under such conditions as the following: They have frequently been subjected to actual slavery and for ages were regarded as fair prizes for the victors in war; they have often been under the absolute control of their husbands, who frequently exercised the right of physical punishment even to the point of death; they have often been sold or bartered by father or husband; they were at times the common property of the tribe and at other periods were compelled to serve as concubines and prostitutes; they have often shared a home with many other wives; rarely have they been allowed to exercise free choice in selecting a husband or have any freedom as to whether or not they should bear children; they have usually been denied the right of divorce, but have often been subject to dismissal at the will of man; they have prevailingly been victims of a double standard of morals; they have been compelled to do the menial and monotonous work of the world and have frequently been regarded as beasts of burden; they have seldom received an adequate economic return for their labor; only a very restricted number of occupations have been open to them; they have usually been denied property rights; they have been subjected to all manner of legal limitations, usually being grossly discriminated against; they were long denied the advantages of education and have been the victims of their own ignorance and superstitions; under various religions they have been denied equal religious and ecclesiastical opportunities; in short, they have lived and died in a man-controlled world.

Countless illustrations of woman's bondage could easily be gathered together. The history of every age is filled with a long list of indignities inflicted upon women. Under the feudal system "women were taught by Church and State alike that the Feudal Lord or Seigneur had a right to them, not only as against themselves, but as against any claim of husband or father. The law known as Marchetta, or Marquette, compelled newly-married women to a most dishonorable servitude. They were regarded as the rightful prey of the Feudal Lord from one to three days after their marriage." In the Pennsylvania Gazette for January 14, 1768, was printed the following advertisement: "To be Sold—a Healthy Young Dutch Woman, fit for town or country business; about 18 years old; can spin well; she speaks good English, and has about five years to serve. Inquire at James Der Kinderen's, Strawberry Alley."

The silver-tongued Demosthenes said: "We marry in order to obtain legitimate children and a faithful warder of the house; we keep concubines as servants for our daily attendance, but we seek the Hetaerae for love's delights." St. Chrysostom, one of the great Church Fathers, described woman as "a necessary evil, a natural temptation, a desirable calamity, a domestic peril, a deadly fascination, and a painted ill." Lessing said: "The woman who thinks is like a man who puts on rouge—ridiculous." Voltaire declared: "Ideas are like beards—women and young men have none." Rousseau said: "The education of women should always be relative to that of man. To please Us, to be useful to Us, to make Us love and esteem them, to educate Us when young, to take care of Us when grown up, to advise, to console Us, to render Our lives easy and agreeable; these are the duties of woman at all times and what they should be taught from their infancy."

The tyranny of man was not so unbearable to American women in 1820 as at many previous periods in history. Girls were beginning to be admitted to public schools. Certain districts allowed girls to attend school in the summer while the boys were on vacation. In 1826 a public high school for girls was opened, but had to be closed within two years because of public hostility. In 1821 the Troy Female Seminary was opened as the first institution in the United States offering "higher education" to women. In 1833 Oberlin College admitted men and women, white and black, on equal terms, thereby becoming the first college in modern times to admit women. During the first decade of the nineteenth century certain legal disabilities of women were removed. In 1809 Connecticut gave married women the right to make a will, this example being followed by several other states within a short time. Mississippi was the first state to grant a married woman the right to control her own property.

In spite of this progress, however, the limitations and restrictions placed upon women were numerous and galling in the extreme. A married woman was under the absolute control of her husband. Practically everywhere in the United States the English Common Law was in force. Under its provisions the status of a wife, as stated by Blackstone, was as follows: "By marriage, the husband and wife are one person in law, that is, the legal existence of the woman is merged in that of her husband. He is her baron or lord, bound to supply her with shelter, food, clothing and medicine, and is entitled to her earnings and the use and custody of her person, which he may seize wherever he may find it. . . . The husband, being bound to provide for his wife the necessities of life, and being responsible for her morals and the good order of the household, may choose and govern the domicile, select her associates, separate her from her relatives, restrain her religious and personal freedom, compel her to cohabit with him, correct her faults by mild means, and, if necessary, chastise her with moderation, as though she was his apprentice or child."

There were still very serious limitations on the property rights of women. "In 1840 the only occupations open to women were teaching, needlework, keeping boarders, typesetting, working in bookbinderies, in cotton mills, and domestic service."

In 1852 the New York Herald ran an editorial which contained the following words: "How did woman first become subject to man, as she now is all over the world? By her nature, her sex, just as the Negro is and always will be to the end of time, inferior to the white race, and, therefore, doomed to subjection; but she is happier than she would be in any other condition, just because it is the law of her nature." It was counted disgraceful for a woman to speak in public or participate in any public demonstration. This feeling was destined to prevail for another half century. As late as 1876 an eminent clergyman declared that the appearance of two women in a church pulpit to speak on behalf of temperance constituted "an indecency in the sight of Jehovah." He went on to say: "It is not allowed women to speak in the Church. Man's place is on the platform. It is positively base for a woman to speak in the pulpit, it is base in the sight of Jehovah." In the early days even the reform movements of temperance and anti-slavery discriminated against women. In 1840 the American Anti-Slavery Society split over the question of woman's right to speak, vote and serve on committees. The World's Anti-Slavery Convention held in London during the same year was put in an uproar over this question of woman's rights on the floor.

The idea was still prevalent that every woman should be under the protection and control of some man. In an exaggerated manner the customary attitude in this regard was expressed by a well-known clergyman in these words: "Wifehood is the crowning glory of a woman. In it she is bound for all time. To her husband she owes the duty of unqualified obedience. There is no crime which a man can commit which justifies his wife in leaving him or applying for that monstrous thing, divorce. . . . If he be a bad or wicked man she may gently remonstrate with him, but refuse him never."

During this period there was very little discussion of women's political rights. The men were almost solidly against the idea of giving women the right to vote, and women's voices were rarely raised in protest against their disfranchisement. The great preacher Horace Bushnell was vigorously opposed to woman suffrage and wrote a book entitled, "Woman Suffrage: The Reform Against Nature." He pictured the dire consequences of giving women the vote in these words: "The look will be sharp, the voice will be wiry and shrill, the action will be angular and abrupt, wiliness, self-asserting boldness, eagerness for place and power will get into the expression more and more distinctly, and become inbred in the native habit." It was just one hundred years after the birth of Susan B. Anthony before the Woman Suffrage Amendment was ratified, placing women on an equal plane politically with men.

Thus we see that when Miss Anthony began her task of liberation, women were stamped with the badge of inferiority. They were still laboring under serious economic, legal and social disabilities, and were without adequate means of protection or redress for their wrongs. Still less were they able to enjoy the advantages and opportunities open to the least deserving of men. A life-long struggle on the part of a band of heroic women was required before the bonds of male domination were broken and escape made possible from centuries of abuse and exploitation.

2. WHAT DID MISS ANTHONY DO ABOUT IT?

Susan B. Anthony was reared in a Quaker home, first in Massachusetts and later in Rochester, New York. Her father was a Hicksite Friend and was an unusually liberal man. She grew up in a society which recognized the equality of the sexes and encouraged women to speak in public. It was the custom of well-to-do Quakers to conduct a school in their own home, so Susan received a much better education than was permitted to most girls of that day. Daniel Anthony was a successful mill owner and believed in giving sons and daughters the same advantages. He was especially desirous of training his daughters for self-support and taught them carefully in business principles.

At the age of fifteen Susan began to teach school, thereby bringing severe criticism upon her father for permitting his daughter to work for wages. Her first earnings were $1.00 per week and board, and ten years later she received only $2.50 per week. Everywhere it was the custom to pay men three or four times as much for exactly the same kind of work. In 1845 the Anthony family moved to Rochester, New York, and a few months later Susan became a teacher in the Canajoharie Academy, where she remained for three years. Although she had many admirers and at least two proposals, she does not seem to have given any serious thought to marriage.

In March, 1849, Miss Anthony made her first appearance upon the public platform, being the speaker of the evening at a temperance rally. Shortly thereafter she returned to Rochester and for the next two years lived at home, taking entire charge of the farm. After fifteen years of teaching, her taste for it was now gone and she was eager to take part in the two great reform movements of the day, temperance and anti-slavery. The Anthony home was a favorite gathering place for liberals and radicals. Here Susan talked with

Garrison, Channing, Phillips and many other notable men and women. During 1851 she was very active in temperance work in and around Rochester. The next year she attended the Anti-Slavery Anniversary in Syracuse and met Elizabeth Cady Stanton and Lucy Stone. As incredible as it seems today, Miss Anthony and the other women delegates were denied the right to speak at a state temperance meeting in Albany in 1852. Whereupon they withdrew and organized a separate meeting of their own. The outcome of the meeting was the appointment of a committee, with Miss Anthony as chairman, to call a Woman's State Temperance Convention. This convention was a great success, Miss Anthony acting as one of the secretaries.

On September 8, 1852, Susan B. Anthony attended her first Woman's Rights Convention at Syracuse, four years after the famous convention had been held in Seneca Falls. Here also she was elected secretary. She had now found her calling in life and devoted the rest of her days to unceasing toil on behalf of woman suffrage. The record of her activities during the next fifty-four years is one of the most amazing in the whole history of reform movements.

For more than a half century Miss Anthony engaged in ceaseless agitation for equal rights. Throughout most of this period she was engaged constantly in lecturing in all parts of the country. She wrote a never-ending stream of articles for the press. Perhaps her most effective activity was that of organizer and director of the suffrage campaign. In this realm she was pre-eminently qualified, and to her more than to any other person the success of the suffrage movement was due. She attended 29 out of 31 annual conventions of the National Woman Suffrage Association. She drafted innumerable resolutions and circulated countless petitions. For forty years she laid siege to Congress, addressing congressional committees during each year of that period. She raised and expended large sums of money for the suffrage cause. For ten years she devoted herself to the task of editing and publishing the massive four-volume

History of Woman Suffrage. Throughout her whole career she carried on a most voluminous correspondence, most of her letters being written personally by hand.

In 1878 Theodore Tilton described the activities of Miss Anthony and Mrs. Stanton in these words: "These two women, sitting together in their parlors, have for the last thirty years been diligent forgers of all manner of projectiles, from fireworks to thunderbolts, and have hurled them with unexpected explosion into the midst of all manner of educational, reformatory, religious and political assemblies. . . . I know of no two more pertinacious incendiaries in the whole country; nor will they themselves deny the charge. In fact, this noise-making twain are the two sticks of a drum for keeping up what Daniel Webster called 'the rub-a-dub of agitation.' "

In response to a question in 1897 concerning the extent of her activities, Miss Anthony said: "It would be hard to find a city in the northern and western States in which I have not lectured, and I have spoken in many of the southern cities. I have been on the platform for forty-five years, and it would be impossible to tell how many lectures I have delivered; they probably would average from seventy-five to one hundred every year. I have addressed the committees of every Congress since 1869, and our New York Legislature scores of times."

We have space here for a mere outline of a few of Miss Anthony's most important undertakings. In 1850 she arranged for the appearance of the first delegation of women before the New York Legislature. During this year she arranged for the World's Temperance Convention in New York. In 1860 Miss Anthony was primarily responsible for the action of the New York Legislature in greatly extending the property rights of married women. During the Civil War she was elected secretary of the Women's National Loyal League and worked unceasingly for universal emancipation. Following the war, she was one of the first to advocate Negro suffrage. She threw herself untiringly into the effort to have women, as well as Negroes, included in the proposed Fourteenth Amendment. In 1867 she was primarily responsible for the organization of the American Equal Rights Association, the Woman's Rights Convention being merged with the new association. She was instrumental in founding The Revolution, a journal devoted to equal rights, and became its Business Manager. She helped to form a Workingwoman's Association and taught women how to organize themselves. In January, 1869, she secured the first Congressional hearing on woman suffrage. In May the National Woman Suffrage Association was organized, with Miss Anthony as a member of the Executive Committee, and in 1872 she was elected President.

In 1883 Miss Anthony made her first trip to Europe, as a result of which a committee was formed to promote an international woman suffrage organization. In 1884 the third massive volume of The History of Woman Suffrage came from the press. The writing of this history was a labor of love and represented an incalculable amount of time and energy on the part of the three authors, to say nothing of the $20,000 expended by Miss Anthony. When the National Association and the American Association were merged into the National American Woman Suffrage Association in 1890, Miss Anthony was elected vice-president at large, and was President from 1892 to 1900. In 1899 she was the chief figure at the International Council of Women in London; and again at Berlin in 1904, at the age of eighty-four.

Miss Anthony was an office-holder in the suffrage movement continuously for more than fifty years. Her whole life was devoted to the suffrage cause. Other women gave part time or periods of time, but few, if any, gave so unreservedly and continuously of time and energy as did Susan B. Anthony. For her the struggle for equal rights took the place of wifehood, motherhood, recreation, leisure. Tirelessly, courageously and efficiently, she spent herself for the great cause.

3. WHAT DID MISS ANTHONY SAY?

The astonishing thing is that Miss Anthony's articles and addresses seem so commonplace to a present-day reader. It seems to us almost incredible that the moderate and reasonable statements and demands which she made should have so infuriated the public. This fact in itself illustrates the reversal of public opinion on the whole question of women's rights.

Miss Anthony's writings are devoted primarily to three subjects: temperance, anti-slavery and equal rights. As we have seen, her first public activities were on behalf of temperance. From the beginning she was also deeply concerned over slavery and was an ardent abolitionist. The striking fact is, however, that after she was well launched in her work, she devoted herself almost exclusively to the suffrage cause. As she herself said on one occasion: "I know only woman and her disfranchised." At another time, upon being requested to participate in the activities of a women's patriotic organization, she replied: "I can give neither time nor money to associations of women for any other purpose, however good it may be." And again: "I shall go on clamoring for the ballot and trying not to antagonize any man or set of men." She once wrote a sharp protest to Mrs. Stanton against involving the suffrage movement in the question of racial inter-marriage, concluding with these words: "Your sympathy has run away with your judgment. Lovingly and fearfully yours."

Although she was always an ardent abolitionist, Miss Anthony deeply resented the idea that following the Civil War women should step aside and wait until Negroes were enfranchised. When urged to postpone agitation for woman suffrage on the ground that Negro suffrage was being endangered, she replied: "I cannot welcome the demon of expediency or consent to be an abettor, by silence any more than by word or act, of wicked means to accomplish an end, not even for the sake of emancipating the slaves."

It was Miss Anthony's deepest conviction that most of

the disabilities and iniquities to which women were subjected were rooted in disfranchisement. Once women gain the vote, she contended, they will be able to remedy prevailing injustices. This point is illustrated in a quotation from an address which she delivered in many of the larger cities of the country between 1870 and 1880: "My purpose tonight is to demonstrate the great historical fact that disfranchisement is not only political degradation, but also moral, social, educational and industrial degradation. . . . Wherever, on the face of the globe or on the page of history, you show me a disfranchised class, I will show you a degraded class of labor. Disfranchisement means inability to make, shape or control one's own circumstances. . . . That is exactly the position of women in the world of work today; they cannot choose. . . . It is said women do not need the ballot for their protection because they are supported by men. Statistics show that there are 3,000,000 women in this nation supporting themselves. In the crowded cities of the East they are compelled to work in shops, stores and factories for the merest pittance. In New York alone, there are over 50,000 of these women receiving less than fifty cents a day. . . . It was cruel, under the old regime, to give rich men the right to rule poor men. It was wicked to allow white men absolute power over black men. It is vastly more cruel, more wicked to give all men—rich and poor, white and black, native and foreign, educated and ignorant, virtuous and vicious—this absolute control over women. Men talk of the injustice of monopolies. There never was, there never can be, a monopoly so fraught with injustice, tyranny and degradation as this monopoly of sex, of all men over all women."

Again and again Miss Anthony expressed the conviction that there could be no real freedom for women until they are financially independent—and she almost invariably went on to say that the ballot is essential to economic independence. "No genuine equality," she said, "no real freedom, no true manhood or womanhood can exist on any foundation save that of pecuniary independence." And again: "Whichever way I turn, whatever phase of social life presents itself, the same conviction comes: 'Independent bread alone can redeem woman from her curse of subjection to man.' "

Miss Anthony resolutely turned her back upon all suggestions for partial woman suffrage. She refused to support any effort to secure the vote for property-owning women, tax-paying or unmarried women. She was uncompromising and refused to budge an inch from her position: Equal suffrage for men and women.

Miss Anthony was a passionate believer in the power of agitation, and her spoken and written efforts along this line were extended for more than a half century. She also recognized the necessity for a continuous process of education among the rank and file of men and women. "There can be," she said, "but one possible way for women to be freed from the degradation of disfranchisement, and that is through the slow processes of agitation and education, until the vast majority of women themselves desire freedom. . . . Therefore, do not waste a single moment trying to devise any sort of insurrectionary movement on the part of the women." On another occasion, she said: "We have been working at the top with the members of legislatures, delegates to conventions, etc., too long; it is now time to begin at the bottom with the voting precincts."

The impression that grows upon one after reading the three huge volumes of Miss Anthony's biography and the six equally massive volumes of the History of Woman Suffrage is that she was possessed by a single idea and that her entire message can be summed up in the single statement: The all-important thing is for women to secure the ballot; then they will have the means of securing equal rights in all realms of life.

4. WHAT HAPPENED TO MISS ANTHONY?

The average person is not hospitable to a new idea, especially when its general acceptance would endanger prevailing rights and privileges. Therefore, we should not be surprised at the decades of opposition, derision and persecution to which advocates of woman suffrage were subjected. And yet one does not know whether to be more amazed at the ferocity with which these earnest women were attacked, or at the utter imbecility of many of the arguments of their opponents.

At the beginning of their crusade, Miss Anthony and her associates were confronted with the almost solid opposition of the male population of the country. Here and there a courageous man advocated their cause, but in the early days the number of such men was exceedingly small. Moreover, the suffragists met with active opposition or stolid indifference from a vast majority of women. "The fact is," said Miss Anthony, "women are in chains, and their servitude is all the more debasing because they do not realize it. O, to compel them to see and feel, and to give them the courage and conscience to speak and act for their own freedom, though they face the scorn and contempt of all the world for doing it!" After several decades of ceaseless effort they could muster only a few thousand active supporters.

As strange as it may seem, among the opponents of woman suffrage just after the Civil War were many leading abolitionists, as well as most Negro men. At this time Mrs. Stanton wrote: "The treatment of us by Abolitionists also is enough to try the soul of better saints than we. The secret of all this furor is Republican spite. They want to stave off our question until after the presidential campaign. They can keep all the women still but Susan and me. They can't control us, therefore the united effort of Republicans, Abolitionists and certain women to crush us and our paper." In describing a convention held in Washington in 1869, Mrs. Ida H. Harper said: "A feature of this occasion was the appearance of several young colored orators, speaking in opposition to suffrage for women and denouncing them for jeopardizing the black man's claim to the ballot by insisting upon their own. One of them, George Downing, standing by the side of Lucretia Mott, declared that God intended the male should dominate the female everywhere!"

Perhaps the most vicious opposition to woman suffrage came from the organized liquor traffic. These men resorted to every contemptible subterfuge of political corruption in their efforts to prevent women from securing the ballot. In their recent book Mrs. Carrie Chapman Catt and Miss Nettie Rogers Shuler cite evidence concerning the opposition of the saloons to woman suffrage, and then say: "From all this it seems fairly clear that the liquor funds spent in the political campaigns of the country ranged from four to ten millions of dollars a year."

Miss Anthony and her friends were subjected to an almost unparalleled degree of abuse and vilification. For a half century insulting epithets of a most extreme character were hurled at them from one end of the country to the other. In 1871 a Seattle paper, in commenting upon an address given by Miss Anthony in that city, said: "She is a revolutionist, aiming at nothing less than the breaking up of the very foundations of society, and the overthrow of every social institution organized for the protection of the sanctity of the altar, the family circle and the legitimacy of our offspring, recognizing no religion but self-worship, no God but human reason, no motive to action but lust. . . . The whole plan is coarse, sensual and agrarian, the worst phase of French infidelity and communism."

In 1866 the New York World made a vicious attack upon Miss Anthony, saying among other things: "Susan is lean, cadaverous, and intellectual, with the proportions of a file and the voice of a hurdy-gurdy." As late as 1899 a Memphis paper referred to her in these words: "Madly she snatches the veil from the face of her maidenly reserve, launches the gunboat of her vengeance, uncorks the bottle of her wrath. . . . Yes, Susan is on tap with a vengeance." At the state convention at Albany in 1854 a Mr. Burnett said: It is well known that the object of these unsexed women is to overthrow the most sacred of our institutions, to set at defiance the divine law which declares man and wife to be one, and establish on its ruins what will be in fact and in principle but a species of legalized adultery. . . . Are we, sir, to give the least countenance to claims so preposterous, disgraceful and criminal as are embodied in this address?"

When Miss Anthony introduced a resolution at the State Teachers' Convention at Binghamton in 1857 calling for the granting to women of "equal and identical educational advantages side by side with her brother man," (co-education) the chairman declared: "Here is an attempt to introduce a vast social evil. . . . These resolutions are the first step in the school which seeks to abolish marriage, and behind this picture I see a monster of social deformity." When women delegates, upon being denied the right to speak, withdrew from a temperance convention in the Brick Church in New York, a prominent clergyman rejoiced that they were "now rid of the scum of the convention."

Not only were these pioneer women called vile names, they were mobbed, arrested and subjected to all manner of indignities. In 1858 at a meeting in Rochester, "Miss Anthony was greeted with a perfect storm of hisses. Finally the demonstration became so threatening that she and the other speakers were hurried out of the hall by a rear door, the meeting was broken up and the janitor turned out the lights." In 1861 Miss Anthony, Mrs. Stanton and several other women arranged a series of meetings in New York State. In Buffalo their meeting was broken up by a mob which included an ex-justice and a son of ex-President Fillmore. "They were mobbed and their meetings broken up in every city from Buffalo to Albany." In Syracuse "rotten eggs were thrown, benches broken, and knives and pistols gleamed in every direction." At Albany the mayor of the city agreed to protect them. He placed policemen in various parts of the hall, "then he laid a revolver across his knees, and there he sat during the morning, afternoon and evening sessions."

In 1872 Miss Anthony, acting upon what she believed to be her rights under the Fifteenth amendment, and in accordance with eminent legal advice, voted in the November election. She was arrested, brought to trial, found guilty of a crime and fined $100, which she refused to pay and which was never collected.

Quite apart from the abuse and persecution to which she was subjected, Miss Anthony's life was filled with hardships. The physical strain incident to constant traveling and frequent speaking was terrific. Her biography is filled with incidents revealing the difficulties under which she labored. In 1875 she delivered sixty lectures in Iowa. "In order to reach the different places she had to take trains at all hours of the night, occasionally to ride in a freight car, sometimes to drive twenty-five or thirty miles across country in mud and snow and prairie winds. . . . Even these ills were not so hard to bear as the cold, dirty rooms, hard beds, and poorly cooked food sometimes found in small hotels. Frequently she had to sit by the kitchen stove all day as not a bedroom would have a fire and the only sitting-room contained the bar and was black with tobacco smoke."

Miss Anthony once described an experience in Kansas in these words: "It is now 10 A. M. and Mrs. Stanton is trying to sleep, as we have not slept a wink for several nights, but even in broad daylight our tormentors are so active that it is impossible. We find them in our bonnets, and this morning we picked a thousand out of the ruffles of our dresses. I can assure you that my avoirdupois is being rapidly reduced. It is a nightly battle with the infernals. . . We speak in school houses, barns, sawmills, log cabins with boards for seats and lanterns hung around for lights." Once she traveled by stage sixty-five miles over an arid desert, and at another time fifty miles over a dangerous mountain trail.

5. WHAT KIND OF A WOMAN WAS MISS ANTHONY?

First and foremost, Miss Anthony was a woman of supreme devotion to a great cause. Her life was utterly consumed in the struggle for woman suffrage. "I know only woman and her disfranchised," was her creed. "This one thing I do," was her motto. Appeals to engage in other worthy movements were regarded as temptations. After a painful experience, as a result of wearing the bloomer costume, she said: "I have felt ever since that experience that if I wished my hearers to consider the suffrage question I must not present the temperance, the religious, the dress, or any other besides, but must confine myself to suffrage." For fifty years she devoted almost every waking hour and every ounce of strength to the struggle for the ballot.

Miss Anthony was gifted with great physical endurance. Her tireless activities would have sent most women to an early grave. One cannot but marvel at the number of things she could crowd into a year—lecturing, writing, organizing, petitioning, exhorting and pleading. In 1857 she wrote: "How happy I am to lay my head on my own home pillow once more after four long months, scarcely stopping a second night under one roof." Seventeen years later she wrote: "I leave home without having had one single week of rest this summer—not this year, indeed, nor for twenty-five years." In her eightieth year her sister said: "Susan has always worked harder than anybody I ever knew, but she is breaking her own record." On February 22nd of that year Miss Anthony wrote in her diary: "I wrote eight letters to Senators this morning, enclosing petitions, and forgot to go to lunch." And this at the age of eighty!

In the midst of our present-day office equipment, it seems almost incredible that Miss Anthony never used a typewriter or employed a stenographer until the very last years of her life. When she was seventy-three she wrote: "The other day a millionaire who wrote me, 'wondered why I didn't have my letters typewritten.' Why, bless him, I never, in all my fifty years of hard work with the pen, had a writing desk with pigeonholes and drawers until my seventieth birthday brought me the present one, and never had I even a dream of money enough for a stenographer and typewriter."

It is not to be wondered at that, as far back as 1859, she confessed: "I am more tired than ever before and know that I am draining the millpond too low each day to be filled quite up during the night," and that in 1881 she again acknowledged: "Yes, we are tired, we are weary with our work."

And yet twenty-two years later she makes the long journey to New Orleans and is still the moving spirit in the annual Suffrage Convention. The year following, at the age of eighty-four, she attended the International Council of Women in Berlin, and was active in all its deliberations. The next year finds her on the Pacific Coast stirring up the women of California and Oregon. One month before her death she attended the Washington Suffrage Convention. What marvelous vitality she had!

Miss Anthony possessed courage of rare quality. To appreciate this characteristic of her life one must remember that she was an exceedingly sensitive person and suffered agonies when made the object of scorn and ridicule. On one occasion she wrote: "Here I am known only as one of the women who ape men—coarse brutal men! Oh, I can not, can not bear it any longer." That was in 1854. Yet during the next five decades we find her courageously going forward with her work in the face of vile epithets and sometimes even of physical violence. In response to the entreaties of a friend, in whose home she was staying in South Dakota, to hurry into the cellar to escape an approaching cyclone, she replied: "Never mind, after my recent experiences a little thing like a cyclone doesn't frighten me." No soldier on the battlefield ever exhibited a finer quality of sheer courage than that manifested in the daily life of this brave Quaker lady. An editor who was not himself a believer in woman suffrage once wrote concerning Miss Anthony: "No man ever had the courage of his convictions as much as she. It takes a bold spirit to stand up against the dangers of gun-powder in the old-time, legitimate way; but it is a braver one that withstands ridicule and that mean cunning which makes wit of every act looking toward the advancement of women."

She earned the right to say: "Cautious, careful people, always casting about to preserve their reputation and social standing, never can bring about a reform. Those who are really in earnest must be willing to be anything or nothing in the world's estimation, and publicly and privately, in season and out, avow their sympathy with despised and persecuted ideas and their advocates, and bear the consequences."

The spirit of unselfishness and self-sacrifice was possessed by Miss Anthony to an unusual extent. She was never concerned for herself, only for the great cause. She lived simply, and every dollar she could earn was devoted to the woman's movement. In one of her early letters she said: "My lunch costs, berries five cents, rusks five, and to-morrow the milk will be three." In 1890 Mrs. Carrie Chapman Catt wrote: "I think you are the most unselfish woman in all the world. You are determined to see that all the rest of us are paid and comfortable, but think it is entirely proper to work yourself for nothing." Ten years later, Mrs. Ida H. Harper wrote: "When Miss Susan B. Anthony lays down the gavel this week as president of the National Suffrage Association, she will have rounded out nearly fifty years in office. The most significant part is that she has never received one cent of salary, but, on the contrary, has put into the cause every dollar she has earned during all that time. When she dies and her slender annuity ceases, it will be found that she has left behind nothing of a money value as the result of her long and unflagging toil. . . . Just one woman in all the world has given every day of her life for half-a-century to bring about this evolution." Mrs. Elizabeth Cady Stanton, her most intimate friend for nearly half a century, wrote: "I can truly say that she is the most upright, courageous, self-sacrificing, magnanimous human being I have ever known."

In her religious beliefs Miss Anthony was a liberal. Although she was a Quaker by birth and training and remained one to the end, she attended the Unitarian Church in Rochester for more than fifty years. In her eightieth year she wrote: "I am thankful for having been born a Friend—a Quaker. To be born into a free religious world is a blessing indeed." She was severely critical of conventional Christianity and frequently complained that many of the churches were on the side of reaction. Concerning prayer she once said: "I pray every single second of my life;

not on my knees, but with my work. My prayer is to lift woman to equality with man. Work and worship are one with me."

Susan B. Anthony would never admit defeat. When the clouds were darkest, she would write: "Never mind, never mind, there will be another time. Cheer up, the world will not always view our question as it does now. By and by there will be victory." Her last words on the public platform were: "Failure is impossible."

6. WHAT WERE THE RESULTS OF MISS ANTHONY'S LIFE?

In 1908, at the 60th anniversary of the first woman's rights convention, the following summary of progress was given: "When that first convention met, one college in the United States admitted women; now hundreds do so. Then there was not a single woman physician or ordained minister or lawyer; now there are 77,000 women physicians and surgeons, 3,000 ordained ministers and 1,000 lawyers. Then only a few poorly paid employments were open to women; now they are in more than three hundred occupations and comprise 80 per cent. of our school teachers. Then there were scarcely any organizations of women; now such organizations are numbered by thousands. Then the few women who dared to speak in public, even on philanthropic questions, were overwhelmingly condemned by public opinion; now the women most opposed to woman suffrage travel about the country making speeches to prove that a woman's only place is at home. Then a married woman in most of our States could not control her own person, property or earnings; now in most of them these laws have been largely amended or repealed, and it is only in regard to the ballot that the fiction of woman's perpetual minority is kept up."

By 1914 eleven states had granted woman suffrage, and by 1918 the number had been increased to fifteen. The Suffrage Amendment passed both Houses of Congress in May and June, 1919, and was ratified by the 36th state on August 24, 1920. Thus we see that just one hundred years after Miss Anthony's birth and fourteen years after her death the women of the United States gained equal rights at the ballot with men. The woman suffrage leaders pointed out with humiliation, however, that twenty-six other countries preceded the United States in giving women the vote, as follows: Australia, Austria, Belgium (municipal), British East Africa, Burma (municipal), Canada, Czecho-Slovakia, Denmark, Esthonia, Finland, Germany, Great Britain, Holland, Hungary, Iceland, Isle of Man, Latvia, Littonia, Luxemburg, New Zealand, Norway, Poland, Roumania (municipal), Rhodesia, Russia, Sweden.

Now that the woman suffrage victory has been won, what is its significance? The most obvious result is the complete refutation of the predictions of dire calamities that would fall upon the nation if women were given the vote. Most of these warnings appear highly ludicrous to us today. On the other hand, the results are as yet far from being as satisfactory as the woman suffrage leaders had anticipated. In at least two regards, Miss Anthony and her friends were perhaps unduly optimistic: first, with regard to the use that women would make of the ballot; and, second, they failed to recognize the limitations of political action in securing economic and industrial freedom for women.

The question has been asked frequently of late, "Is woman suffrage a failure." Yes, in one sense it is. And so is male suffrage, and a far more dismal one at that. Five years of experience with the vote by women is nothing as compared with the decades that men have had the ballot. The truth of the matter is that political life in the United States is in a diseased state. It is wholly unreasonable to cry failure because women in half a decade have not cured age-old ills. On the whole, women have done remarkably well with the ballot, and we may confidently expect great things from them as they gain experience and as society throws off ancient prejudices against women in public life. The gaining of the ballot by women unquestionably constitutes one of the most significant reforms of history.

What was Miss Anthony's part in the woman suffrage victory? By common consent, she played the leading part. By various persons she has been referred to as the Napoleon, the Gladstone, the Lincoln, the Garrison, the Joan of Arc of the suffrage movement. Concerning her ability, her biographer wrote: "As a planner, an organizer, a manager, a politician in the best sense of the word, Miss Anthony was unequalled. . . Almost beyond any other, she had the power to create a following which would remain unswervingly loyal and devoted in the face of repeated disappointments and defeats." One of her associates once wrote: "Without her, the organization would have been utterly broken to pieces and scattered. She is the guiding spirit, the executive power that leads the forlorn hope and brings order out of chaos."

In 1890 her life-long friend, Mrs. Stanton, said: "Sub rosa, dear friends, I have had no peace for forty years. . . . She has kept me on the war-path at the point of the bayonet so long that I have often wished my untiring coadjutor might, like Elijah, be translated a few years before I was summoned, that I might spend the sunset of my life in some quiet chimney-corner." Miss Anthony's biographer wrote: "Thousands of women have said or written to her, 'I was tired, discouraged, wanted to quit—but I thought of you, of what you had borne and how you had toiled for us, and I couldn't stop, I will always keep on.'" In speaking of her part in the suffrage movement, a close associate wrote: "Miss Anthony alert, aggressive and indefatigable, is its nervous energy, its propulsive force."

On the day of Miss Anthony"s death, March 13, 1906, flags flew at half mast across the country. It is estimated that nearly 10,000 persons passed by her bier. Thousands of remarkable tributes were paid to her memory by the press and platform of the country. It was said of her by various persons: "She was the greatest woman this country ever produced. . . . The ages to come will revere her name. . . . The dear friend who has gone from us was one of the century's immortals. . . . We shall never see her like again. . . . She was the most earnest, devoted and resourceful woman of her time. . . . One of the world's grandest women. . . . In the roll of America's great women the name of Susan B. Anthony must always stand at the head. . . . The most persecuted of all women in her early days, Miss Anthony was the most honored of all in the closing years of her life. . . . The most remarkable career among those of American women, perhaps of all women, who lived in the nineteenth century. . . . A career without parallel. . . . A life as perfectly rounded as womanly woman can conceive. . . . She was a maker of history. . . . She has lived a thousand years if achievement can measure the length of life."

CHAPTER 8

FREEDOM FROM INTERNATIONAL ANARCHY

Woodrow Wilson

1. WHAT KIND OF WORLD DID WILSON LIVE IN?

Woodrow Wilson was born the year the Crimean War ended. He was five years of age when the Civil War began. He was elected President of the United States about two years before the World War began. Since he will be judged by history primarily on the basis of what he did or failed to do in the realm of international relations, we shall confine ourselves in this sketch to those phases of his life which had a bearing on his international policy. We shall make no effort, in such limited space, to deal with his domestic policy.

In order to understand the significance of Wilson's efforts on behalf of international peace, we must keep in mind the primary causes of the World War. Among the mighty forces which drove humanity to the slaughter were nationalism, imperialism, militarism, the balance of power idea, secret diplomacy, insecurity, fear, and the divorce of vital religion from international affairs. During most of this time Americans in general labored under the delusion that they were not involved in the affairs of Europe and could, therefore, live their lives in "splendid isolation." Let us notice more in detail the nature of international relations prior to the war.

1. The first notable fact about Wilson's world was the

extent and vitality of *nationalism.* The peoples of the earth were divided into sovereign nations. From the standpoint of world peace, the most dangerous phase of nationalism is its insistence upon absolute sovereignty. Artificial creation that it is, and embracing as it does persons of various races, languages, cultures and religion, it nevertheless demands supreme loyalty from all its citizens, even to the extent of compelling its citizens to slay persons of another nationality, although the slain may be of the same race, speak the same language, be of the same culture and belong to the same church as the slayers. Nationalism is a jealous god and will tolerate none other beside it. It thrives upon self-esteem and self-laudation. It is quick to resent discourtesies and insults. Matters that affect national interest and national honor are everywhere regarded as just causes for war. Nationalism is highly sensitive concerning encroachments upon its sovereignty and deeply resents outside interference of any sort. If anarchy be defined as the absence of law and orderly processes of government, then absolute national sovereignty leads inevitably to international anarchy.

2. Another primary fact about the world in which Wilson lived was the spread of *imperialism.* By imperialism is meant the extension of a nation's control over foreign peoples. This domination may be either territorial or economic in its nature. For two hundred years after the voyages of Columbus and Vasco da Gama there was an intense rivalry for colonies. Spain, Portugal, Holland, France, and Great Britain had acquired colonies in various parts of the earth. During the first half of the nineteenth century the colonial idea began to lose ground everywhere. The era of free trade and laissez-faire was inaugurated. About the time of Wilson's birth economic imperialism began to assume greater importance than colonial expansion. This was due primarily to the fact that Europe was rapidly becoming an industrialized continent.

During the past seventy-five years the European nations have been engaged in a mad scramble for control of the economic resources of the earth and for domination of markets and trade routes. This economic rivalry was supplemented after 1870 by a revival of territorial ambitions on the part of the great powers of Europe. By the time Wilson was elected President in 1912, almost the entire continent of Africa had been seized by European nations, as had also vast areas in Asia and the islands of the sea. In addition to territorial acquisitions, these nations had also gained economic concessions of enormous value in various parts of the earth, and had reached mutual agreement concerning spheres of influence in backward sections. This process of dividing up the treasures of the earth was accompanied by innumerable quarrels between the various nations of Europe. Thus fuel was added to the flames of jealousy and hatred which were already burning furiously because of the inflammability of nationalism.

3. Thus we are led to another factor of prime importance in the international realm, the growth of *militarism*. In a world of sovereignty nations, each of which is self-centered and refuses to acknowledge any law higher than its own desire, and which is engaged in bitter rivalry with other nations for the control of the earth, we should not be surprised to discover the nations arming to the limit of their ability. That is just what the various units of Europe did during the forty years preceding the World War. As a result of the race of armaments these nations spent forty billion dollars upon armies and navies from 1871 to the end of 1913.[1] The higher the arms were piled in one country the more determined became the enemy not to be outstripped in

[1]The rank of the nations in total expenditures for armaments during these forty years was as follows: France $8,568,000,000; Great Britain $8,401,000,000; Russia $7,581,000,000; Germany $7,434,000,000; Italy $3,010,000,000; Austria-Hungary $2,774,000,000. See Harvey E. Fisk, French Republic Finance, issued by the Bankers Trust Company, New York.

preparedness. Therefore, a dual appeal was made to the peoples of the various nations, an appeal to patriotic pride and appeal to fear of other nations. So powerful was this double appeal that the citizenry of Europe endured an almost intolerable burden of taxation and military conscription.

4. But even with this titanic exertion no nation could safely rely on its own arms alone. Therefore, each nation was constantly seeking *military alliances* with other powers against a common enemy. As a result, Europe gradually became divided into two great armed camps. Over against the Triple Alliance (Germany, Austria-Hungary and Italy) was the Triple Entente (France, Russia and Great Britain). Thus was established the famous balance of power. It was believed that peace could be maintained only by keeping this balance undisturbed. Any incident, therefore, that threatened to disturb the balance of power at once became a potential cause of war. All the major nations of Europe were prepared to fight rather than to allow the opposing alliance to gain any significant advantage in the race for power. Professor Mowat, of Oxford, says in this connection: "With the equipoise of Europe so nicely adjusted—Germany and Austria, with Italy in one group, England and France, with Russia in the other—the slightest political tremor made the scales oscillate in an alarming fashion. The international situation was thus delicate and dangerous."

5. In a world of extreme nationalism, greedy imperialism, virulent militarism and unstable balance of power, *secret diplomacy* is the method inevitably resorted to in the effort tc gain a desired end. The use of spies, misrepresentation, deceit, bribery, stealing of documents, fomenting hatreds are commonplaces of the old system. As a result of secret diplomacy, enormous power was placed in the hands of diplomats. A few men, operating secretly, controlled the destiny of a continent.

During the half century prior to the outbreak of the World War, there was a veritable epidemic of secret treaties and private understandings negotiated throughout Europe. Secret diplomacy was invariably accompanied by suspicion and distrust, and sooner or later led to fear and hatred. It created an atmosphere which made impossible the peaceable settlement of the disputes which were constantly arising between the nations.

6. In a world of nationalism, imperialism, militarism, alliances and secret diplomacy, it was inevitable that *fear and insecurity* should everywhere prevail. With national passions aroused by the sight of huge armed forces across the border and with whole peoples at the mercy of propaganda of militarists and diplomatists, whose movements were shrouded in mystery, it was natural that the rank and file of people throughout Europe should be desperately afraid. It was fear, although not fear alone, which caused them to submit to the staggering burden of taxation and military conscription. They were afraid of what would happen if their nation should fall behind in the terrific race of armaments. Upon the fears of the people, militarists and diplomatists built their grand schemes for increasing the power, wealth and prestige of their respective countries, and covered their designs with a smoke screen of high-sounding phrases about "national security," "national honor," and "vital interest." The result was not only the forty important wars of the century, but a never ending succession of crises which were constantly arising to threaten the peace of the world. Again and again from 1871 to 1914 Europe was on the brink of a great war.

7. A final notable characteristic of the world in which Wilson lived was *the absolute divorce between Christianity and international relations in Europe.* For hundreds of years Europe has been nominally a Christian continent and has raged countless wars against Islam. And yet during the period under review little effort was made by the

great powers of Europe to reconcile international practices with the life, teaching and principles of Jesus. It was everywhere believed that it was impossible for nations to be guided by Christian principles. Indeed, in many quarters it was asserted that Christianity was merely a personal religion and wholly inapplicable to affairs of state. The disciples of this doctrine were more numerous and vociferous in Germany than elsewhere, but they were to be found in high positions in all countries. Moreover, even where this doctrine was not consciously held and given audible expression, it was frequently an unspoken assumption and was the basis of national policies.

Summary

We have by no means given a comprehensive review of international affairs in Europe at the time Woodrow Wilson began his work, nor have we given proper emphasis to the more favorable side of the picture. What we have sought to do is to outline the major difficulties and dangers to world peace with which he and his contemporaries were confronted.

A vivid summary of the pre-war situation in Europe has been given by G. P. Gooch, one of two British historians selected to prepare an official diplomatic history of this period from documents in the British Foreign Office, in these words: "The root of the evil lay in the division of Europe into two armed camps, which dated from 1871, and the conflict was the offspring of fear no less than of ambition. The Old World had degenerated into a powder magazine, in which the dropping of a lighted match, whether by accident or design, was almost certain to produce a conflagration. . . . It is a mistake to imagine that the conflict of 1914 took Europe unawares, for the statesmen and soldiers had been expecting it and preparing for it for many years. It is also a mistake to attribute exceptional wickedness to the Governments who, in the words of Lloyd George, stumbled and staggered into war. Blind to danger and deaf to advice as were the civilian leaders of the three despotic empires, not one of them, when it came to the point, desired to set the world alight. But though they may be acquitted of the supreme offense of deliberately starting the avalanche, they must bear the reproach of having chosen paths which led straight to the abyss. The outbreak of the Great War is the condemnation not only of the clumsy performers who strutted for a brief hour across the stage, but of the international anarchy which they inherited and which they did nothing to abate."

2. WHAT DID WILSON DO?

Better blood has rarely ever been possessed by any great leader than that which coursed through the veins of the new born baby in the home of Joseph Ruggles Wilson and his wife, Janet, in Staunton, Virginia, three days before the end of the year 1856. This blood came from a long line of Scotch-Irish ancestors. Not only was the young child, Thomas Woodrow, blessed with an exceptionally good biological heritage, he also inherited the moral and religious traditions of the old Scotch Covenanters. His ancestors on both sides had been staunch Presbyterians for many generations.

His father was a man of very commanding personal presence, a brilliant orator, and a scholar of considerable attainments. He was minister of the Presbyterian Church at Staunton when Woodrow was born. Shortly afterward he became minister in Augusta, Georgia, where he remained until 1870; at which time he became professor of pastoral and evangelistic theology in the Theological Seminary at Columbia, South Carolina. Thus we see that from the ages of two until fourteen Woodrow lived in the Augusta manse. This household was a very religious one. The orthodox theology of the day was received without question. God was regarded as a monarch of indescribable majesty, a stern and unrelenting judge, who could be propitiated only by the shed blood of His Son on the cross. The present life was regarded as a vale of tears, a period of trial and preparation for fairer lands on high. As rigid predestinarians, they regarded all of mankind, save the favored elect, as rushing on to everlasting punishment in the lake of fire and brimstone. Conscience and duty were among the great realities of life. The influence of the church in that community was very powerful. The richest people in the town were of the Presbyterian faith. So the church was conservative not only in theology but with regard to all social questions. Slavery was accepted and defended as a divine institution. The Presbyterian Church finally split over the slavery question, and it was in Dr. Wilson's church that the Southern Presbyterian Church was organized. Dr. Wilson was himself elected stated clerk and served in that capacity for forty years.

When Tommy, as he was then called, was five years old, he saw the Confederate soldiers go away to war against the hated Yankees. At the end of four ghastly years, he saw the beloved leaders Jefferson Davis and Alexander Stephens as they passed through Augusta heavily guarded on their way to prison in the North. He once stood by the side of the great Robert E. Lee and gazed into his face. After the war came the even more terrible days of reconstruction. Rarely ever has a proud and cultured race been subjected to deeper humiliation and more galling treatment that that meted out to the defeated soldiers of the South. Thus we see that the formative years of Woodrow Wilson's life were spent in an atmosphere of religion, war and humiliation.

In 1874 he went away to Davidson College, in North Carolina, but poor health prevented the completion of his course. He was of a very nervous disposition and broke under the strain. So he returned home, which was now in Wilmington, North Carolina, where his father was again in pastoral work. There he spent a year reading serious books. As a result of the rigorous training received from his father, he had an extraordinarily well disciplined mind and was much more mature in his judgments than were most young men of his age. In September, 1875, he entered Princeton University, where his father had been a student. The Princeton of that day was a very religious community. Most of the professors were Christian ministers or earnest Christian laymen. The students were gathered chiefly from well-to-do religious homes. Woodrow's scholastic record was good but not exceptional. When he graduated he barely attained "honors," ranking forty-first in a class of one hundred and twenty-two. But this was because he was not primarily interested in the required classics, mathematics or science. His main concern was literature and the study of government, and much of his best work was done outside the curriculum and classroom. He achieved distinction as a debater and was elected editor of the Princetonian, the college paper. Several able productions were published in the Nassau Literary Magazine, and in 1879 he succeeded in getting the International Review to publish a very able article on congressional government.

From Princeton he went to the University of Virginia to study law. After a year he had such a serious attack of indigestion that he was compelled to return home. Later he finished his preliminary studies in law and received his degree from the University. In 1882 he began the practice of law in Atlanta, as a member of the firm of "Renick and Wilson, Attorneys at Law." But it soon became apparent that he was not cut out for the law, and he entered Johns Hopkins University, where he received his Ph.D. degree. His thesis, "Congressional Government," became a well-known book and ran through many editions. In 1885 he was married to Miss Ellen Axson, beautiful daughter of the Presbyterian minister of Rome, Georgia, to whom he had been engaged for about three years. For the next eighteen years Woodrow Wilson was a college professor, for three years at Bryn Mawr, for two years at Wesleyan University, for thirteen years at Princeton. These were wonderfully happy and successful years. Mrs. Wilson was a woman of great personal charm, as well as an artist of real merit. She and Mr. Wilson were devoted to each other, and each was a constant inspiration and stimulus to the other. He was very popular as a teacher and was also much in demand as a lecturer before important audiences in various cities. His success as a writer was even greater. His writings covered a wide field and included biography, historical works, essays in political science, and several critical reviews. He had access to the leading periodicals of the day and contributed a steady stream of notable articles. Several of his works became standard text-books in colleges throughout the country.

In 1902 Woodrow Wilson was elected President of Princeton University, which had been founded in 1746 by "radical democrats calling themselves evangelical Presbyterians." Prior to his inauguration only clergymen had been elected to the presidency. He had a stormy career in this capacity. He was winning his fight with the Dean and certain trustees, when a wholly unexpected factor intervened. A rich man died and left a sum which was estimated to be ten million dollars, but which actually amounted to three millions, to the Graduate School, naming the Dean as one of the administrators. Three million dollars constitute too heavy odds for any college president to overcome.

In 1910 occurred one of the most astonishing political events in the entire history of the United States. Woodrow Wilson was elected Governor of New Jersey. George Harvey, editor of Harpers Weekly, was chiefly responsible for this event. Harvey had been much impressed by Wilson's address on the occasion of his inauguration as President of Princeton, and in 1906 publicly suggested him as Democratic candidate for the Presidency. The stage was all set for a Democratic victory in 1912. The long impending cleavage in Republican ranks was being precipitated by the personal feud between Roosevelt and Taft. The entire situation demanded that the Democrats nominate a liberal or radical Democrat from an eastern state. Bryan had suffered his third defeat but the Democrats did not dare to name another conservative like Parker. In order to make possible Wilson's nomination it was necessary to get him quickly into politics. Therefore Harvey conceived the idea of having him elected Governor of New Jersey. Here also the stage was set for a change. Boss rule and political corruption had become intolerable. The Democrat bosses, reading the handwriting on the wall, knew they must nominate a liberal. What could be better than to elect a greenhorn college president who was absolutely inexperienced in politics and would therefore be easy to control? And so Woodrow Wilson was nominated and elected.

Then the bosses' disillusionment began. Wilson quietly took the helm and began putting through his own program. He kept the Democratic boss, James Smith, from being reelected to the United States Senate. Soon he gained sufficient support to secure important legislative enactments concerning election reform, employers' liability, public utilities and corrupt practices. His election and legislative record immediately put him in the front line of candidates for the Presidency. His addresses in Wisconsin, Texas and nearer home were received with the utmost enthusiasm. Colonel Harvey and his friends were becoming more and more apprehensive over the extreme liberalism and independence of Wilson. They were getting more than they had bargained for. In December, 1911, an open break occurred and Harvey began campaigning for Champ Clark. At this time, however, Wilson gained two powerful supporters in Colonel House, of Texas, and Josephus Daniels, of North Carolina. House won the Texas delegation at Baltimore for Wilson, while Daniels annexed the two Carolina delegations, and what is more important helped to win Bryan's support for the New Jersey Governor. The real fight at Baltimore was between Wilson and Clark. Bryan turned the tide and Wilson was nominated, winning the November election against Roosevelt, with Taft a poor third.

The only phase of Woodrow Wilson's administration as President of the United States with which we shall deal is his foreign policy. In the light of all that followed, it is astonishing to find that Wilson did not refer to foreign policy in his first inaugural address. He had been elected upon domestic issues and with these he was primarily concerned. And yet from the very beginning he was compelled to deal with one international crisis after another. Immediately after inauguration he was obliged to take account of the Mexican situation. Only thirteen days before General Huerta had become provisional president, by virtue of the assassination of President Madero, and the question of recognition of his government was up for decision. The American ambassador at Mexico City strongly recommended recognition but the President decided not to recognize a government which had come into office by murder. Then began the long period of "watchful waiting," for which the President was so severely criticized by those who desired to see us "go down and clean up Mexico."

Just one month after he became President, Wilson received a protest from the Japanese ambassador against the proposed anti-alien legislation in California. Whereupon he urged the California authorities not to enact discriminatory legislation, and later sent Secretary Bryan as a personal messenger to urge Governor Johnson to withhold approval of the anti-alien land bill. All efforts to this end having failed, he did his utmost to convince the Japanese Government that no national affront was intended by California's action.

Early in the administration, Secretary Bryan, with Wilson's approval, negotiated treaties with twenty-eight nations, whereby it was agreed that the United States and the signatory nations would not under any circumstances declare war prior to arbitration and the report of an investigating commission. In October, 1913, speaking through the newly appointed Governor-General, the President announced his intention to grant a larger degree of self-government to the Filipinos, looking toward the ultimate independence of the islands. In January, 1914, United States Marines were landed in Haiti to help restore order and protect American lives and property. In March the President asked Congress to repeal the provision in the Panama Canal Act which exempted American Coast-wise shipping from payment of canal tolls, and three months later signed a bill to this effect. He also negotiated a treaty with Colombia which awarded that country $25,000,000 for losses through the revolt of Panama in 1903, which revolt was aided and abetted by representatives of the United States. This treaty failed to receive ratification in the Senate.

In April, 1914, the Mexican situation became tense again, American bluejackets were arrested in Tampico but released immediately with expressions of regret. When Huerta refused to give an apology in the form of a salute to the American flag demanded by Admiral Mayo, the President ordered the seizure of Vera Cruz. The fact has since become public that the President "would have preferred to ignore the affair and accept the written expression of regret which was extended," but finally felt obliged to sustain his Admiral. The seizure of Vera Cruz caused great resentment throughout Latin America. Fortunately, the United States accepted the offer of Argentina, Brazil and Chile to mediate the question and the American forces were withdrawn, although not until November 23rd.

The outbreak of the European war came as a complete surprise to the American people. On August 4th the President issued a proclamation of the neutrality of the United States.[2] On the next day he offered to act as mediator if his services should be desired. Secretary Bryan announced that the Administration considered the lending of money by American bankers to belligerent governments as inconsistent with true neutrality. During succeeding months the President drafted a series of protests to Great Britain and Germany against repeated violations of international law and unwarranted interference with the rights of neutrals. That Great Britain repeatedly violated international law in her interference with neutral shipping is not open to question. In one of his notes to Great Britain the President referred to her North Sea blockade as "ineffective, illegal and indefensible." The President made protest after protest but was unwilling to enforce observance of neutral rights by an embargo on arms or by a breach in diplomatic relations. Germany considered this refusal to follow protests with appropriate measures of enforcement as in fact an abandonment of neutrality, since Britain's violations of international law were making possible the successful blockade of Germany. Germany reasoned that if Britain was justified in maintaining the blockade by violations of international law, she in turn

[2]So many things have happened since 1914 that it is easy to forget that at that time the sentiment in favor of neutrality was almost universal in the United States. Only the extreme hyphenates desired armed intervention. Even so belligerent a person as Theodore Roosevelt *after the invasion of Belgium* wrote in the Outlook, of September 23rd, 1914, as follows: "It is certainly eminently desirable that we should remain entirely neutral . . . very probably nothing that we could have done would have helped Belgium. We have not the smallest responsibility for what has befallen her . . . sympathy is compatible with full acknowledgment of the unwisdom of our uttering a single word of protest unless we are prepared to make that protest effective. . . . As for her (Germany's) wonderful efficiency—her equipment, the foresight and decision of her General Staff, her instantaneous action, her indomitable persistence—there can be nothing but the praise and admiration due a stern, virile and masterful people, a people entitled to hearty respect for their patriotism and far-seeing self-devotion. . . . I think, at any rate I hope, I have rendered it plain that I am not now criticising, that I am not passing judgment one way or the other, upon Germany's action."

was justified in breaking the blockade by illegal means. And so she began unrestricted submarine warfare.

This action immediately placed Wilson in an exceedingly difficult position. Whereas Britain's violations of international law merely interfered with American rights, Germany's violations endangered American property and lives, with the consequence that public opinion in the United States soon reached fever heat. Whereas public opinion had been content merely to protest against Britain's excesses, now there was an insistent demand for action, for war if Germany contiued to violate American rights. That at this time the President sincerely desired to keep the United States out of the war can scarcely be questioned in the light of the record of what he actually did during these critical months. Case after case was reported of American property and lives being destroyed by German submarines, and finally on May 7, 1915, the Lusitania was sent to the bottom of the sea, with an appalling loss of life. Instantly there was a violent and insistent demand for war against Germany. That, in the face of this popular measure, Wilson refrained from declaring war for nearly two full years is convincing testimony of the genuineness of his desire to avoid war. Note after note was sent, protest piled upon protest, and, in spite of modification in Germany's extreme policy, the submarine atrocities continued. In December, 1915, the President made an appeal to Congress for further military and naval preparedness.

While the crisis with Germany was at its height, affairs on the Mexican border again became serious. On March 8, 1916, a force of Mexican bandits led by Villa attacked the town of Columbus, New Mexico, and killed seventeen persons. The President immediately ordered General Funston to prepare for action. A punitive expedition under General Pershing crossed into Mexican soil but was unsuccessful in the attempt to capture Villa. The presence of United States troops in Mexico proved to be a constant source of friction with the Mexican

Government. Powerful interests in the United States sought strenuously to induce the President to declare war. Heavy pressure was brought to bear upon Wilson, but with dogged earnestness he resisted all efforts to bring about war. He availed himself of the offer of several Latin American countries to mediate, and the punitive expedition was withdrawn.

In the summer of 1916 Woodrow Wilson was renominated as the Democratic candidate and was successful in the fall election, although by an exceedingly close margin, so close indeed that Mr. Hughes went to bed on election night believing that he had been elected President, and refused to acknowledge defeat until sixteen days later. Early in 1917 relations with Germany grew worse. On January 31st, the German Government, in violation of its pledge of May 4, 1916, and in violation of international law, announced that it would adopt a policy of sinking all ships met in the "barred sea zone." This action made inevitable a break with Germany. The President did not at once ask for a declaration of war, but invited neutral countries to join in a final protest against Germany's action, and then asked Congress for authority to arm ships for entrance into the barred zone.

On April 2nd the President appeared before a joint session of Congress. It was indeed one of the most momentous gatherings in history. A decision was about to be made which would prove to be one of the turning points of history Every seat was filled. Members of the Supreme Court, diplomats of every nation, Cabinet officers and officials of every branch of the Government, waited with breathless interest for the President's words. He was visibly nervous. His face was deadly pale. His fingers trembled. He began to read . . . and then came the fatal words: "I advise that the Congress declare the recent course of the Imperial German Government to be in fact nothing less than war against the government and people of the United States." Four days later, on Good Friday, after a debate in the House which was carried on at times in a spirit of such levity that the presiding officer was compelled to remind the members that they were not "at a vaudeville performance," came the declaration of war.

From that moment the President sought to enlist the entire nation in the one task of winning the war. "Force! Force to the utmost! Force without stint or limit!" became his motto. A total of 4,272,521 men were enrolled in the army and 533,000 in the navy; of whom about 2,000,000 actually reached France. Enormous quantities of food and munitions were supplied to the Allies and undreamed of coffers of gold were placed at their disposal. Vast as was the material and military assistance rendered the Allies it was not more effective in the end than the moral influence of the President's words. His idealistic utterances kindled new courage and new hope in the hearts of the rank and file of people in Allied lands. While, on the other hand, his speeches penetrated to the heart of Germany and were a powerful factor in bringing about the loss of morale which was ultimately so important a factor. In the end the combined physical and moral efforts of the United States turned the tide, and Germany sued for peace. An armistice was arranged on a basis of the Fourteen Points and subsequent addresses of the President.

Woodrow Wilson broke another precedent when he decided to head the American peace delegation to Paris. He felt that so much was at stake that he did not dare to stay away. Before the entry of America into the conflict, as well as throughout the later years of the war, he had been the mouthpiece through which the liberal and peace-loving sentiment of the world had found expression. The fruition of all previous efforts depended upon the outcome of the peace conference. Hence he decided to go to Paris in person, taking with him Lansing, House, White, General Bliss and a large staff of experts, but leaving such Republican leaders as Taft and Root behind—a blunder that was destined to produce incalculable havoc to the President's plans and hopes.

Before the Peace Conference opened Wilson made a brief tour through the chief Allied countries. Everywhere he was received with a degree of admiration and enthusiasm, rarely, if ever, equalled in history. Populaces went wild over him. His presence and words kindled a new hope in the hearts of common people and he was hailed as a veritable saviour of mankind. But alas the victorious nations were in no mood to adopt that magnanimous attitude toward a defeated foe which alone opens the pathway to international salvation. Fear was too intense, suspicion was too deep-rooted, hatred was too bitter, the desire for revenge was too dominant, the trust in force and violence was too complete—and so the leaders in conference assembled refused to follow the President in drafting the kind of peace terms which would make possible the creation of the sort of world for which the hearts of people everywhere were yearning.

The Peace Conference at once developed into a strenuous conflict between two opposing views of the effective way to maintain international peace and justice; one group, for which Clemenceau, the Tiger, was the chief spokesman, cynical of all moral and spiritual forces and confident of the Allies' military prowess, pleaded frankly for a perpetuation of the balance of power system, since for the moment the balance was so heavily weighted in their favor; the other group, led by Wilson, believed that peace could not be maintained nor justice administered so long as the victor stood with his heel upon the neck of the vanquished, but depended ultimately upon a new attitude and a new machinery, that is to say, upon international co-operation functioning through international agencies of justice In this struggle Clemenceau had an enormous advantage, four-fold in its nature: the bitter hatred of Germany and her allies which prevailed everywhere outside those lands, the long series of secret treaties which had been signed between the principal

Allied powers, the intense desire of each of these powers to gain as large a share of the prizes of the war as possible, and the very real danger of anarchy and chaos in many parts of Europe which made it imperative that the peace conference should stay in session until agreements were reached. Against this combination the President was helpless, and while he managed to save a few brands from the burning, his peace of conciliation and idealism was consumed in the flames of national hatred and greed.[3]

Wilson made mistakes, some of them serious in nature; he compromised at points where compromise was fatal. At the crucial moment he was a very sick man, his frail body wracked with pain and his mind torn with confusion and anguish at the thought of the terrible consequences of failure. He cannot be relieved of blame for some of the injustice of the treaty, but he must be given credit for one of the most heroic struggles in the face of terrific odds known to mankind. The terrible fact is that tradition and war had created a situation which was beyond the control of any idealistic leader. Wilson, even if his record had been absolutely flawless, could no more have escaped temporary defeat at Paris than Jesus could escape the cross of cynicism and hatred on Calvary.[4]

---

[3]General Smuts of South Africa, himself one of the outstanding figures of the Peace Conference, said of the Treaty of Versailles: "It was not a Wilson peace, and he made a fatal mistake in somehow giving the impression that the peace was in accord with his Fourteen Points and various declarations. Not so the world had understood him. This was a Punic peace, the same sort of peace as the victor had dictated to the vanquished for thousands of years." Current History Magazine, April, 1921, p. 46.

[4]Concerning this point General Smuts said: "It was not Wilson who failed. The position is far more serious. It was the human spirit that failed at Paris. . . . Even if Wilson had been one of the great demigods of the human race, he could not have saved the peace. Knowing the Peace Conference as I knew it from within, I feel convinced in my mind that not the greatest man born of woman in the history of the race would have saved that situation." Ibid, p. 47.

The most important part of Wilson's program which was salvaged from the wreckage was, of course, the League of Nations. From the beginning the League was his chief concern, and in order to save it, he sacrificed much that was very precious to him. And then, supreme tragedy of all, his cherished League, due to bitter partisanship and his own tragic blunder in tactics, was rejected by the United States Senate. During a swing around the circle, speaking on behalf of the League, the President suffered a stroke of paralysis and during the remainder of his administration he was an almost helpless cripple.

3. WHAT DID WILSON SAY?

No statesman has ever stirred the human race so deeply with his words as did Woodrow Wilson. Himself an idealist of first rank and gifted with a marvelous facility of expression, he lifted the people's conception of international relations to a new level. Four phases of his message deserve emphasis at this point: his fervent belief in democracy, his conception of nations as servants of mankind, his belief in the necessity of international agencies of justice, his undying faith in moral and spiritual forces.

1. Wilson had a passionate conviction that the various peoples of the earth were capable of running their own affairs, and that the real trouble with government was the domination by autocrats, oligarchies and bosses. "I believe in the ordinary man," was the basic article in his political creed. "The select classes of mankind are no longer the governors of mankind. The fortunes of mankind are now in the hands of the plain people of the whole world. . . The countries of the world belong to the people who live in them. . . Every people has the right to determine its own form of government." Wilson's state papers and public utterances were not addressed to statesmen so much as they were to peoples. Again and again he went over the heads of rulers to

the citizens themselves. This was notably true in his appeals to Germany. He carefully distinguished between the German rulers and the German people. Even in his address to Congress advising a declaration of war, he said: "We have no quarrel with the German people. We have no feeling towards them but one of sympathy and friendship. It was not upon their impulse that their government acted in entering this war." And later when the passions of war were rising in the United States, he declared in his Flag Day address: "We know now as clearly as we did before we were ourselves engaged that we are not the enemies of the German people and that they are not our enemies." At the Peace Conference, as throughout his whole career, Wilson was an ardent advocate of the principle of self-determination, self-government.

2. Woodrow Wilson believed that nations should be guided by the same moral and ethical principles which are binding upon individuals. Repeatedly he denounced national aggression and lawlessness in vigorous terms. He constantly declared that the United States had no thought of aggression. "America has no hampering ambitions as a world power. We do not want a foot of anybody's territory. . . . We shall never in any circumstances seek to make an independent people subject to our dominion. . . Conquest and dominion are not in our reckoning, or agreeable to our principles."

On the other hand, the President believed that nations should use their resources and powers in the service of humanity. "It is clear that nations must in the future be governed by the same high code of honor that we demand of individuals. . . . We are at the beginning of an age in which it will be insisted that the same standard of conduct and responsibility for wrong done shall be observed among nations and their governments that are observed among the individual citizens of civilized states. We shall yet prove to the Mexican people that we know how to serve them without first thinking how we shall serve ourselves. . . We can afford to exercise the self-restraint of a really great nation which realizes its own strength and scorns to misuse it. . . We are the mediating nation of the world. . . We have undertaken these many years to play big brother to the republics of this hemisphere . . There is no claim of guardianship or thought of wards, but, instead, a full and honorable association as of partners between ourselves and our neighbors. . . We are trustees for the Filipino people. . . . It is now our liberty and our duty to keep our promise to the people of those islands by granting them the independence which they so honorably covet."

3. Wilson was a passionate believer in international agencies of justice. Again and again he called attention to the futility of depending upon national armaments or upon military alliances for security and justice. On numerous occasions he emphasized the fact that the United States could no longer maintain a policy of isolation. "We thought that the cool spaces of the ocean on the east and west of us would keep us from the infections that came, arising like miasmic mists, out of that arrangement of power and of suspicion and of dread. . . . We are participants, whether we would or not, in the life of the world. . . You can no more separate yourselves from the rest of the world than you can take all the tender roots of a great tree out of the earth and expect the tree to live. All the tendrils of our life, economic and social and every other, are interlaced in a way that is inextricable with the similar tendrils of the rest of mankind. . . Do you not know that the world is all now one single whispering gallery?"

The President saw the necessity for permanent agencies through which the nations could discuss common problems, take counsel as to courses of procedure, and make decisions concerning common action. Therefore, he spent his last ounce of energy in seeking to persuade his countrymen to endorse the League of Nations and the World Court. This is not the place to enter into a detailed evaluation of Wilson's arguments in favor of the League. All we can do at this point is to call attention to one or two statements in which he summarizes his attitude toward the League: "My conception of the League of Nations is just this, that it shall operate as the organized moral force of men throughout the world, and that whenever and wherever wrong and aggression are planned or contemplated, this searching light of conscience will be turned upon them. . . It (the League) is a great method of common counsel with regard to the common interests of mankind. Consultation, discussion, is written all over the whole face of the covenant. . . The voice of the world is at last released. The conscience of the world is at last given a forum, and the rights of men not liberated under this treaty are given a place where they can be heard. . . Settlements may be temporary, but the action of the nations in the interest of peace and justice must be permanent. We can set up permanent processes."[7]

4. Woodrow Wilson had an undying faith in the power of moral and spiritual forces in the international realm. "I have not read history without observing that the greatest forces in the world and the only permanent forces are the moral forces . . . Force will not accomplish anything that is permanent . . . The only thing that will hold the world steady is this same silent, insistent all-powerful opinion of mankind . . . Moral force is a great deal more powerful than physical. Govern the sentiments of mankind and you govern mankind . . . We are depending primarily and chiefly upon one great force, and that is the moral force of the public opinion of the world—the cleansing and clarifying and compelling influences of publicity . . . There is a great wind of moral force moving through the world, and every man who opposes himself to that wind will go down in disgrace . . . Humanity can be welded together only by love, by sympathy, by justice, not by jealousy and hatred . . . There is such a thing as a man being too

proud to fight. There is such a thing as a nation being so right that it does not need to convince others by force that it is right."

Such, in brief, was Wilson's message to mankind. Not always consistent, at times self-contradictory in his utterances, yet no voice has ever carried so far or driven so deeply into the heart of the world the message of faith in democracy, the duty of nations to regard themselves as servants, the necessity of international processes of justice, and the supreme power of moral and spiritual forces, as did the voice of Woodrow Wilson.

4. WHAT KIND OF A MAN WAS WILSON?

Two utterly different pictures of Woodrow Wilson exist in the minds of various people who knew him intimately. The main outlines of both pictures are painted in true colors. The fact of the matter is that two Woodrow Wilsons resided within the one body of flesh and blood. He recognized this fact himself and once confessed to his secretary: "You know, Tumulty, there are two natures combined in me that every day fight for supremacy and control. On the one side, there is the Irish in me, quick, generous, impulsive, passionate, anxious always to help and to sympathize with those in distress . . . Then, there is the Scotch—canny, tenacious, cold, and perhaps a little exclusive. I tell you, my dear friend, that when these two fellows get to quarrelling among themselves, it is hard to act as an umpire between them." On occasions friends and enemies alike have used far stronger language in describing the unfavorable aspect of his character. Not only was he at times stern and forbidding, often he was irritable and quick tempered. On occasions he was unforgiving and even contemptuous of those with whom he seriously disagreed. The manner in which he broke with George Harvey was inexcusable. No sincere admirer of Mr. Wilson has any right to attempt a justification of the way in which he turned his back upon Lansing, Tumulty and House, three supremely loyal friends to whom he was so deeply indebted.

Wilson often referred to the fact that he had a single-track mind, and on occasions seemed to glory in the fact. Many of his most serious blunders were made because of his extreme concentration on one matter to the exclusion of all others. "If he were busy upon a note to Carranza, he might let some monstrously reactionary appointment pass unnoticed. . . Being preoccupied with a problem of preparedness, he allowed the picketing suffragists taken from the White House gate to be treated with brutal indignity at the Washington City jail. . . But amid all these inconsistencies, and they are many and obvious, there is never inconsistency of intention."

Woodrow Wilson was of an intensely emotional and very affectionate nature. The home life of the Wilson family was characterized by an unusual degree of sympathetic understanding and abiding affection. Even after they moved to the White House they maintained the simplicity and freedom of their domestic life. Unlike many previous Presidents, Wilson did not invite persons to his table for the purpose of exerting political influence upon them. Guests were admitted to the Wilson home with care, but once inside they were received with the utmost cordiality. To the very end Wilson retained the warmest affection for many intimate friends. In commenting upon an article which portrayed him as a great intellectual machine, he cried out to Tumulty: "Good God, there is more in me than that! I want people to love me, but I suppose they never will." On another occasion he said: "My constant embarrassment is to restrain the emotions that are inside me. You may not believe it but I sometimes feel like a fire from a far from extinct volcano, and if the lava does not seem to spill over it is because you are not high enough to see into the basin and see the caldron boil."

The death of Ellen Wilson came as a great shock to her husband. They were so utterly devoted to each other that this enforced separation left Wilson in the deepest gloom. He developed spells of melancholy and only an iron will kept his attention on affairs of state. In referring to this period David Lawrence said: "Eight months of tomb-like seclusion in the White House changed the whole temper of the man. His moods in those months were so despondent that the members of his family groped in vain for something that would lift him from the depression into which he had languished." Then by chance he met Mrs. Edith Galt, a charming widow. Soon the romance developed into deep affection, and on December 18, 1915, they were quietly married. Close friends of the family agreed that the love and devotion of Edith Wilson alone made it possible for the President to bear the burden and strain of the last years of his administration. Her faithful care and affectionate presence in the sickroom were the primary means of prolonging his life for four years after the stroke in 1919.

Woodrow Wilson was a deeply religious man. The faith which he inherited as a child, he verified in personal experience. The presence of God in his life was an abiding reality. In the great crisis of his career he turned naturally to the Divine Father for guidance. When he received word that he had been elected President of the United States he said: "I do not feel exuberant or cheerful . . . I feel more like kneeling down and praying for strength to do what is expected of me." The day before he started for the Peace Conference, he said to his secretary: "Well, Tumulty, this trip will either be the greatest success or the supremest tragedy in all history; but I believe in a Divine Providence. If I did not have faith, I should go crazy. If I thought that the direction of the affairs of this disordered world depended upon our finite intelligence, I should not know how to reason my way to sanity; but it is my faith that no body of men however they concert their power or their influence can defeat this great world enterprise, which after all is the enterprise of Divine mercy, peace and goodwill." Just before he sailed for the second time for the Peace Conference in a public address in Raleigh he said: "I do not understand how any man can approach the discharge of the duties of life without faith in the Lord Jesus Christ."

In an impromptu address from the front steps of his home on Armistice Day, 1923, just a few months before his death the ex-President said: "I am not one of those that have the least anxiety about the triumph of the principles I have stood for. I have seen fools resist Providence before and I have seen their destruction, as will come upon these again—utter destruction and contempt. That we shall prevail is as sure as that God reigns." In his Atlantic article he said: "The sum of the matter is this, that our civilization cannot survive materially unless it be redeemed spiritually. It can be saved only by becoming permeated with the spirit of Christ and being made free and happy by the practices which spring out of that spirit." Throughout his lifetime he was a constant reader of the Bible. In referring to the Bible in 1913 he said: "If men could but be made to know it intimately, and for what it really is, we should have secured both individual and social regeneration." For many years he was an elder in the Presbyterian Church.

Few men have ever lived in whom the sense of duty resided with greater impelling force than was true of Woodrow Wilson. In all the major decisions of his life he acted from a sense of duty. Life was a serious adventure to him and he never escaped the feeling that he was a trustee, a guardian of great ideals which should be incarnated in human flesh. In his Cleveland speech he said: "The only thing I am afraid of is not being ready to perform my duty."

5. WHAT HAPPENED TO WILSON?

In referring to the career of Hannibal, a great historian once said: "On those whom the gods love they lavish infinite joys and infinite sorrows." This may be said with equal truth of Woodrow Wilson. No man in all history was ever the object of such world-wide admiration and praise as was Wilson at the end of the war. And yet few men have ever seen their fondest hopes and best laid plans more completely wrecked than Wilson did in 1919 and 1920; when his kind of peace was rejected by the Allies at Paris; his League was spurned by the Senate; and his Administration was rejected by his fellow-citizens to the extent of an unprecedented majority of seven million votes.

It would require a long sustained search to find disastrous consequences of partisan politics that may be compared in extent with the deadly results of the personal feud and political rivalry between Lodge and his associates on the one hand and Wilson on the other. The fault was not all on one side. We have already called attention to serious blunders on the part of Wilson. We are equally convinced that the tactics used to prevent the entry of the United States into the League will be branded by impartial historians of the future as the worst kind of partisan politics. Some of the attacks upon Wilson were not only exceedingly bad form but were wholly lacking in truthfulness. The result of this opposition was to increase the already intolerable burden and strain upon the President to such an extent that in the end he collapsed and never regained his health.

Consider the strain under which this man labored for eight momentous years. He was elected, the first Democrat in sixteen years, upon a liberal or radical economic program, and was therefore compelled to give battle to the entrenched powers of finance and industry. He had hardly taken up the reins before the crisis with Mexico occurred. Then came those anxious days of neutrality in the World War and the long struggle to keep America out of the war; followed by the gigantic problems in connection with the dual responsibility as

Commander-in-Chief of the American forces and chief executive of the American people during those days of upheaval. Then a brief period of exaltation, followed by the Peace Conference, when it seemed as if all the oppressed peoples in the world were being placed upon the President's shoulders.

The climax of all came with the terrific slump in American idealism, and the making of world peace, the football of partisan politics. After all these years of unprecedented and never-ending strain the President determined to carry his cause direct to the people. He started on a long tour across the country. After eight thousand miles of travel and constant speaking he reached the limit. His frail body could stand no more. He had never been blessed with robust health. From childhood he had been the victim of physical weakness. As far back as 1909 he had told intimate friends of his foreboding that if elected to the Presidency the burden of the responsibility would kill him. Following his speech in Pueblo the symptoms of an impending breakdown were unmistakable. The day before the President's headache was so severe that the train was halted between stations, while he and Mrs. Wilson took a long walk. On September 26th at Wichita he rapidly grew worse. The remainder of his schedule was cancelled and his train headed for Washington with hardly a stop. Several days later a clot formed in the blood vessels of his brain, permanently impairing the use of his left arm and leg. For days it was thought he could not live. Then he recovered enough to take care of a few important matters of state. It should not be forgotten that the crisis in the discussion of the League in the Senate came while the President was confined as an almost helpless cripple. The significance of this fact has been emphasized by David Lawrence, an intimate friend and biographer, in these words: "Had he retained his health, Woodrow Wilson, just as sure as day follows night, would have accepted the Lodge reservations to the Versailles treaty and secured thereby for the United States a membership in the League of Nations. He was almost persuaded to do so on his sick-bed but his illness induced a consciousness of incertitude which together with the exclusion of outside advice made him irritable and inflexible."

The last days of Woodrow Wilson were filled with infinite tragedy. Here was a man who had dreamed dreams of international peace and righteousness; who in the spirit of a crusader had led his people in a war to end war and to make the world safe for humanity; who believed in his soul that the League was a gift from God for the healing of the nations; who had given the last ounce of his energy to the task of winning the approval of his countrymen for this great cause; who was rejected by the very people who had once idolized him as their leader and who was spat upon by his political enemies; who was now broken in body and jaded in mind, given to emotional outbursts, frequently in tears, waiting for the end. Let him who would dwell upon the inconsistencies and contradictions in the life of Wilson remember the terrific strain under which he labored. Let him who would ridicule idealism in politics and pour scorn upon the war President as an arch-hypocrite, keep vividly in mind the picture of this pain-wracked and heart-sick old man. As surely as any hero of Flander's field died for his country, so surely Woodrow Wilson gave body and mind and life in the great struggle for international peace and righteousness.

6. WHAT WERE THE RESULTS OF WILSON'S LIFE?

It is too soon to give a complete answer to this question. Everything depends upon which fork of the road humanity decides to follow. The League, for this was Wilson's greatest achievement, may come to an untimely end upon the rocks of national fear and greed, or it may grow in favor and strength until it becomes the medium through which a higher nationalism may find expression in the amicable settlement of all disputes that threaten the peace of the world. But concerning one main point we can be reasonably sure. If modern civilization is to escape deterioration and destruction it will be because international law is substituted for national violence, international government for international anarchy. And the contribution of Wilson toward this achievement will surely be regarded by future historians as far greater than that of any other man of the century. Long after personal bitterness against him has died away, after his inconsistencies and blunders are buried in oblivion, Americans will doubtless delight to place him on the pedestal of fame with Washington and Lincoln, and the world at large will hail him as the foremost figure in the crusade to secure freedom from international anarchy.

Chapter 9

THE PRESENT STRUGGLE FOR FREEDOM

Danger Zones of the Social Order

The blindness, complacency and callousness of the vast majority of people everywhere is one of the most depressing facts of history. With the utmost difficulty have the masses of mankind been aroused to throw off the shackles which have bound them. With a spirit which has at times approached fatalism, they have accepted and endured gross injustice and severe privation. The more fortunate groups have as a rule taken their privileges for granted and have closed their eyes to the inequities and miseries about them. The willingness of people in all stations of life to accept things as they are and their reluctance to change the status quo almost pass comprehension.

So strenuous is the objection to fundamental changes in the social order that the prophet and pioneer have almost invariably been persecuted.

Few of the great reformers of history escaped vilification and violence from the hands of their fellows. Devout and conscientious men not only sanctioned and administered the Inquisition, with its agonizing torture and tragic injustice, but sought to kill those who advocated freedom of thought and speech. Ministers of the gospel not only owned human beings as chattels and defended the institution of slavery, but persecuted abolitionists with great zeal. Rich men of the past not only gained millions from the sweat of toiling women and the blood of little children, but vigorously attacked advocates of a new industrial system. Millions of men and women not only sanctioned the bar-

barities and inhumanities of war, but defamed and imprisoned those who refused to slay their fellows. At whatever period we look, we are confronted with an appalling record of inertia, stupidity and cruelty.

And our own age is no different from any previous one in this regard. What percentage of our fifty million adults and young people at this moment are aware of the extent of injustice and misery in this country, or have even the faintest understanding of the significance of current social problems? Do we not hear on every hand blatant boasting of the glories of our present civilization? Nearly forty years ago Matthew Arnold, after a visit to the United States, wrote: "But now Americans seem, in certain matters, to have agreed, as a people, to deceive themselves, to persuade themselves that they have what they have not, to cover the defects in their civilization by boasting . . . The worst of it is, that all this tall talk and self-glorification meets with hardly any rebuke from sane criticism over there . . . The new West promises to bear in the game of brag even the stout champions I have been quoting."[1]

Every age, however, has had its prophets of doom. And to-day, in the midst of the prevailing optimism, many voices of warning are being raised. Some of the keenest minds of our time are calling attention to the instability of the foundations upon which we are building and are pointing out the inevitable collapse of a social order based upon prevailing attitudes, practices and institutions. Shortly before his death, Dr. G. Stanley Hall wrote: "Not since the fall of the Roman Empire, or at least since the Thirty Years' War, which swept away one-third of the population of Europe, has the Western world faced so many troubles or had so many prophets of disaster as at present."[2] The Literary Review declares: "The plain truth is that as a civilization we are less sure of where we are going, where

[1]Matthew Arnold, Civilization in the United States, pp. 182, 185, 187.

[2]Century Magazine, Vol. 104, p. 830.

we want to go, how and for what we wish to live, than at any intelligent period of which we have full record.[3]

Dean Inge asserts his belief that: "We are witnessing the suicide of a social order, and our descendants will marvel at our madness."[4] George Santayana, formerly Professor of Philosophy at Harvard, says: "Civilization is perhaps approaching one of those long winters that overtake it from time to time."[5] Lord Grey, formerly British Foreign Secretary, is on record as saying: "Recent events have shown us with horrid clearness Europe sliding surely, though it may appear slowly, toward the abyss."[6] Mr. H. G. Wells says: "Destruction is not threatening civilization; it is happening to civilization before our eyes. The ship of civilization is not going to sink in five years' time or in fifty years' time. It is sinking now."[7] Sir Auckland Geddes declares: "In Europe we know that an age is dying. Here in America it would be easy to miss the signs of the coming change, but I have little doubt that it will come."

Mr. Francis Gribble is of the opinion that the historian of the future "will write that, some time in the early part of the twentieth century, the last and most highly organized of the world's civilizations deliberately committed suicide."[8] Ferrero, one of the greatest of modern historians, says: "We are travelling, therefore, step by step back toward paganism."[9] Benjamin Kidd bluntly says: "The civilization of the West is as yet scarcely more than glorified savagery."[10]

In addressing the annual dinner of the Chamber of Commerce of the State of New York, President Nicholas Murray Butler, of Columbia, said: "And, gentlemen, do not forget that it is perfectly possible to destroy civilization.

---

[3]Quoted in the Nation, April 5, 1922, p. 387.
[4]Century Magazine, Vol. 110, p. 374.
[5]Character and Opinion in the United States, p. vi.
[6]Quoted in the New York Times, Oct. 9, 1923.
[7]Quoted in Unity, Nov. 17, 1921.
[8]Nineteenth Century, Vol. 85, p. 888.
[9]Ancient Rome and Modern America, p. 216.
[10]The Science of Power, p. 127.

Civilization has been destroyed before, and it has taken a thousand years to repair the damage done in a generation or two."[11] Glenn Frank, recently editor of the Century Magazine and now President of the University of Wisconsin, writes: "I believe that we shall inevitably enter a new dark age, a period in which civilized values will go into decline and the race be thrust back into the precarious existence of its primitive ancestors, unless we begin with a decent promptness to remove the legitimate grounds for these fears."[12] Professor McDougall of Harvard University, begins his book "Is America Safe For Democracy?" with these startling words: "As I watch the American nation speeding gaily, with invincible optimism, down the road to destruction, I seem to be contemplating the greatest tragedy in the history of mankind."[13]

What shall we say concerning these dire prophecies? The response of the average man to-day, as always, is: preposterous, fantastic, pessimistic, unpatriotic; the result of a deranged mind or a disordered liver. Perhaps this response is a justifiable one. But even the possibility that these warnings may be well founded is sufficient to impel any rational person to go to the root of the whole matter.

In the pages that follow an attempt is made to summarize *the dangerous elements* in five phases of modern life. In this section we are confining ourselves to the effort to discover whether or not we really are threatened with grave and imminent danger to our social order, and if so, to analyze the exact nature of this menace. *We realize full well that there is another side to the picture, and that many volumes would be required to cover all the favorable phases of our national life.*[14] *Without denying that there is a substantial*

---

[11]The Faith of a Liberal, pp. 193, 194.

[12]Century Magazine, Vol. 110, p. 503.

[13]Is America Safe for Democracy?, p. v.

[14]For example, see The Present Economic Revolution in the United States, by Professor Thomas Nixon Carver; see also a pamphlet, Industrial Progress, issued by the National Civic Federation; see also articles: Is America Civilized, by W. C. Abbott, *The Forum,* Oct. 1925; Twenty-five Million Young Americans Go to School, *American Review of Reviews,* Jan. 1926, p. 36; Every Worker a Capitalist, by David F. Houston, *World's Work,* Jan. 1925, pp. 273-280.

basis for optimism now and in the future, and without committing ourselves to a pessimistic point of view, let us proceed with an examination of the evidence of the danger zones in our social order. It is well known that if a rotten apple is left in a full barrel, it quickly spoils all the others. Just now we are engaged in a search for spots of infection in the structure of our society.

1. ECONOMIC DANGERS

We are living under an economic system variously known as the capitalist system, the competitive system, the profit system, the wage system. Two of the major foundations of this system are the doctrines of enlightened self-interest and free competition.

Under modern industrialism, most workers do not engage in independent production, nor do they as a rule own their own tools. The vast majority of them work with machinery designed for mass production in shops and factories. For their labor they receive wages. The man or men who own the plant operate it on a profit basis. That is, they purchase raw materials, pay wages to the workers and salaries to the management, pay interest on the bonded indebtedness, pay rent on the premises, unless owned outright, pay insurance premiums, meet all operating expenses and necessary overhead costs, set aside an adequate amount for depreciation—and retain as profits all that remains of the gross receipts. In the words of Judge Gary, head of the United States Steel Corporation: "The net profits of capital belong to the one who earns or owns the original investment.[15]

What are the results of the profit system, with its motivation of self-interest and its method of competition?[16]

---

[15]Address at Syracuse University, June 13, 1921.

[16]Perhaps the best defense of the profit system is contained in The Present Economic Revolution in the United States, by Professor Thos. Nixon Carver; for indictments of the existing order see Harry F. Ward, The Profit Motive; R. H. Tawney, The Acquisitive Society; Sidney and Beatrice Webb, The Decay of Capitalist Civilization; Stuart Chase, The Tragedy of Waste; Bertrand Russell, Prospects of Industrial Civilization.

The results are neither all good nor all bad. It is easy to exaggerate both the merits and the defects of the existing system. On the credit side must be listed such items as the following: more goods have been produced than under any previous system, and therefore a higher standard of material comfort has been made possible; machinery has lifted heavy burdens from human shoulders and has greatly reduced the amount of laborious work done by hand; the speed of machine production has made available more leisure time; the urge of personal gain has developed in many individuals the qualities of initiative, endurance and daring. These and other merits of the existing system must be admitted, although we shall not enlarge upon them, since they are so frequently proclaimed, and *since our concern in this study is to discover the danger zones of our social order.*

We shall discuss the perils inherent in the profit system under the following headings: (1) Inequality of privilege; (2) concentration of control; (3) industrial strife; (4) waste; (5) dehumanizing of the individual; (6) materialism.

1. INEQUALITY OF PRIVILEGES

Inequality in itself is not objectionable. Few students of social problems advocate absolute equality of wealth and income. The dangerous element in the existing situation is found in the gross disparity in the privileges enjoyed by various groups. A few gain enormous riches, many are unable to secure reasonable comforts, while a considerable number fail to obtain even the necessities essential to health and decency.

The number of very rich people in the United States is relatively small, compared with the total population. It is estimated that there are fewer than 500 families who own as much as 20 million dollars each.[17] According to the latest income tax figures available, those for 1923, the number of annual net incomes as high as $100,000 was 4,182, the

[17]See Dynastic America, by Mr. H. H. Klein, formerly Deputy Commissioner of Accounts of New York City, p. 13.

number as high as $25,000 was 56,466, and the number as high as $5,000 was 625,897.[18] These figures, however, are misleading and do not represent actual net incomes because of various devices adopted for evading taxation. The most complete statistics of income are those prepared by the National Bureau of Economic Research for the year 1918. According to this survey the number of incomes above $100,000 was 7,442; the number above $25,000 was 62,572; and the number above $5,000 was 842,458.[19] That is to say only one head of a family in every 3,406 received an annual income as high as $100,000, only one in every 388 received as much as $25,000, and only one out of every 29 received even as much as $5,000.

On the other hand the number of persons in the United States with inadequate incomes is much greater than is commonly supposed. Evidence on this point may be secured from income statistics and from wage and salary schedules. There are approximately 25,000,000 heads of families in the United States,[20] and yet the total number of income tax returns filed in 1923 was only 7,698,321. Since married men or heads of families with annual net incomes of $2,500 and single men with incomes of $1,000 were required to file returns, it is evident that only about one-fourth of the total number of heads of families received as much as $2,500. According to the estimates of the National Bureau of Economics Research in 1918 the number of incomes as high as $1,500 was 10,512,716, which means that *more than half of all the heads of families received less than* $1,500.[21]

The Cost of Living

An examination of the available data on wages and salaries reveals the fact that the number of poorly paid workers reaches an enormous total. How shall we determine which workers are under-paid Before this can be determined,

[18]Statistics of Income for 1923, p. 4.
[19]The Income in the United States, p. 136.
[20]Statistical Abstract, 1924, p. 29.
[21]The Income in the United States, p. 136.

a study of the cost of living must be made. Fortunately a number of scientific studies into living costs have been made.[23]

The National Industrial Conference Board set the figure for a minimum budget for a family of five in Fall River in October, 1919 at $1,573.90.[24]

Let us examine this budget more in detail, remembering that it was formulated by an employers' organization. The cost of living has decreased since October, 1919. Reducing this budget to the prevailing prices in December, 1925, we get the figure $1,404.80, divided as follows:

Food	$563.92
Shelter	162.37
Clothing	287.82
Fuel, heat and light	75.15
Sundries	315.54
	$1,404.80

That is to say, this budget provides:

Food, 11 cents per meal per person;
Rent, $13.53 per month;
Clothing, $1.10 per week per person;
Fuel, heat, and lighting $1.45 per week;
Sundries of all kinds, $1.22 per week per person.

Any person who has had experience with household expenses will readily admit that it is exceedingly difficult, if not actually impossible, to maintain a family of five in health and decency on such a budget as this. Now let us examine certain wage schedules.

After an extensive survey of the entire country, the National Industrial Conference Board, an employers' organ-

[23] See a valuable book by Paul H. Douglas, Wages and the Family.
[24] For the details of these budgets see Standards of Living, issued by the Bureau of Applied Economics.

ization, reported that the average weekly earnings in all the industries included in their study was $27.13.[25]

Rates of Wages

At this rate a worker earns $1,410.76 during the year, if he is employed continuously. This amount is almost exactly equivalent to our minimum budget. But allowance must be made for unavoidable lost time due to sickness, change of jobs, slack seasons and other causes beyond the control of the worker. On this point Mr. Hoover's Committee of engineers found that: "The clothing worker is idle about thirty-one per cent of the year; the average shoe-maker spends only sixty-five per cent of his time at work; the building-trade workman is employed only about 190 days in the year or approximately sixty-three per cent of his time; the textile industry seemingly has regular intervals of slack time; during the past thirty years bituminous-coal miners were idle an average of ninety-three possible working days per year."[26]

The average weekly earnings of all men employed in the industries of Illinois in November, 1925, were $32.02, and of the women, $18.65.[27] The average weekly earnings of all shop employees in New York State in April, 1925, were: men $30.81; women $16.83.[28] In December, 1924, the average weekly earnings of employees in 453 manufacturing establishments in Massachusetts were as follows: men $28.57, women $16.76.[29] It should be pointed out that these were *average* wages, and that, therefore, many workers received less than these amounts. The Bureau of Labor Statistics has just published the wage rates for common-

[25]Bulletin No. 16, National Industrial Conference Board, quoted in the Information Service of the Federal Council of Churches, Feb. 27, 1926.

[26]Waste in Industry, p. 16.

[27]Monthly Labor Review, Feb. 1926, p. 94.

[28]Monthly Labor Review, July, 1925, pp. 87, 88.

[29]Monthly Labor Review, March, 1925, p. 67.

labor in all sections of the country. The average rate in the various industries studied was 40 cents per hour.[30]

Now what does 40 cents per hour mean in yearly earnings? By working ten hours per day, six days per week, fifty-two weeks per year, at 40 cents per hour, a laborer receives $1,248 annually. Ten hours per day is longer than many laborers work, many have a half-holiday on Saturday, many receive less than the average of 40 cents per hour, many are unemployed for extended periods during the year; which means that many earn considerably less than $1,248 per year—and even this amount is 11 per cent below our minimum budget.

The great bulk of workers in factories, shops and mines are unskilled or semi-skilled, and in the aggregate several million of them earn less than $1,500 per year. Thus we see that income statistics and wage schedules both reveal the fact that enormous numbers of workers do not earn enough to support themselves, a wife and three children in health and decency.

Many Are In Dire Need

Many women workers receive very low wages. In addition to the figures given above we now quote from Miss Mary Anderson, Director of the Women's Bureau, United States Department of Labor: "The Women's Bureau has made investigations of wages paid to women in twelve states, and the highest median earnings, those found in Rhode Island in 1920, were $16.85 per week. The lowest were in Mississippi, surveyed in 1925, and these were $8.60 per week. The next to the highest found in a New Jersey study in 1922, were $14.95, and the next to the lowest, found in Alabama in 1920, were $8.80. In none of the states investigated, with the exception of Rhode Island, was the median wage received by the women as high as the minimum wage set by law in the state of California. The

[30]Monthly Labor Review, Feb. 1926, pp. 87-89.

median means that one-half the women are paid below and one-half are paid above the sum mentioned.[31]

It is easy to be deceived and to assume that the high wages of from $10 to $16 per day paid in certain trades are received by workers in general. Statistics showing the number of automobiles sold and other luxuries consumed, the number of savings accounts, or the number of stockholders,[32] do not affect the validity of the evidence cited which reveals many millions of poorly paid workers in the United States. In these homes comfort and luxury are purchased at the price of child labor or the departure of wives and mothers into factories, shops and offices.[33] In 1920 there were nearly two million married women gainfully employed in the United States, while more than a million children fifteen and under were employed outside the home.[34]

Bad Housing

The fact that there are many millions of men in this country who are unable adequately to support a family creates ominous social problems. Malnutrition and disease are products of low wages. In our great cities and in industrial centers generally the question of adequate housing is a most serious one. The following vivid description of one of our industrial communities has been given by Professor J. M. Clark, of the University of Chicago: "Ride through the industrial district stretching from South Chicago to Gary, and as you view the expanse of ugly flats and barrens, ask yourself why these people are here. Is this a place men would choose to live in? Certainly not, if they were free to move out to those blue, wooded hills beckoning

---

[31]American Federationist, August, 1925, p. 681.

[32]For example see a chapter, Financial Power of Laborers, in Professor Carver's book, The Present Economic Revolution in the United States, pp. 90-122; see also Aren't We All Rich Now? by Samuel Crother in *Collier's Weekly,* Nov. 7, 1925, p. 9.

[33]See Mothers in Industry by Gwendolyn S. Hughes.

[34]The U. S. Census for 1920 estimates that there were 1,060,858 children under sixteen who were gainfully employed. This figure, however, is undoubtedly a gross under-estimate, due to parental evasion and other causes.

in the distance. These people never wanted to live here. But the machines did, and that settled it. If you wish to see who it was that found this site desirable, look yonder at that row of pot-bellied Titans with their grotesquely sprawling limbs, squatting near a feed-trough that looks at least a quarter of a mile in length. Behold, my friends, the only being who actually wanted to live here, out of a total population of a hundred thousand people and six blast furnaces! The rest are here because the furnaces are here and for no other reason. They either were bribed or came under duress of earning their bread, to this place of dreary flatness where there seems no soil wherein the soul of man may strike its roots. Nor is this an isolated case. From Homestead to Hollywood the machines have reared cities after their own needs, the like of which men never saw before."[35]

The rapid rise in rent throughout the country has made it impossible for vast numbers of workers to afford decent homes. Evidence of this fact can be secured in most industrial communities throughout the country. One authority tells us that "one-third of the people of the United States are living under subnormal housing conditions, conditions which fall below the minimum standard, and about one-tenth are living under conditions which are an acute menace to health, morals and family life. The same conditions meet us everywhere—lot overcrowding and room overcrowding, dark rooms and inadequately lighted rooms, lack of water, lack of sanitary conveniences, dilapidation, excessive fire risks, basement and cellar dwellings.[36]

Mr. Berry Parker, an English architect says: "I know Italian, French, Belgian, Dutch and Norwegian slums, and the conditions of life in any slums I have ever seen are better than they are in the slums of New York."[37]

Housing conditions in many cities are steadily growing

---

[35]The Yale Review, Oct. 1922, p. 136.

[36]Edith Elmer Wood, The Housing of the Unskilled Wage Earner, p. 7.

[37]See The Housing Situation Today, by Bleecker Marquette. *American Review,* Sept.-Oct. 1924, pp. 546-555; see also *The Financial Chronicle,* March 21, 1925, pp. 1385-1387.

worse. Justice Edward F. Boyle, of the Children's Court of New York City, in December, 1925, said: "Reports to me show that the evil of doubling up families in small apartments, far from abating in two years, has grown steadily worse; that the male lodger is in the small home in larger number than before with all the attending degrading potentialities to family life and morals; that congestion is growing and spreading; that families are not only crowding themselves with lodgers but in many cases there is a double shift night and day, of lodgers. The peril to health and morals pointed out two years ago is not lessened. If anything, the lapse of time has rendered the situation more acute in these respects." Many new houses and apartments are being built, but the rental rates for most of them are miles above the financial resources of two-thirds of the workers. The situation in New York City is so serious that Governor Smith, prior to making recommendations for legislation, appointed a State Commission on Housing and Regional Planning. This Commission reports that only three per cent of the new apartments constructed in 1924 are within the reach of seventy per cent of the population, and that families with annual incomes of less than $2,500—and that includes more than two-thirds of all families in the city —"are afforded no decent place in which to live, to rear children, and to enjoy a home life."

The fact of the matter is that private enterprise in the housing of the poor in our great cities is breaking down. The costs of construction, including exorbitant rates of interest on mortgages, are so excessive that there is no profit to be made from erecting apartments for cheap rental. And so, under a profit system, such houses are not built. So obvious is this collapse of private initiative that Governor Smith has been advocating a bold plan of state aid to housing.[38]

The serious social consequences of bad housing and overcrowding are visible on every hand. As a result of an

[38]See The Nation, March 10, 1926, p. 245; The Literary Digest, March 13, 1926, pp. 5, 6.

examination of the records of the deaths of 23,000 children in eight cities, Dr. Robert M. Woodbury, of the Children's Bureau, of the United States Department of Labor, found that "the infant death rate where the family is forced to live two in a room or more is two and a half times as high as that in homes which average more than one room to each person."[39] "When people are 'herded together like cattle,'" says Mrs. A. F. Bacon, "there can be no privacy, that prime essential of the home. If a number of persons of low standards of different sexes and ages all live together in one room, it is almost bound to result in vice. When a family of ten, living in three rooms, takes in boarders, modesty and morality are apt to be crowded out."

2. CONCENTRATION OF CONTROL

Extreme luxury for the few and desperate need for the many are not the only serious consequences of vast inequality of wealth and income. The profit system is resulting in an enormous concentration of *power* in the hands of a small minority of our population. The size of industrial and financial units is increasing steadily. The United States Steel Corporation has direct assets of approximately two billion dollars. The Pennsylvania Railroad, the New York Central Railroad, and the American Telephone and Telegraph Company are each capitalized at more than a billion dollars; with the Standard Oil Company of New Jersey, the Union Pacific Railroad, the Southern Pacific Railroad, and the Baltimore and Ohio Railroad falling just short of a billion each.[40]

Do these huge corporations indicate a trend toward concentration of control or toward diffusion of ownership? Many recent articles say emphatically that it is the latter. These corporations are not owned by a few individuals. The American Telephone and Telegraph Company is owned by 343,000 stockholders, the United States Steel Corporation

[39]New Republic, May 13, 1926, p. 307.

[40]See Our Billion-Dollar Corporations, in the *Magazine of Wall Street,* March 31, 1923, pp. 972, 1053.

by 158,940, the Pennsylvania Railroad by 144,228, and so on.[41]

But who *controls* these corporations? This is the important question with which we are concerned at this point. The answer is very clear. Each corporation is controlled by a small group of individuals. Consider the United States Steel Corporation, for example. Actual control rests in the hands of fewer than one-tenth of one per cent of the total number of 158,940 owners. Policies are determined by the Board of Directors of twelve or fifteen members, who are elected by a small fraction of the stockholders. The report of the annual meeting of the corporation in April, 1923, says: "Approximately 100 stockholders attended the meeting. They represented in their own right or by proxy, 2,178,297 shares of common stock and 1,337,311 shares of preferred stock. All directors of the company were re-elected."[42] The degree of concentration of actual control, however, is even greater, as may be seen from the following quotation taken from an address delivered by Judge Gary before the annual meeting of the stockholders on April 19, 1920: "Since the United States Steel Corporation commenced business on April 1, 1901, there have been held, including the present one, nineteen regular and also ten special stockholders' meetings. I have had the honor of presiding at every one, and of voting the major part of all the outstanding capital stock."

Of course it is theoretically possible for vast numbers of stockholders to participate in the management of a corporation. But in practice this does not happen. Professor W. Z. Ripley, of Harvard University, says in this connection: "It is elemental—requiring no proof—that the larger the number of shareholders, the more easily may a

---

[41]See an article, Every Worker a Capitalist, by David F. Houston, in *World's Work,* January, 1925, pp. 273-280; see also statistics of number of stockholders in various industries, in *The Financial Chronicle,* April 1, 1925, p. 1699.

[42]*The Financial Chronicle,* April 21, 1923, p. 1717.

small concentrated block of minority shares exercise sway over all the rest."[43]

The power wielded by these directors is greatly increased by reason of the fact that they are also directors in many other concerns. Some years ago an investigating committee of the House of Representatives found that "one or more of the directors of the Steel Corporation are also directors in terminal, steamship, express, and telegraph companies having a total capitalization of $1,271,778,890; in industrial corporations with a combined capitalization of $2,803,509,348; and in banks and trust companies having a capital surplus, and undivided profits aggregating $3,314,811,178; of $18,-417,132,238 invested in railways of the United States, the directors of the United States Steel Corporation have a voice in the directorates of, or act as executive officers of, railroad companies with a total capitalization or bonded indebtedness of $10,365,071,833."[44]

The Commission on Industrial Relations appointed by President Wilson reported as follows: "A careful and conservative study shows that the corporations controlled by six financial groups and affiliated interests employ 2,651,684 wage earners and have a total capitalization of $19,875,200,000. These six financial groups control twenty-eight per cent of the total number of wage earners engaged in the industries covered by the report of our investigation. The Morgan-First National Bank group alone controls corporations employing 785,499 wage earners."[45]

The report of the Interstate Commerce Commission, of March 25, 1919, shows that there are, in round numbers, some 600,000 stockholders in the class-one railroads, which roads represent 97 per cent of the traffic of the country. This report shows that the majority of the stock in each one of those roads, is held by less than 20 of the big stockholders in each road. The report also shows that less than 1.3 per

[43]See his thought-provoking article, From Main Street to Wall Street, in the Atlantic Monthly, Jan. 1926, pp. 94-108.

[44]62nd Congress, 2nd session, Report No. 1127, p. 210.

[45]Senate Document No. 415, p. 80.

cent of the stockholders of class-one roads control the stock. Commenting upon this report, the late Senator La-Follette pointed out that "the real power which to-day controls the railroads of the United States is the group of a dozen New York financial insitutions. This group of 12 New York banks holds 267 railroad directorships on 92 class-one railroads. With their subsidy branch lines, these railroads constitute to all intents and purposes the transportation system of the United States."[46]

Recently there was a merger of two of the largest banks in New York City, the Chase National Bank and the Mechanics and Metals National Bank, the assets of the new institution being over one billion dollars. This merger is simply the latest of a long series of bank consolidations. "Within the last twenty years 76 banks have gone into consolidations to form twenty greater financial institutions in New York. The combined capital of these banks amounts to $266,600,000, and their aggregate deposits come to $5,-421,835,500 . . . Taken altogether these twenty enlarged banks do business through 118 branches."[47]

Unprecedented Concentration of Power

If space were available similar evidence could be produced revealing the trend toward consolidation in the coal industry, in baking, in department stores, in chain stores, and in fact, all along the line.[48] The combined capitalization of all the corporations in the United States amounts to 70 billion dollars. While these corporations are owned by several million people, they are controlled by a small fraction of the total number of stockholders. As a matter of fact, the corporation is a device which actually results in increased concentration of control. The directors not only control the

---

[46]In the U. S. Senate, February 21, 1921, recorded in the Congressional Record, March 14, 1921, pp. 4779-4781.

[47]See an article Why Big New York Banks Are Consolidating, Literary Digest, June 20, 1925, p. 72.

[48]See the Chain Store, in American Review of Reviews, Sept. 1924, pp. 297-299; see also Bread and Water, in the Nation, November 4, 1925, p. 504.

money they put into a given enterprise, but also vast sums invested by the public. In the whole history of mankind there has never been such a vast concentration of financial and industrial power as we now have in this country.

Mr. Arthur Pound, in an interesting chapter on "The Iron Dukes," says: "The leaders of our greatest corporations, in their powers, and their social significance to industrial society, are modern counterparts of the dukes in the days when dukes had power . . . In our day these men exert immense power. One such may hold power of the purse over hundreds of thousands of workers and their dependents."[49]

In concluding a recent address before the Cleveland Forum, Dr. John A. Ryan, of the National Catholic Welfare Conference, and one of the best qualified students of social problems in this country, said: "As we survey present conditions and the unmistakable trend of political and economic forces, we find a good deal of reason to think that history is about to repeat itself. After more than three centuries, there approaches a return to feudalism. In the Middle Ages, feudalism was based upon military force and the ownership of land. The new feudalism is political and industrial. Not improbably it will be more or less benevolent. The lords of industry will realize, at least for a considerable number of years, that their position and profits will be more secure if they refrain from the cruder and coarser forms of injustice, and permit the dependent classes, both urban and rural, to obtain a moderate share of the products of industry. The masses will probably enjoy a slightly higher degree of economic welfare than has ever been within their reach before. But they will enjoy it at the expense of genuine freedom. They will have surrendered the right, which was once universal in America, to determine their own economic lives.[50]

---

[49] The Iron Man in Industry, pp. 71, 74.
[50] LaFollette's Magazine, March 1926. p. 41.

3. INDUSTRIAL STRIFE

A system based upon self-interest and competition is certain to produce strife. Rivalry in sports or in artistic creation does not necessarily lead to enmity and antagonism. But when the competition is for physical necessities and comforts, of which there is a limited supply, strife is sure to result.

It is evident even to the casual observer that there has been a marked increase in industrial strife in this country during the past two decades. According to the records of the United States Bureau of Labor Statistics, for the years 1916 to 1921, an aggregate of 10,742,738 employes were involved in strikes and lockouts, an average of 1,790,000 per year, the average lost time per man being 30 days.[51]

Both sides in the industrial struggle frequently resort to violence.[52] All sections of the country have witnessed pitched battles between the workers and the hired guards or strikebreakers of the employers. Violence in the West Virginia coal fields has become so chronic that a journalist has written a book under the title, "Civil War in West Virginia."[53]

"In this untamed section of West Virginia" says an Atlantic Monthly article, "two tremendous forces have staked out a battle ground. They are the United Mine Workers of America and the most powerful groups of non-union coal-operators in the country. It is a battle to the bitter end; neither side asks quarter, neither side gives it. It is a battle for enormous stakes, in which money is lavished; it is fought through the courts, through the press, with matching of sharp wits to secure public approval. But more than this, it is actually fought with deadly weapons on both sides; many lines have already been lost; many may yet be forfeited."[54]

---

51 Quoted in The Tragedy of Waste, p. 135.

52 See John A. Fitch, Causes of Industrial Unrest, pp. 223-238.

53 Winthrop D. Lane, published by B. W. Huebsch, New York.

54 James M. Cain, The Battleground of Coal, The Atlantic Monthly, Oct. 1922, pp. 433-440.

The Battle of Passaic

While this section is being writen a bitter industrial battle is being waged in Passaic, New Jersey. On the front page of the New York Times of March 5, 1926, we read: "For a few hours today Passaic, Garfield and Clinton presented the picture of towns behind the fighting area at the front during the war. While an airplane, carrying a news reel photographer, swooped aloft in wide circles, thousands of textile strikers paraded past the mills, scores of them wearing trench helmets, and many equipped with gas masks strapped to their shoulders ready for instant adjustment if the police again used tear bombs. An armored car lumbered slowly through the streets with photographers operating camera lenses at peepholes to picture the events without being molested by the police of Clifton and Passaic, who smashed $3,500 worth of cameras yesterday and attacked photographers and reporters." Two weeks later on the front page of the New York Sun, we read: "A second heated battle between the police and strikers at Passaic, occurring last night, and marked by more ferocity than the former clash in which reporters and newspaper camera men were beaten, today turned eyes to Washington in the hope of some drastic interference to assure peace. Both sides now are asking for investigations. For the second time reporters and camera men suffered as well as strikers, being drubbed with clubs, and photographic machines valued at $5,000 demolished. More vigorous this time was the strikers' resistance, women joining the men in hurling stones and bricks at the mounted policemen. The latter drove their horses into sidewalk crowds, in which were men, women and children, and patrolmen with clubs attacked afoot. After an hour's battle nine men and four women strikers were arrested and five policemen were attended for cuts.[55] On April 8th the situation was discussed under the headline, "Two More Battles in Passaic Strike."

The Spy System

Another disturbing phase of the situation is found in the spread of the espionage system throughout American industry. In their fight against trade unions, many employers have long resorted to the use of spies.

"Investigators for the Cabot Fund for Industrial Research of Boston found that industrial espionage 'operates through the secret service departments of great corporations, the railroads, the United States Steel Corporation, the Western Union Telegraph Company and like corporations. It operates through the spy services of employers' associations; the National Erectors' Association, the National Manufacturers' Association, The National Founders' Association."[56]

Eighty-six pages of the second volume of the Interchurch Report on the steel strike of 1919 are devoted ruption, misleads capital into folly, injustice, and often ous steel plants.[57]

The effects of the spy system have been described by Sidney Howard as follows: "We find that it puts both employer and employee at the mercy of a power which is, at best, unscrupulous; that it lays labor open to corruption, misleads capital into folly, injustice, and often actual crime; that it creates, wherever it appears, a turmoil of unrest and rage; and that it is at the very heart of labor violence."[58]

---

[55] For accounts of the causes of this strike, see The Nation, March 17, 1926, p. 280; and the New Republic, March 17, 1926, p. 98.

[56] "The Labor Spy," a 72-page pamphlet published by The New Republic. (In 1924 this pamphlet was enlarged to a book of 200 pages, under same title.)

[57] "Public Opinion and the Steel Strike," pp. 1-86.

[58] See The Labor Spy, by Sidney Howard, see also John A. Fitch, The Causes of Industrial Unrest, pp. 171-185.

Signs of Increasing Strife

There are ominous trends of the day which seem to indicate that industrial strife will become more intense during the next few decades. (1) The struggle for life in the United States is likely to become terrific as a result of the combination of decreasing supplies of raw materials and an increasing population. Already we are beginning to feel the effects of the operation of the law of diminishing returns. We have been skimming the cream from our economic resources and must soon accustom ourselves to an inferior quality of milk.

(2) We are certain to feel the effects of foreign competition more keenly in the future than we have in the past.[59] Europe is slowly recovering from the devastating effects of the World War, Asia is becoming industrialized, and the world-wide struggle for economic resources is sure to become more bitter.

(3) The United States is becoming more and more industrialized. This means more specialization, more separation into classes, more class-consciousness, more strife. Evidence of a growing class-consciousness is found not alone among working people, but among employers as well. The average Chamber of Commerce meeting or luncheon club of business and professional men is as class-conscious a group as any radical trade union gathering. Moreover, the units in the struggle between employers and workers are becoming larger and the effects of industrial strife are becoming more serious.

(4) The deliberate stimulation of new desires on a wholesale scale is certain to intensify the industrial struggle. By providing universal education for the workers, by all our talk concerning the glories of democracy, and by the appeal of scientific advertising and salesmanship, we have forever destroyed the willing-

[59] See a chapter on, The Coming Tooth-and-Claw Competition, in E. A. Filene's book, The Way Out, pp. 68-80.

ness of workers to live like serfs or peasants. Unless we are ready to abandon popular education, refrain from all references to democracy, and cease stimulating appetites by advertising, we must be prepared to see the workers become increasingly dissatisfied with their inferior status in society and to struggle more vigorously for an equitable division of the privileges of life. If the possessing classes attempt to resist them by force, we shall witness in the United States a rapidly increasing amount of violence and bloodshed in our industrial warfare.

4. WASTE

Self-interest and competition develop individual initiative and daring, but they result in terrific social waste.[60] Mr. Gifford Pinchot, Governor of Pennsylvania, declares: "The people of these United States are the most wasteful in the world—wasteful in living, wasteful in manufacturing, and wasteful in their failure to conserve our natural resources. Ever since the white man set foot upon American soil, he has been destroying forests and making no effective provision for their renewal."[61] Mr. Floyd W. Parsons, editor of the Gas Age Record, says: "The story of the development of life and industry in America is the most amazing tale of the waste of wealth by a careless, improvident people that the world has ever known. We have flooded the air with that wonder fuel, natural gas; covered our land with ashes of burned forests, killed off our wild animal life for the sport that was in it, and robbed our virgin acres of so much of their fertility that in many of the regions farming as a pursuit is about as obsolete as the spinning wheel."[62]

---

[60] See four important books on this subject: Stuart Chase, The Tragedy of Waste, an absolutely invaluable survey; Hoover's Committee of Engineers, Waste in Industry; Sidney A. Reeve, Modern Economic Tendencies; L. F. Bower, The Economic Waste of Sin.

[61] *The Nation*, Oct. 20, 1920, p. 444.

[62] Quoted in Stuart Chase, The Tragedy of Waste, p. 37.

The United States Forest Service sums up its 1924 report with these words: "The central fact is that we are using up our timber four times as fast as it grows, and the end of more than three centuries of abundance is now in sight."[63] Mr. Stuart Chase has estimated that, in one way or another, we are annually wasting 750 million tons of coal, 50 million horse-power from water-power, one billion barrels of oil, 600 billion cubic feet of natural gas, and 5 billion cubic feet of lumber.[64]

Our annual bill for advertising is in excess of a billion dollars, a considerable proportion of which is sheer social waste and in the end has to be paid by the consumer.[65] There are also enormous wastes in distribution. Mr. George W. Alger, writing in the Atlantic Monthly, says: "In New York alone, a fourth of the perishables received at the wholesale markets goes to the public dumps; a third of the oranges and a fifth of the eggs received are rotten and unsalable; annually over seven million pounds of fruit and three million pounds of vegetables are carried by the dump-scows to the sea."[66]

The desire for private gain has resulted in a vast number of middle-men, who add their profits to the ultimate cost to the consumer. The retail trade in the United States reveals anarchy of the worst sort. "By and large," says Stuart Chase, "there is some kind of a retail store —not including automobile establishments—for every 25 families in the country.[67] One-fourth, or perhaps even one-tenth, of this number of stores could serve the various communities more economically. Mr. E. A. Filene, one of the country's most successful merchants, says: "The plain fact is that one of the great wastes of

---

[63] Ibid., p. 256.

[64] Ibid., p. 264.

[65] See the Day of the Advertisement by Edward Bok, The Atlantic Monthly, Oct. 1923, p. 533; see also a chapter, An Analysis of Advertising, in Stuart Chase's book, The Tragedy of Waste, pp. 108-125; see also The Economic Illusion, by Arthur Bertram, pp. 60-71.

[66] Feb. 1921, p. 152.

[67] The Tragedy of Waste, p. 221.

business is due to the incredibly inefficient methods of distribution. Today an article usually doubles in price between production costs and what the consumer pays."[68]

5. DEHUMANIZING EFFECTS

The factory system operated under the spur of self-interest, has many seriously detrimental effects upon the workers. Specialization is being carried to extreme lengths. In many branches of industry the skilled craftsman has been replaced by an unskilled tender of a machine. Much machine work is extremely dull and monotonous.[69] "Thousands of workers perform the same movement countless times a day. An observer tells of a woman whose only task is to take a half-formed hinge and place it in the bending machine fifty times a minute, or 30,000 times a day; another worker cuts out tin can tops by pressing a foot-lever forty times a minute; a garment worker watches twelve jumping needles of a power machine. A social worker tells of a white-haired man whose task is to watch for dents in tin cans as they pass in an endless procession. At long intervals, he uses one hand to remove a can that is dented. All day long he scarcely takes his eyes off the stream of tin cans. During his thirteen years at this job, millions of cans have passed before his eyes."[70]

Concerning the consequences of machine production, Mr. R. Austin Freeman writes: "But that which I wish to emphasize is the intolerable dullness, the dreariness, the soul-destroying monotony of this degrading attendance on a machine; this endless repetition by a rational being of one comparatively simple set of actions. It is not work in any proper sense; it is mere labor.

---

[68] The Way Out, p. 109.

[69] For a defence of machinery, see The Literary Digest, Feb. 7, 1925, p. 24; see also a debate, Can Machines Make Us Free, in the Forum, Oct. 1924, pp. 463-475; see also H. M. Kallen, Education, the Machine and the Worker.

[70] Christianity and Economic Problems, page 58.

And in occupation such as this are the lives of our working men mis-spent. . . . And this labor is not the portion of a few only; drudgery—soul-destroying, wearisome, exhausting drudgery—is the lot of the greater part of the working class. The craftsman grows as rare as the Great Auk; but the laborer remains and relatively multiplies. . . . The machine should have been the drudge of man; in actual fact, man has become the drudge of the machine.[71]

Mr. Arthur Pound, business man, journalist and careful student of industrial problems, writes: "America gave the automatic tool its chance. Its blessings are evident, but, unless controlled by social conscience, it may develop curses equally potent . . . . undirected, it may push the human race into a new slavery, or stampede it into a new anarchy. . . . So far as the great majority of the workers are concerned, modern industry presents this phenomenon—the dulling of the mind—on a scale unequalled in extent, and to a degree unequalled in intensity, by anything on record in history. . . . Our tenders of machines are being starved in their souls. . . . . Certain am I that none but an imbecile could find much delight in sharing the daily toil of our mill-workers, so mechanized has it become."[72]

6. MATERIALISM

The prevalence of the doctrines of self-interest and competition has greatly intensified the spirit of materialism, by which we mean the tendency to test life in terms of material possessions. Never was it so true as today that "things are in the saddle and ride men." In contrast with the creative civilization of ancient Greece and mediaeval Europe or the contemplative civilization of the Orient, ours is a possessive civilization.[73]

---

[71] Social Decay and Regeneration, pp. 176, 286.

[72] The Iron Man in Industry, pp. 34, 35, 51, 166, 208.

[73] See a stimulating book, The Acquisitive Society, by R. H. Tawney.

Never has so vast a proportion of a nation's energy been devoted to the scramble for comforts and luxuries. Concerning this point Mr. James M. Beck, formerly Solicitor-General of the United States, says: "This almost infinite multiplication of human power has tended to intoxicate man. The lust for power has obsessed him, without regard to whether it be constructive or destructive. He consumes the treasures of the earth faster than it produces them, deforesting its surface and disembowelling its hidden wealth. As he feverishly multiplies the things he desires, even more feverishly he multiplies his wants."[74]

Business and industry almost completely dominate our national life, including politics, the press, education and religion. Mr. Edward W. Bok says: "Now Money is King. Business is our God. Commerce Rules. The destinies of nations are discussed from economic angles. . . . . The captain of industry is the man of the day: the captain of the souls of peoples and their futures"[75]

Professor J. C. Van Dyke writes: "We have outrun all the nations of the earth in our pursuit of the golden will-o'-the-wisp. The pace we have set leaves others breathless and ourselves exhausted; but there is no pause. We boast that we are the greatest This and the richest That . . . . but we are not satisfied. We are still pursuing. Is it not true that we have eyes and hands for the yellow glitter only. Is it not true that we are money-mad?"[76]

The average business man is almost completely occupied with financial and industrial matters and spends little time in the reading of history or in the serious study of current social problems. It is a rare business man indeed who has acquired the habit of meditation, reflection and spiritual communion. The professions are increasingly dominated by the commercial spirit.

---

[74] *Fortnightly Review*, Vol. 116, p. 776.
[75] Dollars Only, p. 4.
[76] The Money God, p. 15.

Likewise, the trade unions frequently follow the example of employers in testing life in terms of dollars and cents, comforts and luxuries. The great mass of machine-tenders are victims of such a degree of dullness and monotony that they seek relief in excitement and sensationalism.

The profit system has brought about the astounding state of affairs where it is more necessary to find consumers for goods produced, than to produce goods which are actually needed. Interest charges and overhead costs accumulate by day and by night, expensive machinery must not be allowed to remain idle—and so the manufacturer is compelled to find customers for the maximum output of his plant or run the risk of going bankrupt in the fierce competition of the day. In boom seasons the temptation to expand is almost irresistible, and when slack times come, the effort to dispose of the product of an enlarged plant becomes more terrific. Customers must be found. If the consumers go on a buyers' strike, then "sales resistance must be smashed," as one enterprising manager expressed it. Thus we are confronted with the amazing fact that, at a time when millions of people are in serious need of the actual necessities of life, modern industry does not find it profitable to supply these needs at a price within reach of the purchaser, but instead produces those goods from which a profit can be made, and then moves heaven and earth to dispose of them.

The stimulation of appetites and desires has become a fine art with us. We are spending more than a billion dollars a year upon advertising and are employing directly and indirectly 600,000 men and women, in the gigantic effort to make people want more things.[77] And we are succeeding far beyond our expectations. The desire for things is becoming all-consuming. Things cost money, and so men and women passionately seek

---

[77] See Chase, The Tragedy of Waste, p. 109.

money. If the love of money is indeed the root of all kinds of evil, then we shall certainly reap an abundant harvest of trouble from the seed-sowing now in process.

The disastrous consequences of this exaggerated emphasis upon comforts and luxuries are everywhere visible. "Civilization," says Mr. Raymond B. Fosdick, "has in fact become a great machine, the wheels of which must be kept turning, or the people starve. For millions of human beings it is a vast treadmill, worked by weary feet to grind the corn that makes the bread that gives them strength to walk the treadmill. . . . And with it all has come the speeding up of life, and the spirit of hurry and worry such as our grandfathers with all their lack of conveniences never dreamed of even in their nightmares. The human race lives by schedule, according to a stereotyped routine. Life has become more and more a standardized process, in which there is little of serenity or of leisure. We hurry from birth to death, goaded only to greater haste by our increasingly speedy conveyances, feverishly trying to catch up with the machinery which we have ourselves created.[78]

A vigorous indictment of the present state of affairs is drawn by Mr. R. H. Tawney, in these words: "The burden of our civilization is not merely, as many suppose, that the product of industry is ill-distributed, or its conduct tyrannical, or its operation interrupted by embittered disagreements. It is that industry itself has come to hold a position of exclusive predominance among human interests, which no single interest, and least of all the provision of the material means of existence, is fit to occupy. Like a hypochondriac who is so absorbed in the processes of his own digestion that he goes to his grave before he has begun to live, industrialized communities neglect the very objects for which it is worth while to acquire riches, in their feverish

[78] Our Machine Civilization, p. 7.

preoccupation with the means by which riches can be acquired."[79]

One of the most important questions confronting this generation is this: Shall we continue to spend so disproportionate an amount of time in the kitchen of life, or shall we linger longer in the parlor, the library, and the chapel?

2. INTERNATIONAL DANGERS

War is perhaps the greatest menace now confronting mankind. It aggravates and intensifies most of the evils in modern life. That another great war would be utterly disastrous to mankind is admitted by all competent students of world affairs. Nations have become so interdependent and so interlocked in their relations that there is always the serious possibility that a local dispute may evolve into a world conflict. Desperate but futile efforts were made to localize the war which broke out in 1914. The nature of our modern world is such that we have no guarantee that a local blaze may not be fanned into a world conflagration.

Those who are best qualified to speak are warning us that if another great war comes it will be waged with new and far more deadly weapons than those hitherto used.[80] Two years ago Colonel James L. Walsh, Chief of New York Ordnance District, wrote: "Few persons outside of military circles know to what extent the invention of instruments of destruction has been quickened as a result of the great war lately ended. Since the armistice the range of guns has been doubled, the speed of tractors trebled and the destructiveness of airplane bombs increased tenfold . . . our army flyers can be equipped today with bombs weighing 4,000 pounds and carrying one ton of explosive . . . aircraft machine guns were speeded up from 400 rounds per minute to 1,500 rounds per minute.[81] An automatic cannon has been

---

[79] The Acquisitive Society, p. 184.

[80] See a chapter, The Weapons of the Next War, in The Origin of the Next War, by John Bakeless.

[81] New York Times, March 30, 1924.

invented by John M. Browning which fires one-and-one-quarter pound shells at the rate of 120 per minute. The 16-inch coast defense rifle throws a projectile weighing a ton to an extreme range of 17 miles.[82]

In no realm have more rapid strides been made than in the sphere of aviation. A recent writer in the Forum says: "The last war was a mild experiment in the possibilities of shedding destruction from the air. The flying machine was not one-fourth as efficient at the time of the armistice as it is today. Three airplanes of a type now in existence could carry for a thousand miles, and then drop on their objective explosives weighing more than the Germans succeeded in dropping on London during the entire period of the war,—seventeen tons, in fact. And a majority of the bombs were dropped by Zeppelins. Airplanes were not really efficient for bombing purposes. They are, today. Boundaries are disappearing. Planes now fly at four miles a minute. They rise to heights of thirty thousand feet, and can go higher when occasion demands." [83]

General Mason M. Patrick, Chief of the Army Air Service says: "We have developed automatic pilots so that airplanes can be sent off at a predetermined height and made to drop their bombs at a predetermined point. Or they can be maneuvered by radio with no pilot aboard. They may be carried across a continent by dirigibles and then sent forth on combat missions." [84]

The enormous strides being made in aviation, make the dangers from gas warfare almost illimitable. Commander Burney, of the British Navy and a Member of Parliament says: "Gases now exist that are more than 1,000 times as powerful as anything used in the late war, and on a still day I venture to think that containers carrying gas instead of explosives would kill more people than the same weight of

[82] See the Scientific American, Nov. 1922, p. 319.
[83] July, 1924, p. 67-75.
[84] Literary Digest, Oct. 4, 1924, p. 13.

bombs. There is one gas which is so powerful that the person inhaling it would be killed instantaneously." [85]

Concerning the nature of another great war, Major General E. D. Swinton, of the British Army, says: "It has been rather our tendency up to the present to look upon warfare from the retail point of view—killing men by fifties or hundreds or thousands. But when you speak of gas, you must remember that you are discussing a weapon which must be considered from the wholesale point of view. We may not be so very far from the development of some kinds of lethal ray which will shrivel up or paralyze or poison human beings. The final form of human strife, as I regard it, is germ warfare. I think it will come to that; and so far as I can see, there is no reason why it should not, if you mean to fight. Study the waging of war on a wholesale scale instead of thinking so much about methods which will kill a few individuals only at a time."[86]

In a statement issued on February 1, 1925, Secretary Wilbur said: "If poison gas can be used on one side it can be used on the other, as Germany found out to her sorrow. If disease germs can be used on one side they can be used on the other."

In the issue of September 24, 1924, of Nash's *Pall Mall Magazine,* Winston S. Churchill, now Chancellor of the British Exchequer and formerly First Lord of the Admiralty, sounded the following warning: "It is established that henceforward whole populations will take part in war, all doing their utmost, all subjected to the fury of the enemy. It is established that nations who believe their life is at stake will not be restrained from using any means to secure their existence. It is probable—nay, certain—that among the means which will next time be at their disposal will be agencies and processes of destruction wholesale, unlimited, and perhaps, once launched, uncontrollable: Blight to destroy crops, Anthrax to slay horses and cattle, Plague to poison

[85] Literary Digest, November 17, 1923.

[86] Quoted by Will Irwin, in The Next War, pp. 48, 49.

not armies only but whole districts—such are the lines along which military science is remorselessly advancing."

As appalling as would be the destruction wrought by the weapons used in another great war, we are confronted with an even more ominous peril, namely, the danger of wholesale starvation and widespread loss of life due to malnutrition and disease. The factory system and mass production have made possible a very rapid increase in population. These surplus peoples, amounting to 100 millions in Europe alone, can be kept alive only by the continuous and effective operation of an industrial machine which is world-wide in extent. The free movement of goods—raw materials and finished products—around the world is absolutely essential to prosperity in any one country. Now the ominous thing about modern war is that it seriously dislocates and disrupts production. Even in the last war it is probable that more people died of starvation and disease than were killed by bayonets, bullets and gas. War has now come to be a combat between whole populations and the war zone has been extended so as to include continents.

The present ominous world situation has been created primarily by a combination of industrialism and nationalism. The dominant fact about our age is the rapid spread of industrialism. All the great powers are becoming industrialized. In at least three respects industrial nations are dependent upon other countries, namely, for raw materials, markets, and fields of investment. The United States is now a great industrial power. Fortunate as we are, we must import huge quantities of raw materials. Whereas we consume 77 percent of all the rubber grown anywhere in the world, we produce ourselves only 3 percent. If anything should shut off this supply of rubber, great sections of our industry would be compelled to shut down, millions of men would be thrown out of employment, a financial panic would ensue, and an international crisis would be precipitated. Prosperity in the United States depends also upon our ability to find customers outside our own borders for our surplus supply of goods. Moreover, our foreign investments have increased from less than two billion dollars in 1913 to more than ten billions at the present time, and we are increasing these investments at the rate of a billion dollars per year. To this investment must be added the eleven billion dollars loaned to foreign governments. That is to say, citizens of the United States now have more than 21 billion dollars invested in other lands.

Over against the economic interdependence of peoples is their political division. Humanity is divided in some sixty artificial units called nations. Nationalism is the dominant political fact of our time. Each nation looks upon itself as different from its neighbors and usually regards itself as far superior. Each one proceeds on the assumption that it is an ultimate political unit, that there is no power or agency above it, and that it has the right to determine its own policies and practices without regard to the desires of other countries.

Nationalism and the doctrine of national sovereignty in their present extreme form constitute a supreme menace to world peace. Thus far, with a few notable exceptions, nations have reserved to themselves the final decision in all matters pertaining to national honor and vital interest, refusing to include such questions in treaties and arrangements for the peaceable settlement of disputes. At Locarno the signatories entered into an all-inclusive agreement to settle every dispute between themselves by peaceable means, not excluding questions of national honor and vital interest. But Locarno did not succeed in changing the current conceptions of national prestige or in removing national jealousies. So long as the belief prevails that a nation is the supreme political entity and has no higher duty than to maintain its own prestige and honor and to serve its own interests, that long the peace of the world will be in constant jeopardy. So long as the doctrine of absolute national sovereignty prevails and the citizens of the respective countries maintain the belief that in matters of national honor and vital interest their own government has the right to determine in its own course of action without regard to the feelings and interests of other peoples, that long shall we continue to dwell on the slopes of a threatening volcano.

The nature of our danger stands clearly revealed in the light of recent events in Geneva. That the delegates there assembled acted in a most shameful manner can scarcely be questioned. If the facts were not so well authenticated it would seem incredible that responsible statesmen should be so blind and reckless as to give vent to their mad rivalries on the very brink of the precipice of anarchy and war. With no apparent realization of what they have been doing, these men have been tugging strenuously over the delicate fabric of peace. The mood displayed at Geneva during these eventful days is precisely the mood out of which wars arise. The fact that the Assembly has adjourned without admitting Germany to the League presents us with a situation which is full of peril. An attempt will doubtless be made to gloss over the glaring failure to reach an agreement concerning membership on the Council, but the fact remains that the delegates assembled at Geneva have been gambling with the peace of the world. Whether or not their debauchery is destined to end in disaster remains to be seen. Certainly they have played directly into the hands of the reactionaries and war-makers in every country. A bitter controversy, world-wide in extent, is sure to be waged over the question of representation on the Council. Temper will run high and reckless words will be uttered. A crisis may be precipitated by some threat or by such an explosive speech as that recently delivered by Mussolini over the question of Tyrol. Yes, the whole situation is indeed ominous for the peace of Europe.

Shall the citizens of the United States, therefore, settle back comfortably on the assumption that we are not involved? Is America well out of it? Is this virulent and dangerous nationalism confined to Europe? Is the United States Government less concerned about national honor and vital interest than are the governments of that continent? In no country in the world is the sentiment of nationalism more pronounced than in the United States. No government is more jealous of its right to do as it pleases than our own. We have consistently refused to include questions of national honor and vital interest in treaties with other powers and have always rejected the policy of compulsory arbitration of such questions. In 1919, 36 Senators voted for a reservation which declared: "The United States reserves to itself exclusively the right to decide what questions affect its honor or its vital interests."

No people in the world are quicker to resent insults to the flag or reflections upon the national honor, or more insistent for intervention in other countries when vital interests are at stake, than are the citizens of the United States. The *Maine* is sunk in Havana harbor, the Mexicans refuse to salute the United States flag, an American missionary is killed by bandits in China, property of United States citizens is destroyed in Central America—instantly the passions of our people are aroused and an insistent demand for intervention or war sweeps over the land. British interests force up the price of crude rubber, Mexico restricts the exploitation of her mineral resources, France maintains that she is not morally bound to pay her war debt to us, Japanese citizens purchase land and acquire harbor rights in Mexico, the Japanese ambassador speaks of "grave consequences"—immediately jingoism and hyper-nationalism of the most dangerous kind are everywhere exhibited.

Wherein is the nationalism of Europe different from our own? The chief difference is in the setting of the stage—in geography, in language, in history. The United States is separated from Europe and from Asia by an ocean on either side. On the north are a friendly people and an unprotected boundary line. On the south are nations too weak to be a menace even if they were unfriendly. Moreover, no ancient traditions of hatred and enmity have sunk their roots deep into our national life. The real question we need to ask ourselves is this: What would happen if people of the temperament of our own citizens were brought face to face with the kind of situation which prevails in Europe? What would we do if we were surrounded on all sides by powerful nations, whom we had been taught to fear and hate, and against whom we had fought many times?

It is sheer hypocrisy for the citizens of the United States to throw stones at the diplomatists of Europe, so long as they themselves maintain the attitudes and defend the policies which give rise to international strife and chaos. Exaggerated nationalism is the chief barrier to world peace, and in its erection the peoples of the United States are having no small part.

Before we decide that America is well out of it, let us, therefore, remember: On the one hand, the extent of exaggerated nationalism in the United States and the violent temper displayed by our citizens in tense moments; and, on the other, the extent to which we are already involved in economic and financial affairs of other peoples and the certainty that numerous international disputes will arise over raw materials, markets and investments. In the face of this combination of intense nationalism and world-wide industrialism, to say that America is well out of it is either colossal ignorance or downright deception. The truth of the matter is that we are living in a world where any day some overt act may unleash violent national passions with calamitous effects, as was the case at Serejevo in 1914.

Militarism

The dangers which arise out of the combination of industrialism, with its interdependence, and nationalism, with its division, are greatly intensified by the prevalence of the spirit of militarism in many lands. The word militarism is sometimes used to describe national aggression and expansion by means of violence. This is the definition accepted by most persons who accuse German militarism of causing the World War. On the other hand, militarism does not necessarily connote aggression. What we mean by militarism in this discussion is *the belief that national security can be maintained only by armed force, and the advocacy of military and naval preparedness.* We regard militarism, even when the element of aggression is lacking, as a very grave menace to humanity. We look upon this deification of physical force as the "great pagan retrogression," to use a phrase coined by Benjamin Kidd.

Militarism engenders fear of other people. Armaments lead to counter-armaments. The only way governments can secure the enormous appropriations necessary for the upkeep of modern armies and navies is by appealing to the fears of their citizens. Militarism creates doubt and cynicism concerning non-violent means of maintaining security. Now this fear of other peoples and this paralyzing doubt concerning the effectiveness of international agencies of justice are major barriers to peace.

The spirit of militarism—belief in the ultimate effectiveness of force, scepticism concerning non-violent means, advocacy of military and naval preparedness—is widespread in the United States. Secretary of the Navy Wilbur, in an address in San Francisco, said that we must be prepared against "the aggression of any people influenced, as all people may be, by some extension of the mob spirit, some outburst of passion, or some real or fancied insult. There is nothing so cooling to hot temper as a piece of cold steel."[87]

Rear Admiral Fiske, of the United States Navy, before a very influential audience, recently said: "The plain fact is that international law is largely international humbug."[88] Rear-Admiral Rodgers recently wrote: "The League is a rope of sand . . . This country is rich and is the envy of other nations. We want for nothing and wrongly attribute to others the same spirit that actuates us . . . We cannot maintain our leading position in the world as a great progressive democratic nation with a popular government unless our armed strength is kept in prompt readiness to defend our riches."[89] Officers of the army and navy are speaking constantly upon the public platform in advocacy

---

[87] Quoted in The Nation, Oct. 1, 1924, p. 322.
[88] Annals of the American Academy, July 1925, p. 78.
[89] The Christian Work, Sept. 26, 1925, pp. 261, 262.

of military and naval preparedness and many articles from their pens appear in our various journals.[90]

Military Training

One of the most sinister phases of militarism is found in the vigorous effort now being made to extend military training in educational institutions. It is probably untrue to say that this training makes students bloodthirsty or desirous of going to war. The deadly thing about it is that it is calculated to increase dependence upon armaments and to decrease confidence in non-violent means of maintaining security and justice; that is to say, it spreads the spirit of militarism.

The War Department is avowedly seeking to plant units of Reserve Officers Training Corps (R. O. T. C.) in every college in the country. In December, 1925, the War Department issued a public statement to the effect that it "stands squarely in favor of military training for the greatest possible number of students, considering available personnel, funds and equipment." The extent to which the War Department has succeeded is indicated by the following figures:[91] "During the last school year, that of 1924-25, military instruction was given in *more* than 226 educational institutions in the United States. The exact number is difficult to obtain. Two hundred and twenty-six institutions maintained units of the R. O. T. C., but as just explained, the Secretary of War encourages military training in schools which do not establish R. O. T. C. For the schools with R. O. T. C. Congress appropriated $3,818,020 and the number of students taking military instruction was 125,504.

---

[90] For an interesting account of such activities, see an article, Selling us Another War, in the Nation, Sept. 26, 1923, p. 315.

[91] Military Training in Schools and Colleges of the States, by Winthrop D. Lane with a foreword signed by 55 leading citizens. 32 pages; 10 cents each. Published by the Committee on Military Training, 387 Bible House, Astor Place, New York City. See also a debate on Compulsory Military Training in American Colleges, Current History Magazine, April, 1926, pp. 27-34; see also, "The Other Side of Military Training," in the Survey, Jan. 15, 1926.

To these schools the War Department assigned 768 officers and 1,064 enlisted men to carry on training; it paid their salaries. Before 1916 there were no R. O. T. C. units and the number of officers engaged in military in schools was only 119. Of the 226 R. O. T. C. institutions in 1925, 124 were of college or university rank, 63 were high schools and 39 were what are known as "essentially military schools." According to the Report of the Secretary of War for 1925, the total cost of the R. O. T. C. was $10,696,054 for the fiscal year, 1925.

What kind of instruction do members of the R. O. T. C. units receive? In many colleges the text-book used is the Manual of Military Training, by Colonel James A. Moss and Major John W. Lang, which has had a circulation of more than 320,000 copies. The following quotations are taken from the 1923 edition of this manual: "Bayonet fighting is possible only because red-blooded men naturally possess the fighting instinct. This inherent desire to fight and kill must be carefully watched for and encouraged by the instructor . . . Force him (your opponent) to the ground and break his neck by suddenly throwing the feet well to the rear and falling forward, tightening the arms and pressing the shoulder tightly against the back of the head. This hold when properly executed will break the opponent's neck . . . When the opponent secures a hold from the front, dig the thumbs into his eyes, forcing his head back, and follow up by driving the knee to his crotch . . . Also attempt to grasp one of his fingers and either twist it or break it . . . If the opponent is down, attack with the usual type of kick in his vulnerable parts . . . The principles of sportsmanship and consideration for your opponent have no place in the practical application of this work. . . . The object of all military training is to win battles."

Another phase of militarism is found in the Citizens' Military Training Camps (C. M. T. C.). This branch is designed primarily for young men who are not attending college. The number of men enrolled in these summer courses in 1924 was 32,647, and the total expense of operation was $3,272,768.24.[93]

Summary

Let us now gather together the various elementals in the grave international situation with which we are confronted: increasing destructiveness of war, due to the size of the units involved, nature of the weapons used, and disruptive effects upon production; economic dependence of the various peoples of the earth upon each other and increasing rivalry for raw materials, markets and investments; political division and hostility as a result of virulent nationalism, excessive sensitiveness of national pride, and belligerent temper displayed in hours of crisis; the spread of militarism, with its emphasis upon the necessity of armaments and its depreciation of peaceable means of settling disputes between nations; the progressive industrialization and possible militarization of the Orient—in the aggregate this combination of factors constitutes an exceedingly grave danger to mankind.

At the present moment the great mass of people in the United States are blind and deaf to the signs of the times and are making only the feeblest of efforts to prevent the outbreak of another great war. "The world," says General Pershing, "does not seem to learn from experience. It would appear that the lessons of the last six years should be enough to convince everybody of the *danger of nations striding up and down the earth armed to the teeth.* But no one nation can reduce armaments unless all do. Unless some such move be made, we may well ask ourselves whether civilization does not really reach a point where it begins to *destroy itself* and whether we are thus *doomed to go headlong down through destructive war and darkness to barbarism.*" [94]

---

[93] Report of the Secretary of War, 1925, pp. 5, 6, 152

[94] In an address in New York City, Dec. 29, 1920.

3. RACIAL DANGERS

"I am convinced myself," says Mr. H. G. Wells, "that there is no more evil thing in this present world than race prejudice, none at all! I write deliberately—it is the worst single thing in life now. It justifies and holds together more baseness, cruelty and abomination than any other sort of error in the world."[95] Race prejudice and passion are among the most widespread factors in our modern world. This is not the place to enter into a lengthy discussion of the origins of race feeling. What we are here concerned with are the fact and the consequences that grow out of it.

Since modern nations are, for the most part, artificial political creations, very divergent racial and language groups are frequently included under the same government. In Europe alone, the minority groups total 16 million persons. All over the world minorities are subjected to discrimination, exploitation and sometimes even violence.[96]

The racial problem of the United States is two-fold in character: internal and external. Within our borders are three primary groups which are regarded with suspicion and hostility and which are victims of discrimination, exploitation and occasional violence at the hands of the older white stock, namely Negroes, European immigrants, and Japanese.

Negroes

That the Negroes are an inferior people is regarded as axiomatic throughout the white South and in many other sections of the country.[97] From the many thousands of available selections revealing this conviction, we choose the following extracts from a book written by a Vanderbilt University man, who, after spending three years in graduate

---

[95] Quoted in R. E. Speer, Race and Race Relations, p. 154.

[96] See Noel Buxton and T. P. Conwil-Evans, Oppressed Peoples. and the League of Nations.

[97] For a stimulating article by Professor Boas on racial superiority, see *The American Mercury,* Vol. 3, pp. 163 ff.

study at the University of Chicago, travelled for six years in Africa, Australia, New Zealand, the Philippines and South America, and published in 1923 by the White America Society: "The white race has founded all civilizations . . . The Negro, has not had, and cannot have, a part in progressive civilization. . . . That the colored races do not originate is the most solemn fact of human history, the only fact that bodes ill for the future. . . . A race devoid of creative genius is an unfit type so far as progress in civilization is concerned. . . . Civilization has never survived intimate and prolonged contact with colored races. . . . If we do not remove the Negro, our civilization is to decay. If we do remove the Negro, our civilization is to increase, and our future belongs to God. . . . The white man is the sun that lights the world; the luster of other races is but reflected glory. The white man is in fact what the negrophilist is in theory—the voice of the Almighty upon earth." [98]

Even more extreme are the statements of the Iconoclast Bran, whose writings have had very wide circulation, from which we quote: "We have hunted the black rape fiend to death with hounds, bored him with buckshot; fricasseed him over slow fires and flayed him alive; but the despoilment of white women by these brutal imps of darkness and the devil is still of daily occurrence. The baleful shadow of black hangs over every Southern home like the sword of Damocles, like the blight of death—an avatar of infamy, a decree of damnation. . . . In the name of Israel's God what shall we do? . . . Drive out the 'nigger' young and old, male and female—or drive him into the earth. . . . It were better that a thousand 'good Negroes', if so many there be, should suffer death or banishment than that one good white woman should be debauched." [99]

Discrimination against Negroes is widely prevalent

---

[98] Earnest Sevier Cox, White America, pp. 23, 27, 237, 245, 299, 300, 376.

[99] Quoted by Frank Tannenbaum in Darker Phases of the South, pp. 160, 161; see also The Negro: A Menace to American Civilization, by R. W. Shufeldt, M. D.

throughout the country. In the South segregation is carried to an extreme in separate schools, churches, railway coaches, residential districts, etc. As the number of Negroes in northern communities increases there is a marked tendency toward segregation. Negroes moving into white communities are often subjected to insult, persecution and occasional violence. In Indianapolis, a city ordinance creating separate residential zones for Negroes and whites has been passed and is now before the court. In many northern cities the demand for separate schools is growing.[100]

Violence between Negroes and whites is of frequent occurrence. Numerous cases of atrocious assaults on white women by Negro men are on record. On the other hand, assaults on Negro women by white men are probably even more numerous. Moreover, the treatment accorded Negro criminals has frequently been extremely barbarous and inhuman. Lynching and mob violence in this country constitute a national disgrace. Since 1885 a total of 4,220 persons have been lynched in the United States, of whom 3,182 were Negroes. This is an average of two per week for 41 years! Fortunately the number of lynchings has declined rapidly in recent years. In 1925 the number was 17, one every three weeks, all of whom were Negroes.[101]

The degree of ferocity manifested by white lynching mobs can be surpassed only by searching the annals of savagery. Persons who under normal circumstances are law-abiding and even tender-hearted citizens, exhibit maniacal fury when under the sway of mob passion. Incredible scenes are described by eye-witnesses of lynching-bees and race riots. Some years ago Mr. Ray Stannard Baker made a study of several communities in which lynchings had oc-

---

[100] For numerous illustrations of discrimination—civic, educational, economic and social—see And Who Is My Neighbor? published by the Inquiry, 129 East 52nd Street, New York City.

[101] See The Law vs. the Mob, a leaflet issued by the Federal Council of Churches, 105 E. 22nd Street, New York City; see also Thirty Years of Lynching in the United States, published by the National Association for the Advancement of Colored People, 70 Fifth Avenue, New York City.

curred. Concerning the burning of two Negroes, who had killed a white man, assaulted and killed his wife, and burned three children to death, in Statesboro, Georgia, Mr. Baker wrote: "Men were sent into town for kerosene oil and chains, and finally the Negroes were bound to an old stump, fagots were heaped around them, and each was drenched with oil. Then the crowd stood back accommodatingly, while a photographer, standing there in the bright sunshine, took pictures of the chained Negroes. Citizens crowded up behind the stump and got their faces into the photograph. When the fagots were lighted, the crowd yelled wildly . . . And when it was all over, they began, in common with all mobs, to fight for souvenirs."[102] A member of a mob at Huntsville, Alabama, cut off the little fingers of a Negro victim as souvenirs.

Near Waco, Texas, a young Negro man assaulted and murdered a white woman. He was captured and burned to death in the presence of nearly 10,000 people. An eyewitness describes the scene: "The mob ripped the boy's clothes off . . . Someone cut his ear off; someone else unsexed him . . . He was lowered into the fire several times by means of a chain around his neck . . . About a quarter past one a fiend got the torso, lassoed it, hung a rope over the pummel of a saddle, and dragged it around through the streets of Waco."[103]

Lynching and mob violence are not confined to the South but occur in all sections of the country. Among the most flagrant cases on record are the riots in East St. Louis, Chicago, Omaha and Washington. In July, 1919, a race war broke out in East St. Louis, a city in Illinois just across the river from St. Louis. The following account of events is taken from Current Opinion: "Then hell broke loose. For the greater part of thirty-six hours, Negroes were hunted through the streets like wild animals. A black skin became a death-warrant. Man after man, with hands upraised,

---

[102] What is a Lynching? in McClures Magazine, January, 1905, pp. 299-314.

[103] Supplement to the *Crisis*, July, 1916.

pleading for his life, was surrounded by groups of men who had never seen him before and who knew nothing about him except that he was black, and stoned to death . . . An aged Negro, tottering from weakness, was seized and hanged to a pole. Three million dollars' worth of property was destroyed." A writer in the St. Louis Post-Dispatch said: "I do not believe that Moslem fanaticism or Prussian frightfulness could perpetrate murders of more deliberate brutality than those which I saw committed, in daylight, by citizens of the State of Abraham Lincoln."[104]

The casualties of the Chicago race riots of 1919 were: 38 persons killed, 537 injured and 1,000 rendered homeless. For four days anarchy and violence prevailed throughout large sections of the city.[105] In describing the situation, Professor Graham Taylor wrote: "Armed men of either color dashed through the district in automobiles and beyond, firing as they flew. Two white men, wounded while shooting up the district, were found to carry official badges, one being thus identified as in the United States civil service and the other as a Chicago policeman. White men firing a machine gun from a truck were killed. White and Negro policemen were in turn attacked and badly beaten by mobs of the opposite color. The torch followed attacks upon Negro stores and dwellings, scores of which were set on fire. . . . A colored soldier wearing a wound stripe on his sleeve was beaten to death while limping along one of the main streets."[106]

Some years ago a group of one hundred prominent citizens, including ex-President Taft, Elihu Root, Charles W. Eliot, and Charles E. Hughes, signed an "Address to the Nation" on mob violence, in which they said: "Rarely are the members of a mob sought out and prosecuted even when they have participated in murder, undisguised and in full daylight, and only in a few isolated cases has any lyncher

---

[104] Current Opinion, August, 1917, p. 76.
[105] See The Negro in Chicago, pp. 1-52.
[106] The Survey, August 9, 1919, p. 696.

ever been punished.[107] In a public meeting in New York City, ex-President Roosevelt denounced mob violence as an "appalling outbreak of savagery."

There is no doubt that a dangerous tension exists in many communities between whites and blacks. As Negroes become better educated they become more sensitive and resentful against being treated as inferiors. They are certainly becoming more race-conscious and are acting with more solidarity. They now have 400 publications devoted to their interest. Nearly 8,000 colored college graduates are giving leadership to their various movements. "No sane observer," says Alain Locke, in The New Negro, that truly remarkable anthology of Negro achievements, "however sympathetic to the new trend, would contend that the great masses are inarticulate as yet, but they stir, they move, they are more than physically restless . . . Only the steadying and sobering effect of a truly characteristic gentleness of spirit prevents the rapid rise of a definite cynicism and counter-hate and a defiant superiority feeling . . . Whether it actually brings into being new Armadas of conflict or argosies of cultural exchange and enlightenment can only be decided by the attitude of the dominant races in an era of critical change.[108]

The situation is made even more dangerous by reason of the fact that as Negroes become more aggressive in demanding justice, many white people become more alarmed and more determined to keep them "in their place." Since the migration northward has now reached huge proportions, the problem has become a truly national one. In the opinion of the editor of the New Republic, we are "moving toward race war."[109]

European Immigrants

The presence of an enormous number of foreign-born people in our midst is proving to be a source of great alarm to many native whites. The mingling of great masses of

---

[107] The Survey, August 2, 1919, p. 675.
[108] Pp. 7, 13, 14.
[109] See an editorial, June 22, 1921, pp. 96-97.

peoples of different races, languages and cultural backgrounds even under the most favorable circumstances is certain to cause friction and hostility. There are now in the United States about 14 million persons of foreign birth, coming from 45 different countries. There are 23 million persons in this country one or both of whose parents were born abroad. That is to say, we have with us 37 million first and second generation immigrants. These persons are reading 1052 foreign language publications in 30 different tongues. In New York City church services are conducted in 35 languages, while in the United States as a whole, 42 different languages are used by 26,239 religious organizations. Nearly two million of the foreign-born are illiterate. About seven million immigrants are of voting age.[110]

There is on the part of the native white stock of this country a rapidly rising tide of suspicion and hostility against our foreign-born population. Much of the energy of the Ku Klux Klan, for example, is being directed as an attack upon immigrants, especially the Jewish and Catholic elements. The Klan itself seems to be losing ground, due in part to internal dissension over organizational questions. Nevertheless, there is an abundance of evidence which reveals widespread hostility to these newly arrived peoples. Ignorance, bigotry, and intolerance are creating a situation which is full of peril.

The Japanese in the United States

There are less than 150,000 Japanese in the United States, yet their presence is a source of great fear to the native white stock. Most of the Japanese in this country are concentrated on the Pacific Coast, chiefly in California. Most Californians are convinced that their standards of living and codes of morals are jeopardized by the Japanese. This belief has led to severe measures of discrimination. California, Washington and Arizona have passed anti-alien

[110] See Gino Speranza, Race or Nation, pp. 21, 59, 134, 136, 215.

land laws. California has also abolished the right of Japanese to lease land or to make "croppage contracts."[111]

A foreign-born Japanese cannot become naturalized and is therefore ineligible to citizenship. The law of Congress that limits naturalization to "free white persons" and to Negroes was interpreted by the Supreme Court of the United States in November, 1922, as barring Japanese aliens from becoming citizens, although their children born in this country automatically become citizens. There is no escaping the obvious meaning of this legislation, namely, that, so far as material for citizenship is concerned, Congress regards the Japanese as distinctly inferior to Europeans, Turks, Mexicans and Negroes. This opinion of Congress was again expressed in the manner in which Japanese immigrants were excluded in 1924. While Europeans were admitted on a quota basis, by a majority vote of five to one in the House and ten to one in the Senate, Asiatics were totally excluded from settlement in the United States.[112]

The friendly statement of the Japanese Ambassador to Secretary Hughes that the passage of the exclusion act would lead to grave "consequences" precipitated a violent anti-Japanese outburst in this country.

Fear of the Japanese has not only led to severe economic and political restrictions upon them but also the drastic social discrimination and persecution. Strenuous pressure is brought to bear upon white residents to refrain from patronizing Japanese restaurants, laundries and other business establishments. The presence of Japanese residents in white communities is resented and efforts are often made to drive them out. In referring to the Japanese "invasion," the editor of the San Luis Obispo Tribune, wrote: "It is considered as akin to a scourge of leprosy, unchangeable in its nature, absolutely incurable, unlimited in the extent of its

---

111 See Again the Yellow Peril, by Raymond Leslie Buell, in *Foreign Affairs,* Vol. 2, pp. 295-309; see also, The Development of the Anti-Japanese Agitation, by the same writer, in the *Political Science Quarterly,* Vol. 37, pp. 605-638, and Vol. 38, pp. 57-81.

112 See Grave Consequences, by H. H. Powers, in the *Atlantic Monthly,* Vol. 134, pp. 124-133.

devastation and unquestionably destructive of our Republic as such."[113] When the Japanese started to build a church in Hollywood, anti-Japanese leaders circulated a yellow dodger with these words:

JAPS

You came to care for our lawns—
We stood for it.
You came to work truck gardens—
We stood for it.
You sent your children to our public schools—
We stood for it.
You moved a few families in our midst—
We stood for it.
You propose to build a church in our neighborhood—
We didn't and won't stand for it.
You impose more on us each day until you have gone your limit.
We don't want you with us, so get busy, Japs, and move out of Hollywood!

Many newspapers, the Hearst press in particular, are endeavoring to stir up anti-Japanese feelings. In the New York American of July 23, 1916, appeared an anti-Japanese hymn of hate, from which we quote the chorus:

LOOK OUT! CALIFORNIA! BEWARE!

They lurk upon thy shores, California!
They watch behind thy doors, California!
They're a hundred thousand strong,
And they won't be hiding long;
There's nothing that the dastards would not dare!
They are soldiers to a man with the schemes of old Japan
Look out! California! Beware!

Wider Aspects of the Race Problem

The person who does not recognize the extreme gravity of the race question in the United States is simply blind and deaf. And yet we are faced with another phase of the problem which is potentially even more dangerous, namely, the increasing tension between the Orient and the Occident. Vast territories in the Far East are now under the political control of Western powers, while other Far Eastern coun-

[113] Numerous expressions of this character are contained in The Verdict of Public Opinion on the Japanese-American Question, published by Cornelius Vanderbilt, Jr.

tries are under the economic domination of Europe and the United States.

During the past decade, however, the grip of the West upon the East has been slipping. The prestige of white men is falling rapidly everywhere from Constantinople to Yokohama. The World War laid bare the crudities and inhumanities of Western civilization. Hundreds of thousands of soldiers and laborers came to Europe from Asia and Africa and returned to tell tales of our defects and crimes. The most sensational and vulgar moving-picture films produced in the United States are being exhibited all over the East. Tens of thousands of Oriental students have been studying in European and American universities, many of whom have become exceedingly critical of the ideals and institutions of the West. Missionaries and educators have been proclaiming a message of democracy and brotherhood throughout the East. Numerous books about dangerous doctrines of political and social democracy are being widely read in that vast territory east of Suez, as are also biographies of the great liberators of the West. Rapid strides are everywhere being made in popular education.

The result is that the whole East is seething with unrest and resentment against outside exploitation and domination. Recent events in Egypt, India, and China make it clear that Western political control cannot be maintained much longer by armies and navies. The number of white people residing in these lands is inconsequential in comparison with the hundreds of millions of brown and black and yellow peoples. Japan stands as a warning to the West concerning the possibilities of industrialism and militarism. The whole of the Far East is moving toward industrialism. Many of the ablest leaders in the respective countries are advocating military and naval measures as the only effective means of escaping humiliation and exploitation from the white powers. The extension of popular education and the spread of democratic ideas among a vast population of eight hundred million dark-skinned people, accompanied by insulting, discrimination and oppressive exploitation by white people, are creating a world situation which, if prolonged for many decades, will surely lead to increasing friction and hostility, if not to wholesale violence.

The East, as well as the West, has its jingoes and sensationalists; and there, as well as here, they stir up dangerous passions. The temper of the extremist is reflected in the statements of Achmed Abdullah, a direct descendant of Mohammed on one side and of Genghis Khan on the other: "We taught you to read, to write, and to think. We gave you your religion and your few ideals. We have done more for you than you can ever do for us . . . Stop being liars and hypocrites: and you will cease being what you are today: the most hated and the most despised men in the length and breadth of Asia and North Africa . . . I could mention a dozen instances to prove that you are forcing on the world the coming struggle between Asia, all Asia, against Europe and America, against Christendom, in other words. You are heaping up material for a Jehad, a Pan-Islam, a Pan-Asia Holy War, a gigantic Day of Reckoning, an invasion of a new Attila and Tamerlane . . . who will use rifles and bullets, instead of lances and spears. You are deaf to the voice of reason and fairness, and so you must be taught with the whirling swish of the sword when it is red."[114]

4. POLITICAL DANGERS

Political life in the United States is in a very diseased condition. While there are differences of opinion concerning the seriousness of the malady, all competent observers are agreed that drastic measures are required to prevent further decay and degeneration. The dangerous elements most frequently mentioned are (1) graft and corruption, (2) the ignorance and efficiency alike of the electorate and the legislators, (3) the denial of civil liberties, (4) the indifference

[114] The Forum, Vol. 52, pp. 483-497.

of the voters, (5) the magnitude and complexity of the problems requiring solution.[115]

(1) It is generally agreed that there is less graft and corruption in American politics now than was the case four or five decades ago, or even in 1902 and 1903 when Lincoln Steffins wrote "The Shame of the Cities." Conditions certainly are not as bad now as they were in the days of the old political bosses, Tweed, Croker, McManes, Reuf, and Lorimer.[116] Nevertheless, there is still widespread graft and corruption in American politics. We still have with us the political machine, the political ring, and the political boss.[117] Fraud in elections still prevails on an extended scale.[118] Dishonesty and crookedness are more prevalent in municipal life than in state or national affairs, although even in the latter realm there is an occasional Fall or Daugherty. Professor John R. Commons, of the University of Wisconsin, says: "Great corporations and syndicates seeking legislative favors are known to control the acts of both branches of Congress . . . The people at large have come thoroughly to distrust their law-makers. Charges of corruption and bribery are so abundant as to be taken as a matter of course. The honored historical name of Alderman has frequently become a stigma of suspicion and disgrace."[119]

(2) Perhaps even more dangerous than downright dishonesty is the gross inefficiency of many governmental bodies. A great majority of our state and national legislators are men of average, if not inferior, mental and moral qualities. The number of really first-rate men and women that go into politics is alarmingly small. One writer says

---

[115] For a constructive criticism of American democracy, see James Bryce, Modern Democracies, Vol. 2, pp. 168 ff.

[116] For an illuminating historical account of political corruption in the United States, see James Bryce, The American Commonwealth, Vol. 2, pp. 379 ff; see also Alfred B. Cruikshank, Popular Misgovernment in the United States, pp. 109 ff; and Robert C. Brooks, Corruption in American Politics and Life.

[117] See William B. Munro, Personality in Politics, pp. 42-78.

[118] See Marjorie Shuler, Party Control in Politics and Government, pp. 85 ff.

[119] Proportional Representation, p. 2.

that we have an abundance of well-qualified leaders, "but they are not in politics and never will be under the present vile regime. It is just because they prize honor and reputation that they stay out of politics."

The machinery of government in the United States is frequently referred to as being clumsy and inefficient. Professor Munro says that cities "have had too much governmental apparatus, and it has been too complicated. Mayors, aldermen, councilors, commissioners, members of boards, and heads of departments have had a jumble of duties and powers which nobody could untangle. There has been, in many cities, no concentration of responsibility."[120]

Anyone who has witnessed the scenes in a national political convention must be troubled with doubts as to whether or not this is the ideal way of selecting the most highly qualified men for high office. After visiting one of these conventions, Glenn Frank, wrote: "I think the tragi-comic inefficiency of these quadrennial field-meets of prejudice, passion, and log-rolling symbolizes the decadence of American politics in general."[121] The party system in politics is being severely criticized in many quarters. Certainly there can be little reality in politics under the present dominant parties, with their meaningless names and their lack of clean-cut issues. The average voter has the choice of voting a straight party ticket or of casting his ballot for a long list of persons whom he has never met and concerning whose abilities he knows almost nothing.

(3) One of the most serious political dangers in the United States is the frequent denial of civil liberties.[122] In spite of the popular belief to the contrary, there are very severe limitations upon civil liberties in this country. Trade unionists and members of radical organizations are fre-

---

[120] Current Problems in Citizenship, p. 158.

[121] Century Magazine, Vol. 108, p. 715.

[122] See Zechariah Chafee, Freedom of Speech. See also an article, Repression of Civil Liberties in the United States, by Harry F. Ward, in Publications of the American Sociological Society, Vol. XVIII, pp. 127146. See also Haynes Baker-Crothers and R. A. Hudnut, Problems of Citizenship, pp. 350-397.

quently denied freedom of speech. As a result of the war hysteria, many states passed sedition acts of one sort or another. These acts are often administered by reactionary officials in such a way as to cause great injustice to critics of the present social order. The result of the numerous criminal syndicalist laws has been to drive radical organizations underground and to create widespread contempt for our government. In a dissenting opinion Justice Brandeis says: "In frank expressions of conflicting opinions lies the greatest promise of wisdom in government action; and in suppression lies ordinarily the greatest peril."[123]

Especially in times of industrial disputes are the rights of the workers likely to be abridged by arbitrary officials. In the great steel strike of 1919, according to the Commission of Inquiry of the Interchurch World Movement: "During the strike violations of personal rights and personal liberty were wholesale; men were arrested without warrants, imprisoned without charges, their homes invaded without legal process, magistrates' verdicts were rendered frankly on the basis of whether the striker would go back to work or not. But even these things would seem to be less a concern to the nation at large than the degradation, persistent and approved by "public opinion," of civil liberties in behalf of private concerns' industrial practices."[124] The various publications of the American Civil Liberties Union[125] contain an ominous record of suppression, intimidation and violence against trade unionists and radicals. In view of the extreme probability that the industrial conflict in this country will become more intense in the near future, government officials cannot afford to give the impression that they are tools of the employers.

4. Perhaps an even greater danger than corruption, inefficiency and denial of civil liberties, is found in the appalling ignorance and indifference of the electorate. It is an astounding fact that, whereas men once gave their lives in the

[123] Gilbert v. Minnesota, 254 U. S., 338.
[124] Ibid, Page 238.
[125] 70 Fifth Avenue, New York City.

struggle for the ballot, about half of the qualified voters in this country regularly refrain from going to the polls. From 1865 to 1920 the ratio of the actual to the eligible vote declined from 83.51 per cent to 52.36 per cent.[126] In the campaign of 1924, after a nation-wide effort to get the vote out, half of the qualified voters failed to cast their ballots. In the elections of 1922 at least fifteen United States Senators, from all sections of the country, were elected by less than one-third of the possible votes in their respective states.[127]

Not alone in the indifference of half of the voters do we find a source of danger, but also in the credulity, partisanship and unsound judgment of many of those who do vote. This ominous situation is due in part to the inferior mental ability of many citizens; in part to faulty education or lack of education; and in part to low standards of morals. The Federal Census of 1920 revealed the fact that there were 4,931,905 illiterates in the United States. The actual number is probably greatly in excess of this figure, since no examinations were given and only those persons were counted who admitted illiteracy. In this connection, the report of the Illiteracy Commission of the National Education Association says: "If a careful census were taken in which every individual should be put to the test of reading simple paragraphs and writing simple sentences, the number of illiterates in this country would approximate 10,000,000 and the number of near illiterates would be equally as large."[128]

---

[126]Walter Lippmann, The Phantom Public, p. 16; see also an article, The Vanishing Voter, the New Republic, Oct. 15, 1924, pp. 162-167.

[127]It seems almost incredible that Senator Johnson of California was elected by 29 per cent of the voters of his state, Senator Reed of Missouri and Senator Shipstead of Minnesota by 26 per cent, Senator Copeland of New York and Senator Fess of Ohio by 25 per cent, Senator Dill of Washington by 17 per cent, Senator Ferris of Michigan by 16 per cent, Senator McKellar of Tennessee by 13 per cent, Senator Mayfield of Texas by 12 per cent, Senator Swanson of Virginia by 10 per cent, and Senator Trammell of Florida by a scant 9 per cent! See Nicholas Murray Butler, The Faith of a Liberal, p. 100.

[128]National Education Ass'n., Proceedings, 1923, p. 267.

According to the 1920 census, there were 4,333,111 illiterates of voting age. Moreover, vast numbers of voters who possess the ability to read and write are, nevertheless, grossly ignorant of public affairs and in no sense qualified to vote intelligently. Many other voters lack the moral qualities essential to good citizenship.[129]

5. There is, however, another factor which needs to be taken into account, namely, the magnitude and complexity of political problems in our day. Modern government is compelled to deal with an enormous number of different questions, many of which can be understood only by technicians and experts. The consequence is that an almost incredibly large number of bills are presented at every session of state legislatures and the national Congress. During the period the 67th Congress was in session a total of 14,475 bills were introduced, 1,763 were reported out of committee, and 931 became law.[130] Each year some 10,000 laws are passed by the forty-eight states, while the number and variety of municipal ordinances are quite appalling. The National Budget Committee has estimated that there are now some 2,000,000 laws in force in the United States.[131] Only omniscient men and women could vote intelligently on the multitude of questions confronting our legislators.[132] And yet many of the problems dealt with are of the utmost importance to the social well-being of the citizens at large. Well may a current writer exclaim: "The human mind is appalled at the magnitude of the task of properly governing the enormous population and of safeguarding the immense wealth and interests of the United States. The future political existence of the country and its status as a nation

---

[129]See a disturbing article on The Political Decline of America, by Frank R. Kent, *Harpers Magazine,* Dec., 1925, pp. 14-18.

[130]*Time,* March 24, 1923, p. 2.

[131]See an article, Groping Through the Maze of Our Laws, *New York Times Magazine,* Dec. 16, 1923, p. 6.

[132]For a list of the subjects considered at a single session of Congress, see A. B. Cruikshank, Popular Misgovernment in the United States, p. 271 ff.

may and very probably will depend on the capacity and ability of its legislators and administrators."[133]

That veteran student of government, Lord Bryce, in his presidential address to the British Academy, said: "Sometimes one feels as if modern states were growing too huge for the men to whom their fortunes are committed . . . Enormous nations are concentrated under one government and its disasters affect the whole. A great modern state is like a gigantic vessel built without any watertight compartments, which, if it be unskillfully steered, may perish when it strikes a single rock."[134]

One current writer says: "The Republic does not appear to have enough virile leaders or enough informed and right-minded citizens to save it. This reflects despondency, but it is despondency that springs from logic."[135] Shortly before his death, Frank I. Cobb, editor of the New York World, wrote: "American democracy is now stagnant. The great world stream of popular government has swept past it, leaving it isolated. Enormous material prosperity has paralyzed its initiative and made it timid. A democracy that once dared and dared magnificiently now alternately mumbles about its troubles and mutters about the greatness of the Fathers."[136]

5. MORAL DANGERS

We are not contending that moral conditions are worse now than they were ten, fifty or a hundred years ago. Just here we are not discussing *relative* standards of morals. In this section we shall confine ourselves to the presentation of evidence concerning certain moral dangers *now* confronting us. We shall discuss these perils in the following order: (1) crime and lawlessness; (2) the social evil; (3) commercialized amusements; (4) obscene literature; (5) deterioration of home life; (6) absence of religious education.

---

[133]Cruikshank, p. 270.

[134]Quoted in the *Atlantic Monthly*, Vol. 117, p. 298.

[135]Daniel Chauncey Brewer, The Peril of the Republic, p. 59.

[136]*Harpers Monthly*, Vol. 147, p. 6; see also a debate, Is Democracy Doomed, The Forum, April, 1926.

(1) The citizens of the United States are among the most lawless peoples of the earth as may be seen from the following figures:[137]

Number of Murders per 100,000 *Population*

United States (as a whole)		7.2
77 Cities in the United States		9.9
Memphis	70.0	
Jacksonville	58.8	
Nashville	36.0	
New Orleans	32.5	
Louisville	25.0	
Savannah	24.0	
Mobile	21.8	
St. Louis	21.7	
Pueblo	21.2	
Chicago	17.5	
Detroit	17.1	
New York City	6.4	
Italy		3.6
Australia		1.9
South Africa		1.8
New Zealand		0.9
Ireland		0.9
Spain		0.9
Norway		0.8
England and Wales		0.8
Quebec		0.5
Ontario		0.5
Scotland		0.4
Holland		0.3
Switzerland		0.2

Former Senator Burton of Ohio says: "In the year 1918 there were 222 homicides in the City of Chicago, against 154

[137]See an invaluable study, The Homicide Problem, by Frederick L. Hoffman, published by the Prudential Insurance Company of America, New York City, pp. 97-105; see also *Current History Magazine,* January, 1926, p. 470, and *The Survey,* March 1, 1926.

in all of England and Wales, and six times as many as in the City of London. In 1921 the number in Chicago had reached 352; in 1923, 389; in 1924, 509, a most startling increase." Several cities in the United States have an even higher murder rate than does Chicago, as may be seen from the above table. There were 11,000 murders in the United States during 1924. Robbery is 100 times as prevalent in Chicago as in London. The United States Government has been compelled "to contract for the building of 3,000 specially designed armored cars for use in the mail service."[138] The losses paid by burglary insurance companies has increased 816 per cent in thirteen years.[139] Each year some 30,000 automobiles are stolen in 28 of our cities. In New York City alone there were 30,117 arrests for gambling in a single year. According to Wm. B. Joyce, Chairman of the National Surety Company, the American people lose two billion dollars each year by fraud. Chief Justice Taft has said: "The administration of criminal law in the United States is a disgrace to civilization." Mr. Mark O. Prentiss says: "Today the greatest outstanding menace in America is crime. I am not an alarmist when I boldly state that crime in this country is overwhelming the people and confounding the police."[140]

The manner in which the prohibition laws are being violated is notorious and disgraceful. During a three-year period according to Prohibition Commissioner Haynes, there were 177,000 arrests by Federal authorities for violation of the prohibition law, and the aggregate sentences of those convicted reached a total of nearly 7,000 years. Mr. Haynes reports that "more than 400,000 stills and parts of stills and about 39,000,000 gallons of distilled spirits, malt liquors, wines, etc., have been seized during the last three years. A total

---

[138] Literary Digest, Sept. 13, 1924, p. 32.

[139] See, The Rising Tide of Crime, by Lawrence Veiller, *World's Work,* December, 1925, pp. 133 ff.

[140] See his article, War on the Growing Menace of Crime, *Current History Magazine,* October, 1925, pp. 1-8.

of 11,077 automobiles and 444 boats and launches have been captured." The number of violators who escape is many times greater than the number caught.

Few people realize the extent of our peril from drugs and narcotics. The startling statement is made by Frederic A. Wallis, Commissioner of Correction of New York, that "the United States is the largest user of drugs of any nation in the world."[141] Mr. Wallis continues: "The survey made under the direction of the United States Treasury and recently published showed that there were more than 1,000,000 addicts in this country. Some estimates go as high as 4,000,000. . . . The annual per capita consumption of opium in Italy is one grain; in Germany, two grains; in England, three grains; in France, four grains; in the United States, which does not grow one commercial poppy or coca leaf, the enormous amount of thirty-six grains per capita per annum—practically four times the combined use of these leading European nations. Even India, with its long opium antecedents, uses only twenty-seven grains per capita. . . . It is stated that if the morphine which is derived from these thirty-six grains of opium were dispensed in the usual medical doses of one-eighth of a grain each, it would be sufficient to keep every person in the United States under the influence of an opiate for twenty-nine consecutive days."

It is frequently said that all drug addicts are criminals, actual or potential. So overwhelming is the desire for dope that the victim is capable of any foul deed in order to get money with which to purchase a supply. Nearly 60 per cent of the inmates in the penal and correctional institutions of New York City are users or sellers of drugs. After twenty years of experience with the victims of narcotics, Mr. Wallis expressed the opin-

---

[141] See his illuminating article, The Menace of the Drug Addict, in *Current History Magazine*, Feb. 1925, pp. 740-743. See also Henry S. Spalding, Social Problems and Agencies, pp. 273-283.

ion that "the greatest menace confronting civilization today is drug addiction."[142]

(2) No reliable figures are available with regard to the extent of prostitution in the United States. During recent years there has undoubtedly been a marked decrease in the number of inmates in public houses of prostitution, as well as in the volume of street soliciting.[143] Nevertheless, there is plenty of evidence to show that there is still a vast amount of commercialized vice. In his study for the Bureau of Social Hygiene, Dr. H. B. Woolston says: "We arrive at the conservative figure of approximately 200,000 women in the regular army of vice.[144] Other estimates place the number of prostitutes in the United States as high as 500,000. Moreover, there is undoubtedly a vast amount of illicit sexual relations apart from commercialized prostitution. In the nature of the case the extent of these relations is unknown. Any physician, social worker, judge, clergyman, high school principal or college president, however, can produce tragic evidence of moral lapses.[145] In the aggregate, the extent of sexual relations outside marriage is sufficiently great to constitute an ominous social peril.

The health aspect alone causes grave concern. Social diseases are calamitous in their results. On April 28, 1919, there appeared an advertisement in the New York Tribune over the signatures of Rupert Blue, Surgeon General, United States Health Service, and Royal S. Copeland, Commissioner of Health of New York City, later United States Senator, from which we quote:

---

[142] See a pamphlet, International Control of the Traffic in Opium, issued by the Foreign Policy Association, 1925

[143] See an interesting article, A Revolution in Morals, by James Bronson Reynolds, in the National Municipal Review, Vol. 12, pp. 586 ff.

[144] Prostitution in the United States, p. 38.

[145] For an alarming picture of moral conditions in the high schools, see The Revolt of Modern Youth by Judge Ben B. Lindsey and Wainwright Evans.

"The venereal rate in the American Army was lower than in any army in the history of the world. Yet, from the time America entered the war—April, 1917, to September, 1918—2,295,000 days of service were lost to the American Army through venereal diseases. Of these diseases, only one-sixth were contracted after enlistment. . . . The conditions indicate that the vitality of the nation is imperiled. . . . Out of 770,000 males reaching maturity yearly, it is stated that 450,000 of them, or more than 60 per cent, are infected." A more conservative estimate is given by Mr. Lawrence Marcus, of the National Health Council as follows: "The amount of venereal disease that can be found in the United States on any one day, in all persons, regardless of age or sex, is 8.12 per cent."[146] That is to say, more than eight million men and women are afflicted at a given time. Conclusive evidence is available showing that venereal diseases are responsible for a very heavy proportion of blindness, sterility, still births, invalidism and insanity.

(3) In the realm of commercialized amusements are many social perils. It is evident that moving pictures, theatres, race tracks, dance halls, night clubs and other amusement centers are determining factors in the moral life of the community. Mr. Charles A. McMahon, of the National Catholic Welfare Council, is of the opinion that moving pictures are "daily influencing the masses of our people to an extent not even approached by all our schools, our churches and our ethical organizations combined." The extent of commercialized amusements and sports in the United States is enormous.[147] It is estimated that the daily attendance at moving pictures is approximately 20,000,000 persons. Many of these pictures are of a very high standard, while others constitute a serious menace to morality.

---

[146] Social Hygiene, Vol. 7, p. 451.

[147] See an interesting article, "Billions—Just For Fun," by Walter S. Hiatt, *Colliers Weekly*, Oct. 25, 1924, p. 19.

The latter sort are sufficiently numerous to contaminate the minds of millions of young people. Many of the plays staged throughout the country are of very inferior moral character. There has been an unmistakable deterioration in the moral tone of the theatre in New York City during the past four or five years. Each year the stage becomes more continentalized and presents more and more obscenity and nudity. The daily attendance at shows of the most depraved character in this one city reaches many thousands. Rabbi Stephen S. Wise gives his impression of one of these performances: "It was nothing less than the work of moral scavengers and filth producers. It was the product of moral leprosy. It was the vulgar incarnation of impurity."

(4) One of the most alarming phases of the moral problem is found in the rapid increase in circulation of obscene literature in the United States. Even a casual observer of the wares displayed on the average newsstand can scarcely have failed to notice the alarming increase in the number of sex periodicals. After an extended tour over the country, Mr. Frank R. Kent, the able correspondent of the Baltimore Sun, writes, under the title, "Filth on Main Street," as follows: "The place to fully appreciate its proportions is in the smaller cities and towns with populations ranging from 20,000 up to 100,000—towns, for instance, like Fairmont, West Virginia, where one dealer sells 2,200 copies of every issue of a single monthly exclusively devoted to stories of sex experiences and the nude in art; or like Steubenville, Ohio, when out of 110 periodicals on sale in a single store, 60 were either out and out of a prurient type or bordered on the libidinous line. . . . And not only have we produced a great smut crop of a coarseness peculiarly our own, but the more obscene of the French papers have now been translated into English. . . . When you stop to analyze, scrutinize, and check up, there is here presented more reason for apprehension

as to the future than any other single symptom in America today."[148] Mr. Benarr Macfadden, one of the most prolific producers of sex literature, received $8,866,800 gross from his various publications in 1924.[149]

The rapid rise of the tabloid picture daily must be a cause of concern to all thoughtful people. Someone has observed that these picture sheets are prepared especially for low-grade morons. They contain little serious news, but are devoted to scandal, crime and other sensational items. Mr. Oswald Garrison Villard has analyzed the contents of one of these tabloids, The New York Graphic, and finds that in one week the space devoted to various items was as follows: foreign news 132 inches, editorials 144 inches, beauty shows and contests 554 inches, divorce and annulments 203 inches, crime 183 inches, sex crime 82 inches, sports and radio 1178 inches.[150] A large proportion of any of these papers is devoted to pictures of scantily clad women, divorce principals, criminals, prize-fighters, and other sensational subjects. A recent writer says: "Tabloid journalism in New York is only seven years old. The history of its growth makes a mushroom seem like a century plant."[151] The combined circulation of the picture papers in New York City is now in excess of 1,300,000 daily.

The American novel has also descended in the depths of filth during the past few years. Many current books of fiction rise no higher than the basest levels of sex appeal. Scores of titles of this sort of volume could easily be given. An editorial in the Saturday Review of

---

[148] The Independent, June 20, 1925, pp. 686-689.

[149] See an illuminating article by Oswald Garrison Villard, *The Atlantic Monthly*, March, 1926, pp. 388-398.

[150] *Ibid*, p. 396.

[151] See an article, The Picture Papers Win, by Jo Swerling, *The Nation*, Oct. 21, 1925, pp. 455-458.

Literature says: "The age by comparison with earlier generations is sex mad."[152]

(5) That the American home is suffering from dangerous ailments can scarcely be doubted.[153] An enormous number of mothers are employed in industry and are consequently unable to give adequate supervision and training to their children. In 1920 there were 8,549,511 women engaged in gainful occupations in the United States, of whom 4,966,752 were above the age of 25 and 1,549,379 above the age of 45.[154] The number of married women gainfully employed was 1,920,281. In many industrial communities approximately half of all employed women are married.[155] The absence from home of so many mothers and the consequent neglect of children are having disastrous effects upon moral character.

Science and industry have not only taken many women out of the home into factories, shops and offices, they have greatly reduced the drudgery of home work and have provided more leisure. Now leisure is a good or a bad thing depending upon the use that is made of it. The tragedy is that in so many homes increased leisure simply means an added opportunity to attend degrading commercialized amusements and to engage in other activities that undermine character.[156] Many homes have become mere eating places and sleeping quarters, where the various members of the family spend little time together. "That something is wrong with marriage," says Paul Popenoe, "is universally ad-

---

[152]March 6, 1926.

[153]See George Albert Coe, What Ails Our Youth; for an optimistic article see Boys—Then and Now, by William Allen White, *The American Magazine,* March, 1926.

[154]Statistical Abstract of the United States, 1924, p. 47.

[155]See an important pamphlet, Radio Talks on Women in Industry, issued by the Women's Bureau of the U. S. Dept. of Labor, Bul. No. 36.

[156]See an article, Leisure—What For? by G. W. Alger, *Atlantic Monthly,* April, 1925, p. 483ff; also one on Social Influences Affecting Home Life, by Professor Ernest R. Groves, *American Journal of Sociology,* Sept., 1925, pp. 227-238.

mitted and deplored. The number of celibates, of mismated couples, of divorces, of childless homes, of wife deserters, of mental and nervous wrecks; the frequency of marital discord, of prostitution and adultery, of perversions, of juvenile delinquency, tell the story.[157]

The rapid increase in the number of divorces furnishes ground for grave concern. The mere fact that divorces are increasing does not necessarily mean that conditions are getting worse. It is a noteworthy fact that women of today simply refuse to endure the treatment accorded women in previous generations. This new freedom of women accounts for many divorces. And yet a divorce does mean a wrecked home, however it may be explained or accounted for. The number of these disrupted homes is ominously large. The following table reveals the increase in the divorce rate.[158]

Year	No. Marriages	No. Divorces
1890	542,537	33,461
1900	685,284	55,751
1906	853,290	72,062
1916	1,070,684	112,037
1922	1,129,045	148,815
1923	1,223,825	165,139

The facts are also emphasized by another table:

Year	Number of Divorces Per 100,000 Married Population
1870	81
1880	107
1890	148
1900	200
1906	231
1916	281
1922	330

[157]Modern Marriage, p. vi.

[158]*Current History Magazine*, August, 1925, p. 789; even more alarming figures for certain cities are given in the Revolt of Modern Youth, by Judge Ben B. Lindsey and Wainwright Evans, p. 213.

That is to say, whereas in 1890 there was one divorce for every 16 marriages, in 1923 there was one for every 7.5 marriages, an increase of 125 per cent in 33 years; while the increase from 1870 to 1922 was slightly over 400 per cent. Without entering into a discussion at this point as to whether or not conditions are worse now than in past decades, the evidence is conclusive that numerous divorces disrupt family life and have very dangerous effects upon the moral tone of the community.[159]

(6) Much of our crime and moral confusion may be traced to our failure to provide adequate moral and religious education. Professor Walter S. Athearn has gathered together some alarming statistics concerning this vital matter, as follows: "There are in the United States over 58,000,000 people, nominally Protestant, who are not identified in any way with any church, either Jewish, Protestant or Catholic. There are over 27,000,000 American children and youth, nominally Protestant, under twenty-five years of age, who are not enrolled in any Sunday school or cradle-roll department and who receive no formal or systematic religious instruction. There are 8,000,000 American children, nominally Protestant, under ten years of age, who are growing up in non-church homes. There are in the United States 8,676,000 Catholic children and youth under twenty-five years of age. Of this number . . . . 78.4 per cent are not in religious schools. There are in the United States 1,630,000 Jewish children and youth . . . . of whom 95.2 per cent are not in religious schools. . . . . Taking the country as a whole, seven out of every ten children and youth . . . . are not being touched in any way by the religious program of the Church."[160]

Not only is it true that vast numbers of our children

---

[159]See an article, The Chaos of Modern Marriage, by Dr. Beatrice M. Hinkle, *Harpers Magazine,* Dec., 1925, pp. 1-13.

[160]Character Building in a Democracy, pp. 24, 26.

and young people are receiving no formal religious instruction, the quality of the teaching in most religious schools is very low. The average Sunday School teacher is poorly equipped for the task of training young people in religion. Most religious schools are woefully lacking in physical equipment for religious instruction. Moreover, the amount and quality of religious education in the home is discouraging and distressing. In the aggregate, the people of the United States are making a dismal failure of religious education.

Summary of Present Dangers

Let us now gather together in summary form some of the dangers with which our society is confronted: economic perils due to gross inequality of privilege, with extreme luxury for some and dire physical need for many, disgraceful housing conditions in many cities and industrial communities, concentration of vast financial power in the hands of interlocking directorates, widespread industrial strife and violence, the spy system in industry, decreasing supplies of raw materials, increasing foreign competition, the steady growth of class-consciousness, the deliberate stimulation of new physical desires on a great scale by advertising, industrial waste, the dehumanizing effects of monotonous toil in factories and shops, and the rapid spread of materialism; international dangers arising out of the increasing destructiveness and deadliness of modern war, the growth of industrialism throughout the earth and consequent intensification of competition between the various nations for food, raw materials, markets and fields of investment, exaggerated and irresponsible nationalism, and the prevalence of militarism; racial perils due to discrimination, exploitation, lynching, and mob violence; political perils due to graft and corruption, ignorance and inefficiency, the denial of civil liberties, indifference of voters, and the magnitude and complexity of the problems requiring solution; moral dangers due to crime and lawlessness, a million drug addicts, two hundred thousand prostitutes, eight million victims of venereal diseases, sordid commercialized amusements, the growth of obscene literature, the deterioration of the home, the increase in divorce, the presence of twenty-seven million children and young people who are not receiving systematic religious instruction.

Surely we do not require further evidence to convince us that our social order is afflicted with dangerous maladies. Numerous spots of infection are poisoning our civilization. The very institutions which have been created with arduous toil and great suffering now threaten to destroy us. Can it be that the giant mechanism which we are so busily constructing is destined to crush the human spirit?

In Mrs. Shelley's story, "Frankenstein," the hideous monster says to his creator: "Do your duty towards me, and I will do mine towards you and the rest of mankind. If you will comply with my conditions, I will leave them and you at peace; but if you refuse, I will glut the maw of death, until it be satisfied with the blood of your remaining friends."

"Have all my dreams of greatness ended here?" cries Frankenstein in Milner's play. "Is this the boasted wonder of my science, is this the offspring of long years of toilsome study and noisome labour? Is my fairest model of perfection come to this—a hideous monster, a loathsome mass of animated putrefaction, whom but to gaze on chills with horror, even me, his maker? How, how shall I secrete him, how destroy? I have endued him with a giant's strength, and he will use it to pluck down ruin on his maker's head. . . . My life has been devoted to the fulfilment of one object, now another claims the exertion of its short remainder, to destroy the wretch that I have formed—to purge the world of that infuriated monster—to free mankind from the fell persecution of that demon. This, this, is now my bounden duty, and to this awful task I solemnly devote myself."

6. WHAT CAN AN INDIVIDUAL DO ABOUT IT?

In the face of such grave social problems, what needs to be done? Where can one take hold? What can an individual do about it? A steady stream of literature is pouring from the press in the attempt to answer these questions.[161] It is obvious that we cannot do more in the present discussion than to give mere hints and general suggestions as to possible courses of action. We are, therefore, presenting, in very brief form, a tenfold goal toward which an individual may strive, and which, if attained by a sufficiently large number of men and women, would result in vast improvements in the social order.

1. *Treat every man as a brother and every woman as a sister.* If we, like Jesus, would look upon every person as a son or a daughter of God, with a personality of such infinite value as to be worthy of our love and reverence, many of our most dangerous problems would be solved. Of course, the question always arises in a concrete situation, how should a brother be treated? Frequently this question cannot be answered intelligently unless we are willing to make a scientific analysis of the various factors involved. A general principle in itself is often an inadequate guide to conduct unless supplemented by careful study of ways and means of making its application effective in a given situation. Nevertheless, genuine reverence for personality and deep affection for every human being as a member of God's family would banish such attitudes as condescension, scorn, contempt, disgust, bitterness, hatred and fear; and abolish such practices as prostitution, lynching, capital punishment, violence in industrial disputes and slaughter in battle.

---

[161]At the end of the chapter we have listed a score of the best of these books.

2. *Share privileges with others.* This is an obvious possibility for all of us. We can use less for ourselves and devote more to the service of others, whether of money, time or talents. Everywhere about us are multitudes of people in desperate need, physically, mentally, morally, spiritually. If we would spend upon ourselves only that amount of money and time required in order to make us effective servants of humanity, we would have much more to share with the needy.

One of the most urgent demands of the hour is for greater simplicity of living. The spending of money upon things that are not really essential to efficient service has disastrous social consequences. The consumption of luxuries increases the cost of living and thereby intensifies the struggle of the poor. This is true in spite of the widespread belief that the production of luxuries is socially beneficial because it "makes work" and "keeps money in circulation." The prosecution of the World War made work on a vast scale, kept money in circulation and for a time gave the appearance of increased prosperity, but the net result was colossal social loss, because of the wasteful consumption of the accumulated resources and savings of many decades. The production of luxuries likewise uses up raw materials, human labor, and reserves of capital, which might be devoted to the production of necessities. Until a sufficient quantity of necessities is produced to provide adequately for the physical needs of all, luxury production will continue to be social waste.

Moreover, the pursuit of surplus things requires so much time and energy that one is left without sufficient leisure or strength to meet the insistent needs of others. It is also true that rivalry for material things is a prolific source of bitterness, hatred, and violence. By living as simply as is consistent with physical, mental and spiritual efficiency, we place ourselves in a better position to minister to human needs and to break down the barriers which separate people from each other.

3. *Seek to supplant bigotry and intolerance by sympathy and understanding.* Openness of mind and the willingness to examine all the available evidence are essential to the solution of the complex and dangerous social problems of our day, whether the question under consideration is that of the relations between whites and Negroes, Californians and Japanese, fundamentalists and modernists, employers and workers. There is everywhere a marked tendency to read only those publications and listen only to those speeches which reenforce one's present convictions. Pride of opinion is a marked characteristic of our time. Escape from the imminent perils confronting us will not be possible unless many men and women learn to place themselves in the position of their opponents and look at the question from their point of view. Sympathy is essential to understanding. Those persons, therefore, who desire to have a share in overthrowing existing evils must cultivate the habit of open-minded examination of all sides of a question and reveal a sympathetic eagerness to discover the basis of the other person's attitudes and practices.

4. *Seek to replace economic competition by co-operation.* Before fundamental changes can be made in the existing economic order, it will be necessary to shatter the prevailing spirit of complacency concerning the results of competition for private gain. To this end the moral, as well as the economic, consequences of the strife engendered by selfish competition must be stressed.[162] Millions of people are constantly praying that the Kingdom of God may come to pass upon the earth. We may be sure that if our prayer is answered, the present competitive system will be supplanted by a co-operative commonwealth. If we really desire our

[162] See pages 249 to 253.

prayer to come true, it would seem advisable, therefore, to seek to restrict the field of selfish competition and to extend the area of social co-operation. The strengthening of the co-operative movement and the extension of public ownership are steps in this direction and should be encouraged.

5. *Encourage the extension of democracy.* In a country where popular education is not only advocated but is a matter of compulsion, democratic control is inevitable. Democratic government may be clumsy and ineffective but it is the only possible form of permanent government for an educated citizenry. Oligarchies and dictatorships may wield power temporarily but the days of their rule are numbered. Sooner or later despotic repression results in violent revolution. Moreover, democracy in political affairs is severely handicapped unless accompanied by democracy in industry and finance. It is a notorious fact that men of great wealth dominate the political affairs of the nation. So long as there is a vast concentration of industrial and financial power in the hands of a relatively few men, political democracy will be comparatively impotent, because of the fact that financial power is vastly more important than political power. Financial oligarchies and dictatorship, if prolonged, are just as certain to produce violent revolution as have political despotisms.

For these reasons it would seem to be the policy of wisdom to encourage the extension of democracy, in politics and in industry. To this end we should support such legislative measures as heavily graduated income taxes and inheritance taxes, since they tend to check and limit excessive private fortunes. Democracy in industry is possible only by the effective organization of the workers. So long as giant corporations exist, national trade unions will be needed to equalize the struggle between employers and workers. Efforts to throttle and suppress labor organizations may succeed temporarily, but are likely to lead to violent upheaval in the course of time. The policy of wisdom would seem to be frankly and freely to encourage democratic movements in industry and finance, and to begin now to train the workers in democratic control.

6. *Participate actively and intelligently in civic affairs.* Democracy can be effective only when the more sober-minded citizens take seriously their civic duties. Failure to vote is almost inexcusable, even though time and thought are required in order to cast a ballot intelligently. Political health would seem to depend upon success in breaking the widespread habit of voting a straight party ticket. Moreover, the present alignment in politics is almost meaningless. It is difficult to detect fundamental differences between the two major parties. It may be that the only way to regain political health is by the creation of a new political party, based upon the really vital economic and social issues of the day. If this is found to be the case, then liberal voters may have to stay out in the wilderness for two or three decades before they can gain political control, as was the case with the British Labor Party. Many of our ablest young men and women should dedicate their lives to the purging and elevating of political affairs in this country.

7. *Seek to overcome international anarchy and violence by international co-operation and friendship.* The first step in this direction is the recognition of the fact that the nation is not the supreme political entity and that the welfare of the whole is of more importance than that of any part. Belief in the complete sovereignty of the nation must be modified if we are to avoid another great war. International action must gradually supplant arbitrary national action in matters that concern many peoples. Permanent international agencies of legislation, administration and adjudication are, therefore, urgently needed. Because of this fact, the League of Nations and the Permanent Court of International Justice, in spite of obvious weaknesses due to immaturity

and exaggerated nationalism, deserve the support of all those who would end the measure of international anarchy and lawlessness which has long prevailed.

International organization, to be effective, must be undergirded by understanding and sympathy between the different peoples. To this end a comprehensive program of international education is required. Religion also has a significant function to perform in making men conscious of the essential unity of the human family.

8. *Live creatively.* There are two ways of seeking satisfaction, through possession and through creation. Ours is predominantly a possessive civilization, where success is tested primarily in terms of the abundance of comforts, luxuries and privileges enjoyed. There are many kinds of creation. While there is still a demand for inventors of mechanical appliances, the great need of this age is for creators in the realms of human values and human relations. The man most desperately needed just now is the one who can develop character and teach mankind how to live together without strife and violence. Creativeness in these realms will bring a degree of joy which can never be equaled by feeding physical appetites and passions. Emphasis upon possessions is divisive, whereas the effort to release human values is unifying. To lose all concern for comfort and safety in the eager desire to create character and bring about harmonious human relations is to find the meaning of life and to enter into its richest enjoyment. In every phase of our modern world—in industry, in international affairs, in racial relations, in politics, and in moral life—the door to creative achievement is wide open, and, strangely enough, few enter therein.

9. *Live sacrificially.* The central challenge of Jesus is almost completely ignored by most of his professed followers today. Some indeed are denying themselves, taking up their cross and following the pathway that leads to crucifixion, but not many. And herein is to be

found the explanation of the large measure of failure of organized religion to overcome existing evils. So long as men and women struggle for comfort and luxury and position, that long will they be impotent in the face of the threatening social problems of the day. Deliverance does not come at the hands of comfort-seekers. The cross-bearers alone bring freedom. The measure of a man's service to this generation will be in direct ratio to his willingness to sacrifice himself utterly in some phase of the age-long struggle for the complete emancipation of the human spirit. Unless a man is willing, if necessary, to forsake father and mother, relative and friend, wealth and security, for the sake of suffering humanity, he cannot be a true disciple of that One who, like a grain of wheat, buried Himself in order that new life might spring from the earth.

We ought to remain under no illusions concerning the consequences of taking Jesus' challenge seriously. To follow Him in any of the danger zones of our social order is supremely difficult and dangerous. In industry, in international affairs, in race relations, in politics, in social contacts, to preach and practice the gospel of Fatherhood, brotherhood, love of enemies, forgiveness and the suffering of innocence for guilt, is to run the risk of being branded an impractical idealist, if not a dangerous radical. Such a person is likely to discover what Jesus meant when he said he sent his disciples out as lambs in the midst of wolves. Today, as in the case of the makers of freedom we have studied, men will think they are doing God a service by defaming and persecuting those who seek to lead humanity out of bondage. Thus did they treat William Lloyd Garrison and Susan B. Anthony, Martin Luther and John Wesley, Francis and Keir Hardie; and thus will they treat the men and women of this age who seek to supplant the present social order by one which more nearly approximates the Kingdom of God on earth.

10. *Search for the sources of spiritual power.* If a

person is always to treat every man as a brother and every woman as a sister, to share privileges with others, to avoid bigotry and intolerance, to live simply, creatively and sacrificially in the face of the baffling and menacing problems of the day, he must discover ways and means of drawing upon hidden reservoirs of power. From the record it appears that Jesus found power in at least three ways: He lived close to human need, He withdrew from the multitude for periods of silence and communion with God, and He spent hours in fellowship with the inner circle.

Let a man lose himself in ministering to human need, in seeking to relieve misery and to remove injustice, and he will feel his own impotence and inadequacy for so great an undertaking. Then let him cultivate the habit of withdrawing regularly for periods of silence, reflection, meditation, communion and intercession, and he will come back with renewed insight, vigor and courage. Let him also seek the fellowship of an intimate group of kindred spirits and he will begin to discover what was in Jesus' mind when he said that where two or three are gathered together in His name, there is He also. Above all, let such a man keep himself saturated with vivid memories of the historic figure of Jesus and endeavor constantly to enter into a deeper appreciation of that matchless life and the wonderful words which proceeded from His lips. The man who submerges himself in human need, meditates and prays in the silent watches, cultivates the fellowship of kindred souls, and lives ever in the presence of the Christ, will discover that the illimitable resources of God which flowed into the life of the Carpenter of Nazareth are open and accessible to him also. Freedom awaits the coming of more men and women who have discovered the reservoirs of power.

Makers of freedom must ever be prepared to travel a rough and lonely road. As Joan faces the stake, in Bernard Shaw's play, she cried aloud: "Yes: I am alone on earth: I have always been alone. My father told my brothers to drown me if I would not stay to mind his sheep while France was bleeding to death: France might perish if only our lambs were safe. I thought France would have friends at the court of the king of France; and I find only wolves fighting for pieces of her poor torn body. I thought God would have friends everywhere. . . . Do not think you can frighten me by telling me that I am alone. France is alone; and God is alone; and what is my loneliness before the loneliness of my country and my God? I see now that the loneliness of God is His strength: what would He be if He listened to your jealous little counsels? Well, my loneliness shall be my strength too: it is better to be alone with God: His friendship will not fail me, nor His counsel, nor His love. In His strength I will dare, and dare, and dare, until I die. I will go out now to the common people, and let the love in their eyes comfort me for the hate in yours. You will all be glad to see me burnt; but if I go through the fire I shall go through it to their hearts for ever and ever. . . . O God that madest this beautiful earth, when will it be ready to receive Thy saints? How long, O Lord, how long?"

Appendix

BIBLIOGRAPHY

Stuart Chase, The Tragedy of Waste
John A. Fitch, Causes of Industrial Unrest
Arthur Bertram, The Economic Illusion
R. H. Tawney, The Acquisitive Society
Bertrand Russell, Proposed Roads to Freedom
J. A. Hobson, Incentives in the New Social Order
Paul H. Douglas, Wages and the Family
Carl D. Thompson, Public Ownership
G. S. Watkins, Introduction to the Study of Labor Problems
John Bakeless, The Origin of the Next War
Sherwood Eddy and Kirby Page, The Abolition of War
Arthur Ponsonby, Now Is The Time
R. L. Buell, International Relations
Wm. S. Culbertson, International Economic Policies
C. J. H. Hayes, Nationalism
Irving Fisher, America's Interest in World Peace
Moorfield Storey, The Conquest of the Philippines
J. H. Oldham, Christianity and the Race Problem
Alain Locke, The New Negro
Geo. Albert Coe, What Ails Our Youth
A. Herbert Gray, Men, Women and God
Judge Ben B. Lindsey, The Revolt of Modern Youth
Samuel Dickey, The Constructive Revolution of Jesus
V. G. Simkovitch, Toward the Understanding of Jesus
Sherwood Eddy, The New Challange to Faith: or, What Can I Believe in the Light of Modern Psychology, Philosophy and Science?